HERE IT IS

PAUL ROOS

WITH JENNIFER MCASEY

HERE IT IS
Coaching, leadership and life

VIKING
an imprint of
PENGUIN BOOKS

VIKING

UK | USA | Canada | Ireland | Australia
India | New Zealand | South Africa | China

Penguin Books is part of the Penguin Random House group of companies
whose addresses can be found at global.penguinrandomhouse.com.

First published by Penguin Random House Australia Pty Ltd, 2017

1 3 5 7 9 10 8 6 4 2

Cover design by Alex Ross © Penguin Random House Australia Pty Ltd
Photography: front cover by Julian Kingma, back cover by Getty Images/Sean Garnsworthy,
front endpaper by AFL Media/Scott Barbour, back endpaper by Getty Images/Adam Pretty
Typeset in Sabon by Midland Typesetters, Australia
Colour separation by Splitting Image Colour Studio, Clayton, Victoria
Printed and bound in Australia by Griffin Press, an accredited ISO AS/NZS
14001 Environmental Management Systems printer.

National Library of Australia
Cataloguing-in-Publication data:

Roos, Paul, author.
Here it is / Paul Roos; Jennifer McAsey.
9780143787044 (hardback)

Roos, Paul.
Australian football coaches – Biography.
Football players – Australia – Biography.
Leadership.

Other creators/contributors:
McAsey, Jennifer, author.

penguin.com.au

To Tami, Dylan and Tyler
What a wonderful journey

Contents

Prologue

In 2016, I left the Melbourne Football Club and coaching for good. For the past 35 years I'd been deeply involved with three clubs as a player and coach.

I'd captained a club, notched up 350 games, played in a Grand Final, coached the Swans to their first premiership in 72 years, and helped a club that was at rock bottom to get back on its feet.

These are all things that matter to me, but now as I reflect back on my career it isn't those public achievements that are at the front of my mind.

In November 2016 I received an email from Robert Jackson, who was the strength and conditioning manager at Melbourne while I was coach.

It's a pivotal role at any sporting club, and Rob is one of the best. He's worked at a couple of National Rugby League clubs and three AFL clubs, worked under six different senior coaches in total.

Rob explained he'd often been asked the difference between each of the coaches and had always answered they were mostly cut from the same cloth, with their own quirks.

The coaching mantra in most clubs, and one that he lived

by, was basically, 'It's not about being liked, it's about being respected.'

He had always been the 'tough guy' trainer who demanded perfection, penalised players for being late or not hitting gym targets, and he didn't hesitate to yell when he felt frustrated.

I understood what Rob was saying. I had grown up playing under some great coaches, but many had a similar approach. They didn't have time to get to know you, and often it was motivation by fear.

But Rob said that when I came to Melbourne the dynamic changed, and he'd changed too.

Rob wrote:

> You walked into the club and one of your key messages was, 'Clubs are built on relationships – between coaches, between players, between football and admin.'
>
> You made a point to us all: 'Know each other, have a conversation, actually show some care about each other, 'cos we are going to have ups and downs, but the only thing that'll make you get up and help your teammate, put your body on the line, work that extra hour . . . is knowing that they would do the same for you and that you care.'

Rob said he had taken my message on board and started asking players about their families, their hobbies, what music they liked. 'I did everything I could do to understand more about what makes these players real people,' he wrote.

'Real people.' That phrase was an echo of something I'd heard three years earlier, in 2013, when I had first contemplated taking the Melbourne coaching job.

At the time, the team was languishing near the bottom of the ladder and the whole club was hurting. I had a private meeting with the senior players, to get a sense of what was wrong and whether they were prepared to take responsibility.

Jack Watts spoke up. I had never met Jack but, like most AFL followers, I knew he was a former number one draft pick who had not been able to live up to expectations. He'd been much maligned, and unfairly had come to symbolise Melbourne's failure.

Jack spoke bluntly about the way he felt the players were treated at that time: 'Roosy, I just want to be treated like a human being.'

It wasn't something I ever thought I'd hear a player say.

At that point, before I took the Melbourne coaching job, I was fairly certain I could help those boys. Footballers, like everyone else in society, want to be cared for and want to care about other people. They want to enjoy going to their workplace, and they want to be treated with respect.

Jack's comment affirmed to me that this team needed an emphasis on relationships, nurturing, strong direction and understanding. Someone needed to try to figure out why Jack Watts was playing the way he was, why he hadn't been able to reach his potential.

I got excited about taking on the challenge, because it was clear that the Melbourne coaching role was much more about leadership and relationship-building than football skills and drills.

If there is a thread that runs through my playing and coaching career, it has been woven by forging strong relationships at every club I've been at. To me, that is the only way you can get the best out of people and ultimately have success in life.

At the Swans, we built a premiership-winning side, but only because we had all bonded together – players, coaches and key staff – to create a culture where respect for each other, hard work, humility, honesty and discipline were valued above all else.

Rob told me that when other coaches or interns or students or corporate guests ask him, 'What's the difference between the coaches you've had?', he's now got a slightly different answer: 'The greatest lesson I've learned is that all coaching should begin with understanding the true importance of building relationships.'

Rob's email had a profound effect on me. If there is anything I wanted to be remembered for after nearly four decades of life in football, it is just that. No matter what club you're running, the local netball club or an elite AFL club, strong, genuine relationships must be the foundation.

You must invest in people and gather good people around you. There will be many times when you challenge each other, but at the end of the day egos ruin footy clubs and bad relationships ruin football clubs.

You need to have people you trust, people you want to go into battle with, in all positions, and you must stay true to your values.

To coach effectively, you have to be like a parent to your players. After all, at most AFL clubs the players and coaches spend more time with each other than with their own families.

I feel very fortunate that I started my senior football career at the Fitzroy Football Club. I turned up there as a laid-back 17-year-old, with very little idea about being a serious athlete.

Football was only part-time in those days, but thankfully, Fitzroy had a group of senior players who were as professional as you could possibly be in the 1980s environment. Players such as captain Garry Wilson, our superstar Bernie Quinlan and Laurie Serafini were strong, positive role models for me and the other young players.

They were humble and respectful, they trained very hard and they set standards of behaviour which they expected the team to follow. They developed a player-driven, values-based club culture long before it became fashionable, and I'll be forever thankful to them for showing me the right way to go about my football and my life.

From that foundation, I was able to establish myself and build a career that spanned 356 games. At the end of my playing days at the Swans, in 1998, I sat down and wrote a list of 25 things I liked and disliked about coaching and playing. I wanted to make sure I never forgot what it was like to be a player.

When I look back at those notes now, they are really about treating people with respect, as well as building a positive environment where players can learn and grow.

In this book, I set out the full list publicly for the first time, and hope my tips may help leaders in all walks of life as they work to achieve their own ambitions and guide others to thrive.

That list became the basis of my coaching at both the Sydney Swans and the Melbourne Football Club.

At both clubs I was lucky enough to work with players, coaches and administrators who were prepared to focus on the things that I believe matter: honesty, accountability, positive communication, close relationships and hard work. At both clubs, people were prepared to put aside their own egos for the greater good of the team and the club.

If I can sum up what I want to achieve from this book, it's to try to put an old head on young shoulders. I'm outlining my experiences as a player and coach, and the lessons I've learned, with the hope they may help fast-track someone else on their journey.

I know for sure that if I had been a coach before I was

a player, I would have been a much better footballer and teammate.

I would have understood that every player in the team is important, and that even if you're a good player, you have to sacrifice yourself to make the team better.

Of course it's not possible for most people to coach or manage first. So whether you are a footballer, athlete, business leader, teacher or simply a young person trying to find your path, I hope this book can provide some insight, and help you find purpose and success.

It might surprise people to know that success for me has not been measured in premierships, or the numbers of wins and losses over a long career in football. Success has been measured in the strength of friendships; the creation of close teams where everyone is valued; in setting high standards and living them day-to-day; and staying true to my principles – even when the ball didn't always bounce my way.

Part One

1998–2002
From Footy Boots
to Coaching Blueprint

CHAPTER 1

Never forget how it feels to be a player

In my 356th and last game of football, coach Rodney Eade gave us a rousing pre-game address. We were playing Adelaide in a do-or-die semifinal at the SCG, and 'Rocket' Eade wanted us to imagine we were all on a train together, riding it side-by-side to victory.

I'd heard hundreds of pre-game speeches in my 17 seasons at the top level and Rocket's were some of the better ones.

But I certainly didn't have a first-class seat on that train. I'd started the game on the bench and by late in the second quarter I was still there, jiggling my legs and jogging up and down the boundary line to stay warm.

At half time I joked to teammate Stuart Maxfield that I couldn't find my ticket for the train, and asked if he knew where to get one.

It was a light-hearted moment on a sombre night as we went down to Adelaide. Not exactly the way I wanted to end my career, but I wasn't complaining.

I was 35 years old and, until that final year with the Swans, I'd hardly ever sat on the bench since I'd made my debut as an 18-year-old with Fitzroy back in 1982.

I had achieved almost everything I dreamed of as a young

boy growing up in the eastern suburbs of Melbourne. In 1996, I had played in a Grand Final with the Swans; I'd been named All-Australian captain and been an integral part of two great clubs. There wasn't a premiership medallion on my trophy shelf, but I was incredibly grateful to have made a living for so many years playing the game I was passionate about.

As I reflected on my playing career, I soon realised that the last half of that 1998 season, when I sat on the bench so often, had actually been a gift and something I was thankful for.

The interchange bench was different back then. It wasn't a place for players to rest and be rotated on and off the field as it is now; rather, it was mostly a place where the team's fringe players dwelled.

Spending time there was a real eye-opener for me. It proved to be pivotal in forming the philosophies that were to become the foundations of my coaching career. I believe in my last 10 games I learned as much about coaching and player psychology as I had in the previous 340 games.

I saw what sparked players and what crushed them.

Until that time, I'd never had to worry about being picked in the team, never been anxious about whether I'd get a chance to make a contribution on the field. I was fortunate to be a good player at Fitzroy and the Swans and, to be truthful, I'd never worried too much about the fringe players in my teams. Suddenly, I was one of them. Sitting on the bench alongside players desperate to get a chance, I began to understand how different was their experience and their mentality.

When the bench players did get on the field, they were nervous and would often make a skill error or stuff-up. Next minute, the coach was telling the runner to drag them off the ground and they were back on the bench.

Seeing this up close was at times distressing and didn't make sense. It was counter-productive to drag players for mistakes. Those players could never build their confidence under a system like that, common at every club.

In change rooms across the country, from junior clubs to the top teams, you often saw a sign pinned to the wall: 'A champion team will always beat a team of champions.' But from my experience that wasn't how it worked. The stars were feted and the rest often just made up the numbers.

It occurred to me that it would be easier to build a successful side if every player in the team, all 22 of them, felt they belonged and had a role to play.

Those 10 weeks gave me real empathy for the players who weren't stars. I started to think that if I ever became a senior coach, I'd want them to feel part of the team. I mulled over how to build their confidence and make them feel valued, so all players could work together for a common cause.

There were other things I questioned as I contemplated life from the bench and looked back over my career. I scribbled down notes during the year, random thoughts about what I liked and disliked about coaches, and how I might go about it if I was in charge.

I wondered why players weren't given more responsibility for how their team operated. After all, it was *their* team. Even though I had been captain at Fitzroy, I was rarely asked my opinion on the players, or how we trained, or how we could improve.

So, a month after I retired from football, when the memories were still fresh, I sat down at my desk.

I wasn't sure what my next move would be and I needed a break from football. But in the future I might become a coach and I never wanted to forget what it was like to be a player, never wanted to lose touch with the players' perspective.

I had real insight into what could motivate players to perform better and I didn't want that to fade over time.

The headline at the top of the A4 page was simple: **'Coaching notes – October 1998'**. I didn't know it at the time, but that simple list was to become my coaching blueprint, the bedrock for me when I took over at the Swans and later at the Melbourne Football Club.

It wasn't written as a criticism of my previous coaches but rather as a touchstone to guard against losing empathy for players. I'd taken a lot of positives from my coaches at Fitzroy: David Parkin and Robert Walls and Robert Shaw, among others.

But as I wrote, I had in mind that a new era of professionalism was unfolding. The time was right to do things differently. For the first time in the history of the game, a majority of players didn't have to work outside football. Playing football *was* their job.

So how should coaching change to make the most of that increased access to players? What sort of workplace and working conditions should professional players expect? I knew it would be important to create an environment where players wanted to come to 'work', and where they felt important.

Football had long been a brutal sport, survival of the fittest the common theme both on the field and off. But times were changing in the mid to late 1990s. I believed that motivation by fear and thrashing players on the training track were not the ways of the future. The modern workplace was evolving and so was footy.

With all those issues in mind, I put my thoughts to paper. Most of the points I wrote weren't related to a specific incident but had formed in my mind over time.

Not all are pertinent now, but the majority are still relevant and were put into practice every day I coached. Being human, I admit I wasn't always able to stick to them religiously, but they remain my coaching creed.

Always remember to enjoy what you're doing.

Coaches were a moody lot in my experience, and their moods were very predictable. When we won they were bright and if we lost a black cloud was parked above their head. You'd walk into the rooms after a loss and you knew the coach would be cranky. The worst part was that it would affect the whole week.

None of us liked to lose, so I understood where it was coming from, but that didn't stop me thinking it was unhelpful. Of course we were all disappointed after a loss and there's no way you'd be smiling in the rooms after the game. But it wasn't enjoyable having to walk around on eggshells for days after a loss.

Four-time premiership coach Leigh Matthews has made the point that even the best coaches lose on average once every three weeks, so that's a lot of dark moods.

The coach's grumpiness made most of the players edgy and it was unpleasant to be at the club. But if we were losing, surely we really needed to be there so we could spend time working on our game? Basically, if the mood lasted too long past game day, it wasn't constructive to improvement.

If my coach wouldn't engage with me or the other players because he was still in a dark mood from last Saturday's loss, what was the point of that?

My view was that once you turned up back at the club on Monday and had done the game review, it was time to move on. You were there to work and educate the players.

Because footy was becoming more professional, players were going to spend more time at the club, so a positive mood had to be more conducive to learning and progressing.

We were lucky enough to be doing what we loved, so why not try to enjoy it as much as possible? I appreciate it can be hard to enjoy footy when you're at a club that is struggling. I knew all about that – at Fitzroy, we didn't play any finals in my last eight seasons at the club.

For me the key was simply working hard to maintain my own personal standards and taking responsibility for myself. If you don't have high standards, there's little a coach can do. I didn't need to talk to the coach every week to improve, but it was certainly better if I did have constructive discussions with him, especially if things weren't going to plan.

Coach's attitude will rub off on the players.

When the going gets tough, it's more important than ever that the coach appears as confident and relaxed as possible. If he's stressed, players will adopt the same mentality.

I'd seen the negative side of this adage so often in my time at Fitzroy. Then, when Rodney Eade took over as coach of the Sydney Swans in 1996, my second year at the club, it was a revelation.

The Swans had finished last on the ladder in 1994 and I joined at the end of that season. In 1995, the tide started to turn at the Swans. Under veteran coach Ron Barassi, we won eight games and finished 12th. Barassi had coached the club for three years and worked hard to instil the right work ethic and stabilise the team. In the decade before Barassi took over, the Swans had seven different coaches.

Eade was a new-generation coach and he had a new attitude. Early on in his tenure, he had great rapport with the players and knew how to create the appropriate mood. It rubbed off on the players and we defied the pundits to play in a Grand Final.

We'd walk into the rooms before a big game and Rocket would crack a joke or rib you about your shirt or your shoes.

That really impressed me. It indicated his confidence in us, his belief that we were going to enjoy ourselves and have a good day.

I formed the view that it was crucial a coach knew how to handle and absorb pressure, and shield the players from it to some degree. I believed successful coaches needed to have a strong sense of self, be confident and calm, and convey that to the team.

Never lose sight of the fact it's a game of football.

Like so many other kids in Melbourne, I'd played footy since I was about eight. It was a big part of my childhood, though I was equally passionate about tennis and basketball.

Fitzroy officials first noticed me when I was 15 and, by the age of 16, I was playing in the club's under-19 side. Football was about to take over my life and over the next decade it was the centre point of my world.

But in late 1988, an event occurred that began to change my perspective. I was on a post-season footy trip to the US with Fitzroy teammates when I met Tami Hardy at a bar in San Diego.

Over the next few years, Tami and I travelled back and forth from California to Australia and we married in October 1992.

Meeting Tami and her family meant I spent a lot of time in the US, where hardly anyone knew Australian Rules football existed, let alone cared about it.

Brett Stephens, my former teammate at Fitzroy, also influenced me. He retired in 1993 and became a fitness instructor on the international tennis circuit, working with 14-time Grand Slam winner Pete Sampras.

Brett had been a fanatical footballer – he'd taken it seriously to the point of being neurotic about his routine. Then he went on the tennis tour and he came back and said, 'Roosy, it's not that big a deal out there in the world, it's a game of footy', and that really struck me.

Going overseas for extended breaks became very important to me, not only to see Tami's family but because the trips helped me disconnect from the all-consuming nature of football and recharge.

I also wrote that point down because I wanted to make sure that if I ever did coach, I had a reminder to keep the job in perspective and never get carried away with my importance. It was a note to self: keep your life in balance and don't ever be defined by the game.

The coach's job is to set strategies, team plans, team rules, team disciplines and give specific instructions to players at breaks – don't just verbally abuse.

I can't count the number of times coaches yelled at my teammates and me.

There was one particular time I'll never forget. The coach raced down the terrace onto the ground, stormed over to one of my mates and let go with a torrent of meaningless abuse. 'You're a c---, you're a c---, you're a c---.' And then the coach walked away.

How helpful to the player was that hysterical behaviour? No help whatsoever. He still didn't know exactly what he'd done wrong and the chances of him being confident and motivated to perform well had just evaporated.

Coaches spent so much time yelling and screaming and coming up with punishments. I don't hold this against any of my coaches, it was just the way it was. They'd been treated like that and the cycle went on.

Most coaches weren't full-time, and neither were the players, so they didn't have time to come up with detailed strategies and instructions. But that's what we craved as players. We wanted the coach to tell us what we should be doing, to explain what he wanted. It was a waste of time shouting at us about the things we'd already buggered up.

I came to believe the coach should be there to give solutions and to educate players. If I was to coach, I wanted the players to be clear about our team plans and team rules.

I also figured that if players helped make the rules under the guidance of the coach, then they would be far more likely to understand them and stick to them.

I'd seen too much unrestrained, destructive emotion at football clubs. But I understood it was easy to get caught up in the heat of the moment. That's why I wanted to put this down on paper, so I'd always have a reminder to keep myself in check.

After game, don't fly off the handle. If too emotional, say nothing, wait until Monday.

Not only did the abuse flow at quarter time, half time and three-quarter time, we often copped it after the match as well. Players were humiliated in front of their teammates and I'd borne the brunt of it too. The attacks could be vicious personal insults and they achieved nothing.

I felt strongly that humiliating people was not the right way to get the best out of them and didn't want to fall into that emotional post-game trap. There were many times I didn't speak to the players at all after a loss. If I was too emotional I would wait until the Monday match review, when I was more clear about the message I wanted to get across to the players.

Good communication skills.

League coaches were often aloof, taciturn characters when I played. Many of them were hard men who thought actions spoke louder than words.

But I thought that, if I ever did the job, I would make a point of communicating with the players as much as possible and keeping my door open. Someone told me about a coach who was so distant players had to make an appointment to talk to him.

I felt if a coach wasn't prepared to interact with the players and get to know them on and off the field, then he couldn't be effective. Times were changing and coaches and players were spending many more hours at the club, so they had to have a relationship and be able to talk to each other.

David Parkin, who had coached Hawthorn and Carlton to premierships before he became my coach at Fitzroy in 1986, was an early role model. Parko, also a university lecturer, was committed to giving players feedback. Every week he'd mark your performance and write comments for you. It was a different era and his time with us was limited, but I always respected the amount of effort he put into communicating with us.

The players had to feel you were on their side, that you were an ally and were interested in them. That you would treat them as you would want to be treated was another of the points I wrote down. It's a simple message, but not always easy for a coach. I knew at times they had to deliver harsh, blunt messages. But I believed it was better to be honest and upfront when those moments came.

Players don't mean to make mistakes, don't go out to lose; never drag a player for making a mistake.

These thoughts crystallised in my last season as a player when I became more acquainted with the younger and less talented players on the team.

I wasn't as important to the team – didn't feel as valued – and realised that's how a lot of players felt during their entire careers. I could see that talent was being wasted because some players never had anyone back them. They lived on edge and didn't get a fair chance to prove their worth.

I decided it would be more effective to show faith in those players. It didn't mean I'd never take a player off the ground. If they were undisciplined or broke team rules, there might be no option. But if they committed a skill error such as dropping a mark or missing a handball – that would never be reason for me to drag them if I became a coach. From what I'd seen, all that achieved was a big dent in their confidence. No one made a skill error on purpose.

I'd give them a chance to make it up to the team rather than dragging them to the sidelines and making them feel worthless and embarrassed. That didn't help the team at all.

Weekly meetings with team leaders; make players more accountable for training, discipline, team plans – it is their team too.

We'd be stronger if every player felt part of the plan.

During my playing days, players were rarely consulted and had little or no say in the way their team and their club was run. The coach was the font of all knowledge. The players were adults and I'm sure many had strong views on the game, but we were expected to do what we were asked, without question.

I was captain of Fitzroy for six years, but even that role didn't mean you were included in discussions about the team. I was only consulted in my later years when the club was going down the financial drain and the administration was desperately trying to keep players from leaving.

So, as a man in my 30s, being treated like that didn't make any sense to me at all. It also stopped us from taking responsibility when the side wasn't performing well. If we had no say, we didn't own the problem.

Surely it would be productive to set up a system where the coaches met regularly with the senior leaders of the team? I knew many of my teammates were capable of making worthwhile contributions to the way the team operated; they wanted to, but were never asked.

If I was coach, I wanted players to feel empowered and have more of a vested interest in their team, the way we trained and played, and the standards we set.

Motivate players by being positive.

When coaches criticised me – which wasn't uncommon, of course – I learned early on that it was more effective if they also gave me a piece of positive feedback as well.

I knew it wasn't possible for a coach to always look at the world through rose-coloured glasses, but there had to be a balance between constructive criticism and positive reinforcement. Again, it was about building relationships and treating players with respect.

Team bonding and camaraderie is important for a winning team.

During my time at Fitzroy, from 1980 to 1994, we had some of the worst facilities in the competition. But there was a great group of people at the club and we were a close-knit bunch. That unity helped us overcome challenges. We wanted to play with each other, and we wanted to help each other out on the field.

It was the same when I went to Sydney at the end of 1994. Most players came from interstate and were living away from extended family and friends. We supported each other, the young players and the older ones, and I saw how important that unity was as we defied the critics to make the Grand Final in 1996.

My list of coaching notes contained 25 points in all, though a few of them are closely related. The first 24 were written in October 1998, and the final one was added after a trip to the US in 1999.

Here is the full list:

1. Always remember to enjoy what you're doing.
2. Coach's attitude will rub off on the players.
3. If coach doesn't appear happy/relaxed, players will adopt same mentality.
4. Never lose sight of the fact it is a game of football.
5. Coach's job is to set strategies: team plans, team rules, team disciplines, specific instructions to players.
6. Good communication skills.
7. Treat people as you would want to be treated yourself.
8. Positive reinforcement to players.
9. Players don't mean to make mistakes – don't go out to lose.
10. 42 senior players – all different personalities, deal with each one individually to get the best out of him.
11. Never drag a player for making a mistake.
12. Don't overuse interchange.
13. Players go into a game with different mental approach (1998 season coming on and off the bench).
14. Enjoy training.
15. Make players accountable for training, discipline, team plans – it is their team too.
16. Weekly meetings with team leaders.
17. Be specific at quarter, half, three-quarter time by re-addressing strategies – don't just verbally abuse.
18. Motivate players by being positive.

19. After game don't fly off the handle. If too emotional, say nothing, wait until Monday.
20. Surround yourself with coaches and personnel you know and respect.
21. Be prepared to listen to advice from advisers.
22. Keep training interesting and vary when necessary.
23. Team bonding and camaraderie is important for a winning team.
24. Make injured players feel as much a part of the team as possible (players don't usually make up injuries).
25. Training should be game-related (e.g. San Francisco 49ers, backs versus forwards, training against clock).

I put the list in my desk drawer for safe keeping, unsure when, or if, I'd ever need it. At that stage of my life, coaching was still nothing more than a list of ideas and theories, several years away from being tested.

CHAPTER 2

Taking tips from the pros

Whyat is the best thing an American sports fan and recently retired Australian footballer could do with his time?

In 1999, the year after I finished my 18-year playing career at Fitzroy and the Swans, I had my own version of a gap year. I'd promised Tami that we'd spend time with her family when my career ended, so we packed up our house and, with our two young sons, Dylan and Tyler, we relocated to the US.

It wasn't only about family fun. I also used the visit as an opportunity to do a study tour of some of the most famous NBA (basketball) and NFL (gridiron football) sporting clubs in the US. Sports there were already fully professional and years ahead of Australia in terms of player development, training routines, match analysis, recruitment and facilities.

In the 1990s, the main football codes in Australia were in the process of transition from semi-professional to fully professional.

For example, during my time at Fitzroy from 1980 to 1994, I'd been to uni for a short time, and then worked in insurance, sales and real estate. When I came to play for the Sydney Swans in late 1994, it was the first time I didn't have to work outside football, though that still wasn't the case for all players.

However, times were changing. By the late 1990s, very few players had to supplement their income with extra employment outside football.

If players and coaches were going to be full-time professionals, what would our week and our year look like? What could we achieve that we had not had time for previously? If we were going to devote so much extra time to football, it needed to be productive.

Going to the US and visiting top NFL clubs such as the Denver Broncos, the San Diego Chargers, the San Francisco 49ers and the Chicago Bears, as well as NBA clubs including the LA Lakers and Chicago Bulls, would give me a glimpse into the future.

I had my own views on how a professional environment at an AFL club could be structured, but I wanted to test those out against the reality of life at the premier American clubs.

I had a few contacts in US sport and they really helped open doors. One of these was Darren Bennett, who had played for the West Coast Eagles and Melbourne in the early 1990s.

Darren was a close friend of my former Swans teammate Kevin Dyson, as they had previously played together at Melbourne. Kevin gave me Darren's number and I got in touch with him.

Darren had gone to the US in 1994, where he did a trial at the San Diego Chargers and his kicking was so impressive they put him on the roster. Darren played for the Chargers from 1994 to 2003 and became one of the best punters in the NFL during that time. He was named in the NFL's 1990s All Decade team and was later named in the Chargers' Hall of Fame.

He organised for me to meet senior coaches and fitness staff at the Chargers.

I was also fortunate to have an opportunity to meet key staff at the LA Lakers, arranged through my old Fitzroy teammate Brett Stephens. Brett was working as fitness coach with US tennis champion Pete Sampras, who was a massive Lakers fan and had some great connections within the organisation. Through Brett and Pete, I was able to spend time at the Lakers.

During the visit I ran into their legendary coach, Phil Jackson, who was in the gym. Phil was most accommodating, as he had coached Luc Longley (the first Australian to play in the NBA) and Luc had introduced Phil to Australian Rules football, so he knew a bit about our game.

I had a great experience at the Lakers, and meeting Jackson, though it was only for 15 minutes, was a highlight.

As far as coaches go, Jackson was the top of the tree in my eyes. His books on coaching and teamwork had a strong influence on me. Jackson also applied holistic and spiritual elements to his coaching, another aspect of his leadership that appealed to me.

Jackson was the coach who famously taught Michael Jordan, the greatest basketball player ever, to be a team player when they were together at the Chicago Bulls. Jordan could do everything on a court. Like a lot of athletes who are supremely talented and a notch or two above everyone else, he had a tendency to be a one-man show. Most don't know any other way – they can do it all, so why wouldn't they?

Jackson got in Jordan's ear at the Bulls and convinced him that being a team player would be far more beneficial in the long run for his own career and legacy. The logic went like this: it's great to be a superstar, but it doesn't mean that much if you don't win titles.

Jackson persuaded Jordan to bring his teammates into the game and be part of a culture where every player on the court had a contribution to make, even if Jordan had more talent in his little finger than they did in their whole bodies.

Jackson's message resonated with me, because I know it's human nature for elite players in any sport to be a bit selfish – there are very few players who are naturally completely selfless. The trick is convincing them what is best for the team is also best for them.

Jackson's way acknowledged the individual but took that to a higher level where the individuals together became a stronger unit. For Jordan to be the greatest player of all time, he needed his teammates.

In the Bulls' case, it paid off handsomely. Under Jackson, and with Jordan in the side, they won six NBA titles – in 1991, 1992 and 1993, and then in 1996, 1997 and 1998. We all know how hard it is to achieve 'three-peats' in any elite competition and the Bulls did it twice.

Jackson then went on to coach the LA Lakers and was at the helm when they won five titles between 2000 and 2010. He holds the NBA record for the most combined championships as a player and a head coach – two as a player and 11 as a coach, for 13 titles in total.

The coach's mantra about team play was key for Michael Jordan, who would later be quoted saying, 'Talent wins games, but teamwork and intelligence wins championships'.

It certainly rang true for me in the context of the AFL. The players considered the best in the competition were generally those who had been part of premierships. A title elevates a player. Conversely, the great players who were never part of winning teams have always had a question mark over their career.

Clearly basketball is different from football because there

are only five players on court at a time, while in footy there are 22 in the team, but the principle was the same. I really believed that a team-first attitude was the best way to win titles, and you didn't need to be chock-full of superstars to achieve it.

The greatest challenge for any AFL coach, from my experience, was to get 22 players to unite as a collective and play together.

Jackson's approach was pivotal as I mulled over how you would get everyone, even the players who dominated, to play for the team. How do you convince them to forgo a few possessions or a goal to actually make the team better? That was the psychological side of football and meeting Jackson cemented the impact he'd already had on my thinking.

But my trip to the US was also informative when it came to more technical aspects of the game, notably training and technology. The technology used in America at the time was sci-fi stuff compared to what we were doing at home in Australia.

I was able to sit with assistant coaches and watch them analyse games via computer in real time as they were fed copious amounts of data about their players. Nothing like that was happening in Australia, where statistical analysis was still basic.

But the real eye-opener for me was the way teams conducted their training sessions. I watched the San Francisco 49ers train with a purpose and intent I'd never seen before. Their sessions were conducted with military precision.

They started with small groups of players, just the linebackers together, and then the running backs together, followed by the wide receivers. As training progressed, they built up to full game simulation and it was spectacular to watch.

At that stage, training in Australia was not a lot more organised than kick-to-kick, circle work and lane drills. The first session of the week, on a Tuesday night, was focused on running, and the training was often harder than games.

The emphasis was on fitness and there was very little footy practice related to strategy or any sort of game plan. The best teams were those with the fittest, most talented players. At Fitzroy, our coach Robert Walls had introduced innovative kick-in drills, but until the 1990s most coaches didn't have a lot of time to come up with tactics.

When I watched teams train in the US, it prompted so many ideas. I realised we could put a lot more time into organising training, giving it real substance.

The American clubs were filming their training sessions and their drills were specifically designed to replicate moves they wanted to make during games. We hadn't been doing that at all.

Everything was aimed at improving their skill level or their ability to make important plays at critical times in a contest. At the 49ers, training was structured down to the last minute. After 45 minutes, the full offence was playing against the full defence. Everything was planned and had a purpose. There was no wasted time. When the whistle went, they all knew where to go.

I remember shaking my head, blown away by how efficient their sessions were. They knew exactly what they were doing and what they wanted to achieve from every session.

It made a huge impression on me and I knew we could make training in Australia much more effective. After visiting the 49ers, I scribbled a 25th and final point on the coaching notes I'd written the previous year: **Training should be game-related (e.g. San Francisco 49ers, backs vs forwards, training against clock).**

I also visited the Chicago Bears, who trained at a facility worth $80 million. It had two outdoor fields – one was heated – and an indoor field with cameras at both ends. The vision feeds went straight back to their IT guys, who made them available for the coaches to analyse.

We were never going to have facilities like the Bears, but that wasn't the point. These experiences led me to two conclusions. The first was that we should be training as we wanted to play. The second was that development of players could be fast-tracked if we filmed training sessions. Players would be more accountable and the vision could be used as a learning tool.

I knew that in the future training could no longer be mainly a fitness exercise. We had to start treating it as the players' version of the classroom, where we could demonstrate and educate. Training, and any time spent at the club during the week, needed to have a teaching component. That way we'd get a lot more out of it than we had in the past.

There was still more to learn from my US tour. A meeting with the recruiters at the Denver Broncos NFL team also had a huge impact on my philosophies.

For several years, I'd believed clubs should consider a young man's character, as well as his football talent, when assessing potential players through the draft or trades. I'm not just talking about talent. I'm talking about work ethic, honesty and discipline.

It was an idea formed during my years at Fitzroy where, by lucky coincidence as much as anything, we had an outstanding bunch of players. When I started at the Lions, the senior players such as captain Garry Wilson, Bernie Quinlan and Laurie Serafini, all trained very hard and set an example for the team to follow.

A few years ago, David Parkin, who was my coach from 1986 to 1988, wrote an article about the Fitzroy players and his time at the club. Parkin, who coached Hawthorn and then Carlton to a total of four premierships, said his Fitzroy experience was one of his best even though he didn't coach the team to a flag. What he loved about the club was working with a high-quality group of players, and he listed how many Fitzroy players had gone on to become successful in business or in the football industry after they finished playing.

Of course, I'd also seen a number of guys at Fitzroy who were hugely talented but didn't have any discipline and it was the same at every club. The senior players tried to help, but nothing was effective if they didn't have a strong work ethic and their own drive and determination.

The Denver Broncos were in the midst of a hugely successful run when I visited the club in 1998. They had won the Superbowl in January 1998, beating the Green Bay Packers, and they were to go on and defend their title, beating the Atlanta Falcons in January 1999.

Their recruiters knew how to build a winning team and I wanted to find out as much as I could about their approach.

The Broncos' scouting director during those two Superbowl victories was Ted Sundquist, and he supervised both pro and college recruiting. He landed some great players for the Broncos and had a reputation for being very active in drafting, signing free agents and trading players.

When I asked how much weight they gave to a footballer's character, as opposed to pure athletic talent, the Broncos staff were blunt – they valued character very highly. If they had two guys who were similar athletically, the Broncos would always go for the one with better character.

They sought players who'd been dux of the class, scholarship holders, or heavily involved in the community. They tried to build their team around those players, even though the NFL environment was often egotistical and individualised.

It was common sense that character should be part of the criteria, but for so long football scouting in Australia had been dominated by talent and tradition. It was easy to forget how important work ethic was and turn a blind eye to that trait when a talented larrikin came along.

It was powerful to hear how deeply the Broncos delved into a guy's college degree, what he was studying, what he did outside college and the people he hung around with. They showed me hard evidence of the benefits of that policy and it validated what I had been thinking.

That became another pivotal moment for me. By the end of the year, I knew our training and coaching had to have a much stronger focus on educating players. And before those players came to the club, their character should be a key consideration in drafting and trading discussions.

It was time to head back to Australia. In 2000, I took a role as a part-time defensive coach at the Swans, under Rodney Eade, and I also worked as a host on the Sydney Olympics coverage for the Seven Network.

I was still tossing up whether I would pursue coaching or the media more seriously, but I was leaning towards coaching. I enjoyed creating dossiers for the players, providing them with detailed information on their own strengths and weaknesses, and their upcoming opponents. The education side of coaching appealed, and in 2001 the Swans' deputy CEO, Col Seery, offered me a full-time assistant coaching role.

Treat people as you would want to be treated yourself.

Many of the guys I had played with at the Swans were still on the list, so it was interesting to transition from teammate to coach. Coaches had mostly been combative during my time, but I believed that wasn't the best approach in the modern era, and particularly as the players knew me so well.

I was close with many of them. I couldn't just say, 'I'm a coach now, I can't be your mate.' I didn't want to take on the hard-nosed persona of so many coaches. Obviously, I was no longer one of the boys, but I wanted to retain my strong relationships with the players. My view was that we were in this together, and 'coach versus players' wouldn't work.

I decided the key to my new role as a full-time assistant coach was to be true to my values. If the players did like me, that was great, but my main aim was to coach them fairly, to be honest and respectful with them.

Good communication skills.

When I was a player, it was frustrating that 'Joe the Boot-studder' would come and say you might be dropped that week, or tell you that one of the coaches reckoned you'd played like a busted arse.

The communication had to be better than that, and it had to be face-to-face.

The 2001 season was a roller-coaster. We won the first three games, beating the Adelaide Crows, West Coast Eagles and the Kangaroos. Then we lost five games in a row, won a few more, then finished in a slump, losing three of the last four home and away games.

We finished seventh, with 12 wins, and scraped into the finals. We played Hawthorn, but were up against it. Our midfield was anything but fighting fit – Daryn Cresswell had a fractured bone in his hand, Paul Williams had a fractured bone in his foot and captain Paul Kelly had hamstring niggles. By half time Kel had strained his hamstring and was out of the game. The Hawks ran over the top of us in the second half and thrashed us by 55 points.

You could feel the pressure building at the end of 2001, especially around Rodney Eade. He'd done a fantastic job since he was appointed in 1996 and had taken us to the Grand Final in his first year. There had been so many high hopes, but we hadn't been able to reach another decider. So, it was one more year without that elusive flag.

The struggle to win premierships changes people. The tensions were coming to the surface. Over the previous year or two, Rodney's coaching style had altered, and I could understand why that happened. When he'd arrived at the club, he was a breath of fresh air, but losing the 1996 Grand Final naturally affected his mood.

He gradually became tougher on the players. In round five of 1998, we were eight goals up at three-quarter time in a game against the Bulldogs, but they rallied and we won by only two goals. After the game, he wouldn't let us sing the song. When we got into the showers, I thought, *stuff that*, and I started singing 'Cheer, cheer, the red and the white', and all the boys joined in.

I believed you had to respect the competition and value winning, no matter the margin. It was very hard to win any game, and we'd got there, even if it wasn't pretty. Even Rocket had to laugh as we came out of the showers.

But after another frustrating season in 2001, he was doing it tough. There was no discontent from the players, no talking behind closed doors, but he was putting pressure on himself, and he was feeling it from the club administration.

They were panicking. We had good players such as Paul Kelly and Andrew Dunkley nearing retirement, and we hadn't won a premiership. AFL football can be a combustible beast, especially if success doesn't come easily. It's like the kettle has been turned on, it's boiled and liquid is spurting from the spout but it hasn't been turned off to release the pressure. It just keeps boiling and boiling, and the heat keeps rising and rising.

That is what happens for a coach if you get close but don't win a premiership, and that was the situation at the Swans.

Part Two

2002–2005
The Bloods Rule

CHAPTER 3
Catapulted into coaching

Sunday morning, 16 June 2002. The Swans had lost to Geelong at the SCG the previous day. We'd been four goals up in the last quarter, and then Geelong kicked five goals. We went down by two points. That made it six losses in a row. It was a perfect storm in footy terms.

The players were called in to the club early on Sunday morning. Coach Rodney Eade was not in a friendly mood. 'Okay guys, we're doing the scarecrow.'

The scarecrow was a challenge I'd rarely seen since the early 1980s, when our coach at Fitzroy, Robert Walls, used to dole out the physical punishment after a bad day.

The scarecrow goes like this – you all stand there holding your arms straight out sideways from your body, and you can't let them droop. The pain starts in your neck and shoulders, and pretty soon it burns badly. Guys eventually collapse down onto their knees, with their heads on the ground, but still holding their arms up. If your arms sag, you're out. Footballers are competitive by nature, and no one wants to be the first one to give in. It usually takes about 15 minutes until there is only one man left, and he takes the dubious honour of being the winner. The Swans players were not happy about doing the scarecrow on a Sunday.

They weren't even supposed to be at the club. They were due to have the week off, as we had a mid-season bye the following weekend. Adam Goodes was heading interstate to see family, and other players had organised a few days out of town. But the loss to the Cats had stung the club administration and the coach, and the mood in the rooms after the match was edgy and tense. I recall the CEO at the time, Kelvin Templeton, a former star player at Footscray and the 1980 Brownlow Medallist, told Rodney Eade the players should train the next morning as punishment.

As an assistant coach, I was in the meeting. All the coaching staff protested, but the club's management held firm, so Rodney called the training session.

At a club function later that night, I remember talking to a couple of the senior players, including Stuart Maxfield. They were blunt – they weren't going to turn up the next day. This was as close to player revolt as I'd seen since I joined the Swans at the end of 1994.

I was equally blunt in return. I said, 'Whatever you do, whether you agree with it or not, you better show up.'

Thankfully they turned up, but the players felt it was a knee-jerk reaction from the club and not the way to turn around their form. I could see their point of view and, to be honest, I don't think Rodney really wanted to haul them in either.

As they toughed out the pain of the 'scarecrow', I remember thinking that nothing good was going to come from this exercise. It was going to turn out badly.

And sure enough . . .

Ever since the start of season 2002, there had been signs of fracture at the club. I knew a fair bit about fractured football clubs due to my last eight years at Fitzroy. Late in the 1986 season, with the club carrying huge debts, we were faced with the choice of merging with a Melbourne-based club or relocating to Brisbane to become the Brisbane Lions. The players were keen on heading to Brisbane because we could stay together.

As it happened, that deal fell through. The next decade was a constant struggle for the Fitzroy Football Club and all involved. Our facilities were sub-standard. Promises from club bosses of better days just around the corner were never fulfilled.

It was a downward spiral. By the early 1990s, champion Fitzroy players like Gary Pert and Johnny Blakey had been discarded and loyalty was a long-forgotten concept. There were constant contract disputes and concerns we wouldn't get paid. At the end of 1994, I'd finally had enough and accepted a contract with the Swans.

The atmosphere at the Swans in early 2002 was nowhere near as dire as those Fitzroy days, but there were similarities. In particular, there was a lack of unity and divisions were creeping in. It wasn't the fault of any one person, but the lack of success since the Swans' Grand Final appearance in 1996 was causing frustrations to boil over.

There were competing ideas and philosophies and people were pulling in different directions. As well, differences inside the club were being played out in the public eye through the media. A number of things that should have been kept behind closed doors were leaked to football journalists.

Rodney's contract was due for renewal at the end of 2002 and there were persistent questions from the media about his future. Chairman Richard Colless had refused to guarantee Eade a contract extension.

For years, I'd believed a coach had a shelf life at one club of seven or eight years, an idea that really gelled when I wrote my coaching notes in 1998. Rocket had started coaching the Swans in 1996, so that made 2002 his seventh year at the helm. No matter who the coach is or how good they are, it's generally time for fresh ideas and a fresh voice. Leigh Matthews, who played in four premierships and coached four, has expressed a similar view.

Rodney had done a fantastic job. He had come to the club at the end of 1995 when we'd finished 12th, with eight wins for the year. He had taken us to the Grand Final the following year and we'd played finals every year except 2000.

Rodney had been very upbeat in his early days as coach of the Swans. Every time we walked into the rooms before a game, he'd joke and communicate with every player. Several points on my coaching notes were a direct result of his manner when he first started – in particular, that **a coach's attitude will rub off on players.**

He was a brilliant strategist and had an extraordinary ability to read the game from the coaches' box. He had introduced multiple midfield rotations and at times we'd won games simply because he'd created so much confusion for opposition coaches. His football brain was razor-sharp.

Rocket, as we called him, had a terrific run but just couldn't get the team over the hump, couldn't win a premiership. His general mood had darkened during the previous couple of years. At times, he delivered vicious sprays to players who he thought had stuffed up, and it was clear the pressure was getting to him. I remember half a dozen times he would start or finish a speech by saying, 'I'm not here to make friends.' I worried he was spoiling some of the great relationships he had built at the club.

The start of season 2002 was hectic in lots of ways. The big news was that Tony 'Plugger' Lockett was making a comeback. At 36 years of age, the greatest goal-kicker ever had decided he had more football left in him. He'd retired at the end of 1999, the season he kicked his 1300th career goal and broke Gordon Coventry's 62-year-old goal-kicking record. Now he was back.

He wasn't our only big, bustling forward at the start of that year. Barry Hall, like Plugger before him, had been traded to the Swans from St Kida. A junior boxing champion, Barry had a formidable reputation as an on-field hard man. So now we had two imposing spearheads.

We started the season against the defending premiers, Brisbane, up at the Gabba. It was a tough ask and Plugger's comeback was derailed when he suffered a corked thigh that was so bad he couldn't walk. But Hall was proving his worth. He bagged four goals in the loss to Brisbane and seven in a round two thrashing of Carlton.

Captain Paul Kelly, the heartbeat of the side, was back after a bad run of injuries. But he and Eade were not always seeing eye to eye as the coach tried playing him in the forward line rather than the midfield.

We had an inconsistent start to the season with three wins, two losses, and a draw against St Kilda from the first six weeks.

Then it got worse. The defeats kept coming, week after week.

I could sense things were starting to go pear-shaped. The CEO was looking over his shoulder; the chairman was looking over his shoulder; the coach was worried about getting a new contract and whether he had the support of the board.

I learned early in my career that the CEO should be a CEO, the chairman should be chairman, the board is the board, the coach should be in charge of the team – and when it all gets mixed together that's when things fall apart.

If Richard Colless wasn't showing confidence in Rocket and Kelvin Templeton was not backing him either, then it became difficult for the coach to fulfil his role. The players aren't silly, they know when there's a lack of unity between the administration and the coach. The friction was palpable.

As the mistrust grew, Rocket wasn't communicating openly with the players. It seemed to me the players felt he was no longer their ally; he was the coach and they respected him, but he was no longer in it with them.

In his autobiography, *Swan Song*, Paul Kelly said that period was tough for the players. They were doing their best but kept 'snatching defeat from the jaws of victory'.

The media scrutiny intensified and the tension rose. A destructive chain of events was unfolding.

When I look back, Rocket's biggest mistake was that he didn't leave before the season started. He had several opportunities to coach elsewhere. He has since said that, in hindsight, he'd probably run his race with the Swans at the end of 2001 but didn't take up an offer from Fremantle because he believed he should serve out his contract in Sydney.

Timing is everything in football . . . and it was reaching midnight for Rodney.

A week after the scarecrow session and the bye, we were back at the club preparing for our round 13 match against Fremantle.

I was sitting in my office on Monday when I had a phone call from Channel 10 sports reporter Stephen Quartermain, who said he'd heard Rocket was going to give it away and I was probably going to take over. It was news to me.

Then the phone rang and it was my great friend Johnny Blakey, who at the age of 36 was still playing for North Melbourne. 'The big story down here in Melbourne is that Rocket is about to give it away,' Johnny told me.

Rodney was in the next office to mine, but outsiders knew before me. That typified what was going on at the club at the time.

There was only one thing to do. I walked into Rocket's office and said, 'Mate, I've just had two phone calls . . . Are you giving it away?' He told me it was true, he was resigning.

Rocket had planned to tell the players the next morning, but the word was out. Paul Kelly and most of the players found out when they got home from training that night. He was the captain and he had teammates ringing him to ask what was going on. He had to ring a club official himself to find out.

As Kel said at the time, it really would have been much better to hear it directly from the coach. Once again, confidentiality was broken, news had leaked from the club and the divisions were laid bare.

It was a momentous day, as Tony Lockett also announced that his comeback was over. He had managed only three games and was giving it away after a discussion with deputy CEO Col Seery.

A press conference with Rodney Eade, Richard Colless and Kelvin Templeton was held the next day to announce what everyone already knew.

Later, Richard was insistent that Rodney had resigned – he had decided to jump before he was pushed. There was no doubt about Rodney's tactical nous, but the chairman felt they needed a coach with different personal skills.

The board was going to consider all options over the next few months. But who was going to coach the team for the rest of the season?

The three assistant coaches, Steve Malaxos, John Longmire and I, met with Col Seery. We thought about rotating the coaching role for the rest of the year, but eventually they asked me to do it.

I had a decision to make and, momentous as it was, it had to be made quickly. Richard Colless made it clear there were no long-term guarantees – the appointment was only until the end of the season.

I spent hours discussing it with my wife Tami. I would be taking on a team that wasn't high on confidence, with only three wins from the first 12 rounds. There was a question mark over their talent level. It was a big gamble. If things went well, this could be the start of my coaching career. If they didn't go well, my reputation could be tarnished and my coaching career could be over in 10 weeks. If I really wanted to be a coach, was I actually jeopardising my chances by stepping in as interim coach?

In the end, I was swayed by the strong relationships I had with the players. I'd played with many of them and we were close. I decided to give it a go. I'd been an assistant coach for 18 months and now I was taking the mantle.

As is the case whenever a coach leaves mid-season, there was a bit of a shambles. I turned to my sheet of paper. My coaching notes, written nearly four years before, were about to be put to the test.

Always remember to enjoy what you're doing.
Good communication skills.
Positive reinforcement to players.
Never drag a player for making a mistake.

That's where I started. Just a few days away from playing the Fremantle Dockers at the SCG, I didn't have time to implement new game plans or strategies. It was simply going to be about mindset, attitude, teamwork and relationships.

The crux was the environment and the energy I wanted to bring, the energy the players would feed off. Would they go into games thinking, *Well, there's only 10 weeks to go, bugger it, we'll have a new coach next year anyway*? Or were they going to get energised by me?

At my first meeting with the playing group, I told them we weren't going to change much on the field. But I wanted the off-field atmosphere to be very different, to lighten the mood and make it positive.

'We need to enjoy what we're doing. We're playing footy, not splitting the atom,' I said. 'We need to want to come to work and have fun.'

My message was focused on building their confidence. I emphasised that I would back them – I wouldn't drag them off the field if they kicked the ball out of bounds on the full, or missed a goal.

That can sometimes be a challenge, but the coaching staff remained strong on it, refused to yell at them, and the players responded well. We wanted to correct the errors and teach those skills at training, rather than humiliating them and sapping their confidence during a game.

Taking over as coach at that stage of the season also gave me licence to play the younger guys, to get some fresh talent on the field and give them game time. Luke Ablett and Leo Barry came into the side and they relished the opportunity.

That first week, Paul Kelly said that the change had released a new energy and freedom among the players. Kel gave Rocket credit for bringing the club out of the wilderness, but said perhaps every coach has a use-by date.

The captain said the players felt enthusiasm and confidence they hadn't experienced for some time. In Kel's words, they went into the Freo match like excited kids, eager to get a win.

Gutsy midfielder Jude Bolton, still one of the emerging players at that stage, had been low on confidence. He was afraid of doing the wrong thing and it made him introverted on the field. Jude says it was a relief that we backed him to lift when he made a mistake, rather than benching him.

Brett Kirk, previously in and out of the team, began to thrive, as did Adam Goodes, who had been ridden hard by the coaches in previous seasons. It helped enormously that I already knew each of the players well and understood how to get the best out of them.

It wasn't a criticism of Rodney Eade that the players sparked. Whenever a coach is changed – it doesn't matter if he's been the most popular coach in history or the worst coach in history – there is a sense of newness, of excitement.

I wanted to try to harness that excitement and translate it into how the players performed in games. I wanted to hand them more responsibility, to see them pull together and realise their own power.

We beat Fremantle by 77 points in my first game as coach. A good start, though no one was getting carried away. We followed that up with three losses in a row, but we were competitive and the players had a more positive frame of mind. Then we beat Carlton, North Melbourne and St Kilda. In round 21, we played at the MCG against Melbourne, who were sitting sixth on the ladder and heading for finals footy.

We shocked the Demons with six goals in the first term and another six in the second. At half time, we were eight goals up. As the players were about to head back onto the field after the half-time break, I grabbed Kel and Daryn Cresswell, our other star midfielder. I drew them in close: 'Boys, if we can kick the first two or three goals here, we can go on with it. Kel, you can do it. Cressa, you can do it. Take charge!'

We went on to win by 11 goals. I focused on those one-on-one conversations with the key drivers in the team, persuading them they could make things happen and that they could influence others in the team.

But it wasn't just about the older players. I wanted every player to understand they were valued and could make an important contribution. They couldn't all be as talented as Kel or Cressa, but I wanted to help players bridge the gap, help them understand what role they could usefully play.

And then it was the last home and away game of the season, round 22 against Richmond at ANZ Stadium in Sydney. Kel had announced his retirement, as had Andrew Dunkley, our tenacious key defender who I'd played along-side in defence for four years. There was a lot of love for those two players. It was to be their last game and, as far as I knew, it could also be my last game as a coach.

Rumours had begun swirling that Western Bulldogs coach Terry Wallace – who still had two years left on his con-tract – had done a deal with the Swans and was going to be the next coach. And the rumours went into overdrive when, early in that week, Wallace shocked the footy world and stepped down as coach of the Dogs with one game left in the season. The Bulldogs made it plain they thought he had quit because he had another job lined up, and it did seem strange he would resign while still under contract if that wasn't the case.

However, the Swans management denied any deal. I was asked about it and replied honestly that I would be shattered if the Swans had already spoken to Terry directly, as chair-man Richard Colless had assured me that hadn't occurred.

The media asked Kel during the week if I should be appointed permanent coach, and he backed me for the job, but added that of course he didn't make the decision.

It was a challenging week, but I was determined to put all the speculation and distractions aside. I had to be single-minded, because my primary aim was to keep the team focused on sending Kel and Dunks off with a win and ending the season on a positive note.

We were down at half time against the Tigers, but I was confident the players would pull out something special for their retiring mates – two players who meant so much to the club. In the second half, we kicked 12 goals to Richmond's five and won by 40 points. We'd won six of the 10 games I'd coached, including five of the last six.

At the end of the game, Kel and Dunks walked a lap. It was their moment as they soaked up the adulation of the Swans fans. I was on the ground too, clapping as they finished their lap and walked back to where their teammates were waiting.

Then all of a sudden, I was in the middle of a mob of Swans players. I still don't know whose idea it was, as the players enveloped me and chanted '*Roooos*'. It took me completely by surprise. It was a funny moment in one way, being in the middle of a big group bear hug, and I was thinking, *What are these guys doing?*

It was surreal, but it was also moving. I'd really enjoyed coaching the group, and it seemed clear they too had gained a lot from the past 10 weeks.

But I didn't have much time to dwell on it or contemplate its significance. The talk and speculation about Terry Wallace continued in the media. I still had work to do, as our reserves were in the finals, and I'd organised a trip to Melbourne to watch a few finals games with some of the players as a way of furthering their footy education.

The club announced it would hold talks with Wallace as well as me and over the next 10 days I tried not to worry about it. I got on with the job of wrapping up the season, though it wasn't always straightforward.

A group of supporters started a campaign they called 'Choose Roos', and the local newspapers got behind it. In the second week of September, the fans came to the club and presented us with a petition signed by 700 people, urging the administration to retain me as coach.

It was flattering and showed a passion for the Swans among Sydney people that had not always been evident. But I still wasn't sure how it would pan out. And with the Swans unable to commit to me, I had to look at other options. My priority was the Swans job, but I also held informal talks with the Western Bulldogs.

We had a new football manager, Andrew Ireland, who had joined the Swans from Brisbane. A former Collingwood player, he had been the long-term CEO at the Lions and had helped steer them to their first premiership, in 2001. They were looking good for back-to-back flags, and Andrew had been lured to the Swans by Richard Colless.

I didn't know Andrew well, but we held discussions about the job, and then I was given a challenging task – if I wanted to be considered, I would have to front the board and present a long-term vision for the club.

After my 10-week stint as coach, I wanted to go on with it. I'd had the chance to put a few of my ideas into action, and I had a healthy rapport with the players. I could see there was enormous potential in the group. I truly thought we could achieve something together, and that drove me to pull out all stops to get the job.

I had a couple of days to put together the very first PowerPoint presentation of my life, outlining my vision for the Sydney Swans . . . a club which had not won a premiership since 1933, 69 long years ago.

CHAPTER 4

The manifesto

I was faced with a challenging task if I wanted to become the next coach of the Sydney Swans. To be honest, I'd much rather spend an afternoon trying to beat Wayne Carey to the ball than grappling with a computer and putting together a PowerPoint presentation.

But it had to be done, so I turned to Anthony Cahill, the head of IT at the club – a former school teacher and a very smart man with an amazing IT brain. He's also a really knowledgeable football person. Over two days, he worked hard to help me transform my ideas into a manifesto for the Sydney Swans' future. His assistance showed me the strength of the relationships I already had with the fantastic staff at the club.

As I look back now, I'm glad the Swans' board wanted me to present my coaching vision. I knew we needed significant change and I had so many thoughts running around in my head. Setting it out in a presentation clarified my opinions about pre-season training, about developing players, about recruiting. My ideas were translated into a logical, clear action plan. It gave me a guide for the road ahead.

It had taken about 15 hours to put together the 47-slide presentation covering coaching philosophy, training philosophy, game plan, recruiting and business plan.

It talked about areas where we needed to improve, looked at the individual players and the way we wanted to play. I tried to set out where we were at the end of 2002, where we wanted to get to and how we could get there.

The title was simple: 'Sydney Swans, 2003 and Beyond'.

I arrived at the Swans' headquarters on Driver Avenue at the SCG on Monday, 16 September and went to the boardroom to present to the coaching sub-committee – Chairman Richard Colless, Colin Seery, who had been elevated to CEO, Ricky Quade, who was on the board and had previously coached and played for the Swans, and our new head of football, Andrew Ireland.

This is the first time I've publicly revealed the contents of this key document, which outlined in detail the path we would take to transform the team.

The first page was titled 'Vision' and contained a clear statement of my intent.

> My aim is to inspire, teach
> and lead the Sydney Swans
> to become winners!

In the introductory slides I went through my record as a player. A total of 356 games, five best and fairest awards; captain of Fitzroy, captain of Victoria, and twice named All-Australian captain. Next I outlined my coaching experience, and tried to show that, while I might be a fledgling coach, I'd worked hard to broaden my knowledge.

I detailed my visits to major sporting organisations in the US, to the Denver Broncos and San Francisco 49ers, among others. I spoke about the Australian football coaching clinics I'd conducted in America. And I couldn't leave out a little-known fact – my very first coaching gig was in 1999, in charge of the US Australian Football Association National Team against Canada, in Chicago. (We won.)

My competitor for the Swans job, Terry Wallace, had been an AFL coach for six and a half years, taking over the Western Bulldogs job halfway through 1996 when Alan Joyce was sacked. Wallace had quickly rebuilt the Dogs and coached them to preliminary finals in 1997 and 1998, and they also played finals in 1999 and 2000. I was up against a coach with big runs on the board.

When I did that study tour to the US in 1999, there were very few coaches in Australian football who had gone overseas to observe and learn from other professional sports.

Those experiences had been invaluable to me and were instrumental in shaping my ideas about the future of coaching and team success. I wanted to impress upon them that I might not have the experience of Terry, but I had a point of difference and didn't want to do things the way they'd always been done. I had new ideas and plans.

I moved on to my General Philosophy for the club.

United
Everyone on board
All involved
All have an important role
All heading in the same direction

> **Excellence**
> Lead by example
> No shortcuts
> Attention to detail
> Desire for success

The first thing I wanted to emphasise was that the club had to be united to make real progress. There was no doubt there had been significant divisions during the past two seasons. I'd lived through the dark days of a flailing footy club at Fitzroy and seen coaches come and go, trying desperately to turn things around.

It had forged my belief that just appointing a new coach wasn't going to make the difference. You had to have common purpose and synergy between the chairman, the CEO, the football manager and the coach. Everyone in the room that day knew it too.

Richard Colless had been chairman of the club since 1993. He took over at the lowest ebb – the Swans finished last on the ladder in 1992, 1993 and 1994 – and he had led the club out of that quagmire. We'd made the Grand Final in 1996, but hadn't reached the pinnacle. Season 2002 had been especially frustrating and worrying for Richard and he knew better than anyone that we had to heal the fractures.

Towards the end of Rodney Eade's time as coach, there was interference from the administration in the running of the team. At one stage, the then CEO, Kelvin Templeton, had come down to training to take marking practice. Kelvin was a former Brownlow Medallist and one of the best centre half-forwards of all time. But for him to leave his upstairs office and appear at training was unsettling and unnerving for the coaches and players. The intentions were good, everyone was desperate to win a premiership, but we were divided about the best way forward.

That sort of thing had to stop. There would be rough times ahead – all football clubs ride a roller-coaster – but if I was to become coach, everyone had to look after their own job and be as one. We had to ride the roller-coaster together.

The 'Choose Roos' campaign at the end of the season was a sign of the public and player support for me to be appointed coach, and helped convince the board I could be a uniting force for the club.

I spoke about attention to detail, and leaving no stone unturned to create an environment where excellence was the minimum standard.

In the US, I'd witnessed the incredibly professional standard of training and analysis. There was so much more we could do to improve. I spoke about changing the way we trained, breaking down our drills so they were more targeted and skill-oriented. We had to use our time more effectively to develop every player on our list.

Developing a strong club culture
Sense of belonging
Sense of history
Pride in working for the Swans
Positive environment

I also wanted to forge a culture where players didn't take shortcuts, but committed themselves to every aspect of the program. When I began playing in the early 1980s, you had to take shortcuts in your preparation because you couldn't do it all – you worked outside football, so there was no way you could go to the physio, get massage, do your weights, do all the training you should.

Now we had the time, so we talked about how a week would look for a fully professional footballer. The coach had to set the scene, to show guys what a professional athlete looked like.

Culture was not a word often used in football clubs at that time, but it was about to become a buzz word.

Until the 1990s, the AFL had largely been a talent-based competition. The teams with the superstar players would generally win. But with the competition evened out by the draft and the salary cap, clubs were looking to find an edge in other ways.

If we could establish great values, customs and habits at our club – a culture – that all the players bought into, surely it would forge a stronger club. That could give us an advantage over other teams.

We discussed building a culture where we maintained elite standards and kept each other honest, took no shortcuts and treated each other with respect.

Understanding and appreciating the history of the South Melbourne/Sydney Swans football club was integral to building a new culture.

In 2002, the players had a well-equipped, professional workplace, which was a far cry from the conditions experienced by the Swans players who had been the pioneers in Sydney 20 years before. Their club had been bitterly divided and during 1982 half of the players still lived in Melbourne and flew up for games.

Ricky Quade knew all this better than anyone. He finished playing in 1980 and was appointed coach at the end of 1981, trying to manage a team with players living in two different cities. Rick has described in the past how they were promised the world if they went to Sydney, but instead had a training ground with potholes and no gymnasium. Players were given the phone book and the newspaper classified section and told to find their own housing. Now our players were set up in houses, were paid well, and had all the support they needed.

It was a disjointed history, and we felt we were starting to lose this connection to the past, to South Melbourne and to champions like triple Brownlow Medallist Bobby Skilton, and 1970 Brownlow Medallist Peter Bedford.

We didn't want a squad of spoilt brats who were being provided with these fantastic facilities and opportunities but had no idea what came before them.

This idea resonated with Richard Colless, who often spoke of what he called 'the cause'. I didn't necessarily agree with the term, but I agreed with his philosophy. Of course great athletes pushed themselves, but their ambition could reach greater heights if they were playing for something bigger than themselves. It would become more than just me, me, me.

We wanted players to understand the Swans' history and, by doing that, start to work together with a common purpose and direction. At a club that hadn't won a premiership since 1933, that could be a powerful driver if we got it right.

The players might respond well if they felt a greater sense of belonging, and had something to fight for. It had to be a privilege to wear the red and white jumper.

Encourage
Leaders
Positive reinforcement
Knowledge & understanding of the club

Confidentiality
Keep things in-house
Controlled access to the media

I spoke at length during my presentation about the need to develop more leaders among the playing group. It was three weeks since Paul Kelly and Andrew Dunkley had retired and there was talk of a leadership vacuum.

We could solve that problem if we got all the players more involved in shaping their club. It went back to my coaching notes: **Make players more accountable for training, discipline, team plans – it is their team too.**

I explained how I wanted to ask players what they wanted to achieve, and then honour and value their input. Players should have more ownership of discipline, game plan, meetings and training. We had to start treating the players as shareholders of the club, not just employees. I wanted to set things up so they would be invested in their club.

This was a new idea, but Richard Colless and the others in the room responded well. It aligned with Richard's 'cause' – if the players had a bigger say in the workings of the club, they would care more and be more wedded to it.

We then talked about confidentiality, which was a touchy subject. During 2002 there were endless leaks of information from the club to the media as relationships had soured. Everyone cared about the club but wanted to push their own agenda. We had to put an end to that. If we were to be united, it was vital to keep things in-house.

My next slides were about respect, loyalty and honesty – again getting back to the basics of my coaching notes: **Treat people as you would want to be treated yourself, no matter who they are or what role they are in.**

Our moral compass and radar had been askew in that tumultuous time during 2002. The fundamental human values can get lost in a high-pressure environment like a football club. I was saying, 'Just because we're a football club it doesn't mean we lie to each other or talk behind people's backs or don't look people in the eye and tell them they're in or out of the team.'

We had to strip the club right back and decide what we stood for. Forget wins and losses – what kind of values and behaviour did we want to have at our football club? We had to reshape our football club, rebuild the culture and make those traits a priority.

There had been a few media stories questioning whether the club was honest with me about their dealings with Terry Wallace. I believed what Richard and Andrew had told me, but we needed to reaffirm that those values would be at the core of our relationships if I was appointed coach.

Then it was time to get down to the nitty gritty – my Coaching Philosophy.

Provide inspiration
Face of the club
Coaches and players set the tone
Coaches and match committee lead the club
Make tough decisions

Share and accept ideas
Players and staff to own the shared aims of the team
Greater interaction and input
Foster a challenging environment

Teaching Environment
Team training
Game plans
One-on-one skills
Individual player meetings
Football education

Identify weaknesses

Correct weaknesses

We were entering an era where the coach could no longer worry just about the football team. He had to be the face of the club, the public leader. I was prepared to take on that responsibility and make sure the players also did what was needed.

During my 10-week stint as interim coach, I had been very open with the players, telling them we had to work closely with sponsors and members and supporters. The reality was they made the money for us and we spent it, that's the way a footy club works. We had to respect where the money was coming from, and respect the people who made that possible.

However, we also had to be very focused on our main aim – to remember that winning football games was our chief priority.

I quoted Patrick Head from the Williams Formula One team: 'If we can be successful on the track, other things, particularly commercial aspects of the company, tend to look after themselves.'

We'd always meet our obligations to sponsors and corporate partners, but I believed they'd be more satisfied too if we were performing on the field.

One of my key points was that coaches had to start seeing ourselves as teachers, there to educate players. That would mean assessing the strengths and weaknesses of each individual player and working on whatever they most needed, be it marking, kicking, positional play, spoiling, or tackling.

I wanted to redefine what a coach and coaching group looked like, and I outlined how we would try to improve each and every single player on our list – again a reference to my coaching notes of 1998: **42 senior players – all different personalities, deal with each one individually to get the best out of him.**

Some aspects would be common to all. They must know the game plan, but when it came to coaching and teaching, midfielder Brett Kirk had different strengths and weaknesses to our key forward Barry Hall. We had to break it down and be more specific. There was no point training them exactly the same way. We had to make a measurable improvement in skill and learning during the time we spent with players, as teachers do with their students in a classroom.

I was interested in skill acquisition, in finding cutting-edge ways to improve skills and measure that gain. We had been to the Australian Institute of Sport and I wanted to see if any of their sports scientists could help us improve in this area.

I was also keen to see if we could devise drills to sharpen players' on-field decision-making. We had to start unpacking how to improve every skill a good player needed.

This was part of a pledge that as coaches we would have a thirst for new knowledge. We'd also be trying to reinforce our strengths and address our own weaknesses.

We were fortunate to be based in the Sydney Cricket Ground sporting precinct, which also includes the nearby rugby/rugby league/soccer stadium. In summer, we trained on the same field as the Sydney Roosters NRL team and the NSW Waratahs rugby union side.

All this made us open to outside influences. It seemed sensible to share knowledge and ideas, to learn from other professional sports if they were relevant.

After I took over from Rodney Eade mid-season, we had legendary rugby league coach Wayne Bennett come in and speak to the players. Our club doctor, Nathan Gibbs, was a former NRL player and he knew Wayne, who was coaching Queensland's State of Origin team at the time.

Wayne had an incredible effect on the players. It was like Clint Eastwood – one of my absolute heroes – had come to talk to the players. They were overawed.

He asked the players when the club had last won a premiership. Someone answered that it was back in 1933. In his laconic way, Bennett responded. 'Well, you must be doing something wrong then. You better start doing things differently, because what you've been doing hasn't been working that well.'

That message really hit home to the players. It was another sign that we needed to shake things up and reassess how we went about all aspects of our program.

I've since heard several players, including Paul Kelly and

Luke Ablett, comment on how significant Wayne Bennett's address was for them. Kel, who had played a lot of rugby league until he was 15, was like a little kid in his presence. Wayne asked him a question and Kel just froze, he was so in awe.

Wayne is an imposing figure with so much respect in the sporting world. He doesn't say much, but whatever he says makes sense and has a powerful impact. We couldn't have hoped for a better speaker. That talk was important in setting the environment for significant cultural change.

I also addressed my Training Philosophy. Not only did we have to be better teachers, but we also had to get better at analysing the game so we could make training more relevant.

I put up a slide illustrating how far and how fast Adam Goodes – then a very promising 22-year-old with 87 games under his belt – ran during an average game.

It showed Goodesy was covering around 13 kilometres per match and it was broken down into walking, jogging, striding, sprinting and maximum effort. He was walking for 3.5 kilometres, sprinting for 1.4 kilometres and at maximum effort he covered 1.3 kilometres.

I explained that from now on I wanted the work we did on the training track to relate directly to what a player needed to do during a game. It was the last point on my coaching notes:

Training should be game-related (e.g. San Francisco 49ers, backs v forwards, training against clock)

Our fitness department would be required to closely analyse games and devise a program so we weren't wasting time. If that was what Adam had to do during a match, we had better be training him so he was capable of that, and more. Again, training had to be more individualised because Adam's game running patterns were different from those of other players.

I broke training down into post-season, pre-Christmas,

post-Christmas and in-season and outlined how we would tackle each phase.

One of my bugbears was that too many players went away for the eight- or 10-week post-season break without a proper review of their standing. I wanted to send every player off with a clear idea of his strengths and weaknesses, plus a plan for him to follow during the break.

Of course they needed a rest, but they still had to come back in reasonable shape, ready to hit the track. It was time to change the mindset about the post-season break. Previously the pre-season had been focused on regaining fitness. But if we were to really improve on the field, I wanted players to come back ready to concentrate on skill development and game-related training.

It was then time to talk about my game plan. I outlined how I would mould a team that played one-on-one football, with every player accountable for his opponent. Every player had to contribute.

Pressure/Aggression (Finals Football)
Tackling (80% effective)
Hard ball gets

Hard Running/Superior Workrate
Handball receives (88–103 per game)
Uncontested marks (51–63 per game)

If that was our game plan, there were two fundamental skills that had to underpin it. I spoke to the sub-committee about 'ground balls' and 'tackling'. Tackling had always been a big part of the game but, in general, AFL players weren't particularly good tacklers. But in Sydney, we were surrounded by league and union players, and we saw how well they tackled. They really stopped opponents in their tracks. During the last part of season 2002 when I was in charge, our coaching group had started to analyse our tackling more closely. We broke it down to effective tackles, and non-effective tackles, where the opponent was tackled but still managed to break away or feed the ball to a teammate.

Once we'd analysed these stats, we put them against our win–loss record. We found that if 80 per cent of the tackles we laid were effective, then we won 80 per cent of the time. It was a significant correlation.

And there was a similar impact when it came to ground balls. It wasn't a phrase commonly used in the game at that time, but what we meant by that was picking up the ball and securing it, then passing off to a teammate.

The key was securing the ball and not fumbling it. Fumbling was a real curse. It was common sense in a way, but it had really struck me while I was watching a pre-season game at the start of 2002. I noticed that almost every time a player fumbled the ball, it led to a goal for the opposition or at least a scoring opportunity.

I logged the number of times our players fumbled the ball during a match. If we had 13 or fewer fumbles per game, then we also won 80 per cent of the time.

It all tied in with our one-on-one mentality. If we were going to play that style, we had to win our own ball and secure it. If a player fumbled, his teammate was more likely to be out of position, away from his opponent, because he'd anticipated receiving the ball. The fumble mucked up the chain.

If our opponents did get the ball and our player didn't make the tackle, it would put a lot of pressure on our defenders, because they were likely going to be one-out with their opponent and the ball could get through quickly.

Clean gathering of the ground balls and effective tackling would be our bread and butter. Those two stats were to become our key indicators in games for years to come – and something we carefully guarded from other clubs.

Those skills were the defensive basis, but on the offensive side I wanted us to work harder than other teams. I wanted to train the players so they could run harder, and for longer, than ever before, out-running their opponents and ensuring we always had numbers at the contest.

It had already started happening during the last 10 weeks of the season when I was stand-in coach. I pointed out that our handball receives – a measure of how much players run and help each other – had gone up in that period from 88 per game to 103 per game. Uncontested marking, where a player runs hard to get himself into space to receive the ball clear from any opponent, had also risen, from 51 to 63 per game. These were areas we could improve even further.

The game style I was proposing was going to be demanding. We weren't going to flood the backline, as was common among AFL teams of that time. Flooding is a term that describes when a team sends extra players into defence to crowd the opposition forward line and make it harder for them to score. Flooding teams don't tackle as much. They basically allow the ball to get down to the opposition forward line, and then try to have the weight of numbers to get it back. They often rely on a poor kick by the opposition landing in the lap of one of those extra numbers in the backline. I wanted our players to be right beside their opponents, and tackle them as soon as they got the ball, no matter where they were on the ground. Flooding teams don't try to tackle and get it back straight away, which was our game plan.

The figures I presented were a sign I wanted the team to be clean in their ball handling, to run and work hard offensively, and to tackle if we didn't have the ball. To be hard to play against. That summed up how I wanted to coach, because that was the football I believed won finals.

I also provided evidence that as a coaching group we'd work hard to prepare our players for games and give them strategies to counter the opposition's strengths.

At the back end of 2002, we'd won five of the last six games. We'd beaten Melbourne and North Melbourne, who both were about to play in the finals that year.

I explained the way we'd been able to nullify Melbourne's preferred way of playing, particularly at the kick-ins and the centre bounces, where they got an advantage from the ruck work of Jeff White. It had worked so well that their coach, Neale Daniher, said that after they played us they realised they were too one-dimensional.

I wanted our team to play a certain way, but also to take away two or three key strengths of the opposition. We had studied Melbourne, put strategies in place to counter them, and that resulted in a win for us. I wanted to show that I already had some runs on the board. While the main emphasis during my 10-week stint as interim coach had been to build the players' confidence, I'd also implemented a few basic game plan changes.

There were a multitude of ways we could improve the players on our list. As coaches, we would work tirelessly to better the hand we were dealt. But it was also vital that every year we used the recruiting period to add as much talent as possible.

I explained my views on recruiting, and started with a slide comparing our best 22 players to the standout team in the competition at the time, the Brisbane Lions.

B:	Fixter 6	Schauble 6	Barry 7
	Johnson 8	Michael 7	White 7
Hb:	Kennelly 6	Saddington 7	Mathews 7
	Scott 7	Leppitsch 8.5	Ashcroft 7
C:	Fosdike 7	Cresswell 7	Maxfield 7.5
	Pike 7	Black 9	Lappin 9
HF:	Bolton 5.5	Goodes 7.5	Nicks 6.5
	Headland 7.5	Brown 7.5	Power 7
F:	O'Loughlin 8	Hall 7.5	Stevens 5
	Hart 6.5	Lynch 8	Bradshaw 6
Ruck:	Doyle 6.5 / McDonald 6		
	Crouch 6.5 / Voss 10		
	Williams 9 / Akermanis 9		

I/C:	Ball 7	Seymour 6	Kirk 6	O'Keefe 6
	Charman 6	McCrae 6.5	Scott 6.5	Notting 7

The Lions, under coach Leigh Matthews, had won the 2001 premiership, and were raging favourites to go back-to-back in 2002. We needed a benchmark and there was none better than the Lions. How did our team compare to theirs, and how could we become not just as good as them, but better?

The Lions were an incredibly talented side. They had so many players I rated eight or above. Captain Michael Voss, a midfield machine, rated 10 in my book. The freakishly talented Jason Akermanis was a 9; Simon Black, one of the cleanest ball handlers in the game, was a 9, as was their other key midfielder, Nigel Lappin.

Their backline, led by Justin Leppitsch, rated 8.5, was hard, tough and creative. My old Fitzroy teammate, Alastair

Lynch, was the pivot at full-forward and rated 8. When I look back now, I probably under-rated a fair few of their players, as they were still in the middle of a run that resulted in four consecutive Grand Final appearances for three flags.

When I ranked our players, I calculated we totalled 141.5, compared to 162.5 for the Lions. We were 15 per cent behind them in terms of talent. We were in the game to win premierships. To do that, we had to find ways to make up that deficit.

Of course, ranking us against the Lions was not entirely accurate. But I knew the Swans board members were generally analytical people who liked measurable analysis. The 'us against them' slide was a snapshot to show we had to improve our players and fill some gaps.

When I look back at it now, it was vital we were able to improve and develop players from within. Our manic midfielder Jude Bolton was ranked 5.5, Barry Hall was 7.5 and Leo Barry was 7. Brett Kirk was on the bench and rated 6. Ryan O'Keefe was the same. Luke Ablett, Amon Buchanan, Adam Schneider and Lewis Roberts-Thomson weren't even in the best 22 and weren't ranked. Three years later, they were all premiership players. Kirk, O'Keefe, Hall, Jude Bolton and Barry were all 9s by then.

But at the time, that comparison was a way of putting the rest of my presentation in context. It was saying that, if we can get the culture, the training, education, development and game plan right, there is a lot of room for improvement in our players.

I was assessing their current talent, but arguing that if we got the best out of our people then we could bridge the gap. Everything was interdependent.

In the 1980s, when the most talented teams won the premiership and there wasn't much time for development, you might have looked at our team and thought we could never win a flag. My presentation put forward a different story: if we put the programs in place, have a plan and stick to it, we can get there.

Recruiting more effectively was a key plank. This is when I first raised the idea of much more targeted recruiting. Instead of simply trying to nab the best player on the market, we had to start looking at recruiting players who would meet our particular needs.

I spoke about seeking out players from other clubs who were under-achieving and starved of opportunities. We also had to look dispassionately at the national draft, to consider the depth of young talent and decide whether it might be wiser to trade picks for more experienced players. This was to become the blueprint for our recruiting over the next eight years.

My plan for success was twofold. As coaches, we would work hard to develop our current list, and then at the end of every year we'd prioritise particular recruits, try to fill any holes and get a better list for next year.

That was and remains the nub of my philosophy on building a successful team. I argued it was nonsense to talk about a club having a premiership window, as if it opens and then shuts again and you have to go down to the bottom of the ladder. Every year we would take the same approach and that would give us a chance to be consistently good every year.

Rather than the idea of having a set premiership model or formula, it was a process of building the strongest list possible every year. If we looked at our strengths and weaknesses and went from there, at some stage we'd win a premiership.

Which leads to the conclusion of my presentation. I decided

bold was best, to bring out my inner showman. Maybe it was a nod to George Costanza from *Seinfeld* – You've got to give them something and then leave the room as quickly as you can.

> I will inspire, teach and lead
> the Sydney Swans to be
> winners and ultimately deliver
> a Premiership!
> Paul Roos, September 2002.

I said I'd deliver a premiership. It was a leap of faith, but I truly believed a premiership would come if we stuck to a specific plan, concentrated on processes rather than outcomes, and stopped meandering. Sometimes you have to visualise something and say it out loud to make it happen.

When I look back now at this presentation, it reinforces how many elements go into building a successful team. So much needs to go right. Many of the ideas about leadership, player empowerment, education, game-related training and recruitment are now commonplace, but at the time they weren't generally how clubs worked.

If I had put this presentation together after I finished coaching, people would have said, 'Well, that was what you found out.' It was the chicken and the egg. The fact I wrote this three years before the premiership makes you realise how important these things turned out to be. Much of what we set out to achieve came to fruition.

But that was later. My presentation had run for nearly five hours. I walked out of the boardroom that day and still didn't know if I'd secured the job.

Soon after, Richard Colless offered me the job, a two-year deal. I said I'd get back to them . . . and he nearly fell off the chair. I'd also had interviews with the Bulldogs and North Melbourne, and I told him I needed a bit of breathing space.

To be honest, I was a bit pissed off that the Swans had made me jump through hoops, so there was a bit of defiance. It had been an emotionally draining few weeks with the Wallace controversy in the background. I took a bit of time, because I needed to make sure I trusted Richard and Andrew Ireland and the board, and that they trusted me.

I'm very big on trust. Richard understood that. He said it publicly once and it's true – 'Once you lose Paul's trust, you don't get it back.' It was good for all of us to sit back and make a clear, rational decision.

But in my heart I knew I had trust in Richard and Andrew and the board. We spoke again, and a two-year contract became a three-year contract. It had to be a two-way street. I didn't want to get halfway through the first year and get the sack. I was fully committed to the cause, and I wanted them to be clear they were committed to me.

On Thursday, 19 September 2002, the club held a media conference to announce I was the new coach.

Richard told the media the board had voted unanimously to appoint me to lead the team and the club. He said it was about 'heart and soul', and the board had loved the coaching presentation with its emphasis on honesty and unity.

My message was for fans to be excited, but patient. We would rebuild the club and the team and that would take time. 'We are not going to win 22 games of football,' I said. 'We are going to have some pain along the way.

'It's all about trying to develop, and trying to get players to a certain level that we believe can compete consistently to win a premiership.'

The hard work was about to start.

CHAPTER 5
Player power

A new era was beginning at the Sydney Swans. As senior coach, I now had the opportunity to put my ideas into action. I had promises to keep, most importantly to myself and to the players. I had a clear path. The coaching notes I had written four years before and the 40-page plan I'd presented to the board in September were my guides.

One of the first things I wanted to do was find ways to empower the players, and foster their input into how the team and club was run. To do that, it was crucial to develop leadership capabilities and ensure they felt comfortable speaking up.

Make players more accountable for training, discipline, team plans – it is their team too.

I constantly reminded myself to focus on strong, honest relationships built on trust. The board, senior management and coaching staff were determined to stand together and unify the club after a rocky period. I had to lead the way. I didn't want to become an autocrat, a yeller or a control freak, or talk behind people's backs, no matter how stressful or frustrating coaching became.

Treat people as you would want to be treated yourself.

As the players returned for pre-season training in early November 2002, it was apparent people both inside and outside the club were worried about a perceived lack of leaders among the group.

To some degree it was understandable. The 2002 season had seen a changing of the guard in more ways than one. Not only had coach Rodney Eade resigned mid-season, but so had veteran midfielder Wayne Schwass and Tony 'Plugger' Lockett. Then, at season's end, our captain Paul Kelly and vice-captain Andrew Dunkley had hung up their boots.

Kel had played 234 games for the Swans; Dunks had racked up 217 games. Plugger's tally after his comeback was 281 (for St Kilda and the Swans), and Schwatta had played 282 (for North Melbourne and the Swans). We had lost a combined total of 1014 games experience.

I sensed a real panic around Kel's retirement in particular. There was a perceived void and everyone was asking, who is going to lead this footy club? Daryn Cresswell, Stuart Maxfield and Paul Williams were the most experienced players remaining at the club, but at that stage there was no definite captain-in-waiting.

Kel, or Captain Courageous as he was often called, retired as one of the most widely admired leaders in the AFL. A country boy from Wagga Wagga in NSW, he was a plumber by trade. He had not taken up Australian Rules until he was 15 and when he first came to Sydney to play for the Swans he thought it wouldn't be long before he was back at home and back working on the tools. How wrong he was.

Kel made his debut in 1990, and became captain in 1993 when the club was in the middle of a 26-game losing streak. He led the team out of that black hole and then won the 1995 Brownlow Medal. He was tenacious, had a brilliant burst of speed, was a fantastic tackler and inspired teammates with his fearless on-field acts.

Never a big talker, Paul Kelly to me was almost the last of the 'doers', a captain who led by his actions. It wasn't natural for Kel to call a meeting with his teammates. His attitude was more along the lines of: 'What do we need a team meeting for? Doesn't everyone try?'

The reality was that not everyone did try as hard as Kel. As difficult as it was for him to understand, not everyone played at 100 per cent all the time like he did. Kel's way was beautifully simple – 'You run down the race behind me, watch what I do, and if you can do what I do, then we'll win.'

But there were very few players of Paul Kelly's calibre at any club. So when a young player was drafted, he might say, 'He's one of the greatest players, I can't do what he does, so what am I going to do? I'll just leave it to him.'

The danger was that you get a big discrepancy in the contribution to the team; someone like Kel gets more frustrated because others can't do what he does, the young players get frustrated because they feel a bit hopeless and can't do what Kel does and the cycle goes on.

The tradition in football clubs had always been to give the captaincy to the best-performing player. When I started at Fitzroy, the captain was Garry Wilson, then it was Matt Rendell. At the Swans it was Kel.

They had all been fantastic captains, but times were changing, and I could see weaknesses in that system which relied so heavily on one individual. There was a leadership evolution under way. It was becoming apparent that the best player did not have to be the captain of the football club.

With Kel gone, I felt one of my most important roles as coach was to define what leadership is, and help all our players become better leaders. We had to develop a structure that helped them understand they all had to contribute if the team was to be a strong unit.

We wanted them to realise they had a part to play even if they were one of those fringe players I had sat with on the bench in my final season.

It was about bridging the gap, agreeing what role they could usefully carry out and how they should behave, even if they were never going to be as talented as Paul Kelly or Tony Lockett.

With footy becoming a full-time occupation, there was a danger you could get the young, inexperienced guys over in one corner and the superstars sitting over on the other side. How could we give them a common cause?

As well, during my last few years as a player I had wondered why players weren't given more ownership of their team. They were the ones who had to get out there on the field, so they should have more involvement in the whole process.

Those philosophies were the foundation of player empowerment and the overhaul of the culture at the Swans. We were going to do things differently.

But how should we go about making significant changes? In September, while I was in Melbourne with some of the younger players watching the teams who were still in the finals train, I ran into Ray McLean at the airport – one of those chance meetings that would prove life-changing.

I didn't know Ray well, but was interested in his organisation, Leading Teams, which at that time was working with Collingwood and had previously been at St Kilda and the South Australian footy club Central District, as well as NRL and rugby union teams.

I'd heard that Ray, a former teacher who had gone on to design leadership programs for the Australian military, was a very effective communicator. He had a proven track record for implementing systems to develop better leaders and improve team culture, bonding and performance.

After I was appointed coach a week or so later, I contacted Ray to find out more about his Performance Improvement Program. Our ideas were in sync. Ray's program emphasised the importance of team members being accountable and honest with each other, and leadership being a shared responsibility.

His principles were based on empowering players. They had to establish and then drive their own standards and discipline code. It struck a chord because that was a version of my early days at Fitzroy when I'd played under great role models such as Micky Conlon, Laurie Serafini, Garry Wilson and Bernie Quinlan. We didn't call it 'culture' then, but that's effectively what those leaders at Fitzroy had created.

They were a very honest bunch who trained and played to high standards. To earn their respect, you emulated them. If you mucked up, they'd let you know. That constructive feedback from my teammates was far more effective and powerful than another roasting from the coach. This was the heart of the system I wanted to enshrine at the Swans.

So, in November 2002, we took all the players and coaching staff on a pre-season camp to Coffs Harbour in northern NSW. Ray was the facilitator, the perfect person to put structure around these ideas.

The first stage, in a sense, was simple. As a group, the players had to diagnose the problems, to be honest about the things that were holding them back from success. What shortcuts were we accepting, what counter-productive behaviour had we been letting each other get away with? What habits did we have that were not serving us well? On one hand, easy questions – but being honest with each other in an open forum was both confronting and powerful.

Ray asked the players how they believed they were perceived as a team, and how they actually wanted to be perceived. One of his key ideas is that a team needs a trademark, an identity that sums up how they want to see themselves.

Stuart Maxfield and Brett Kirk, who at that time was 25 but had played fewer than 50 games, were both candid. Other clubs viewed us as under-achievers, they said, and a team that wouldn't always fight to the bitter end. We were a team that relied on too few players.

Stuey and Brett weren't the only players to have their say. Straight away I was really pleased with how many players were prepared to put forward their views. Seemingly introverted young players started to come out of their shell. Leo Barry, on the verge of 100 games, was a strong, intelligent voice. Ben Mathews, a quiet achiever from Corowa in southern NSW, emerged as a young leader. Experienced players such as Jason Ball and Paul Williams made valuable contributions. We encouraged everyone to express their thoughts. Players dropped their guard and spoke up.

It was like an awakening for the group. Matthew Nicks, who made his debut in 1996 and had played alongside Kel and Dunks and Plugger all his career, said it felt like the group was blossoming. Everyone was on a more equal footing.

I felt the players had genuinely embraced the opportunity to take more responsibility and ownership of their team. They were excited and the discussion flowed easily.

The standout speaker, though, was Maxfield. He told the group they were kidding themselves if they thought they had trained as hard as they could or showed maximum effort every time they played. He made it clear that what we had been doing was not good enough. His views were brutally honest, but he had the respect of all the players because of the way he drove himself.

Over the course of the camp, the players came up with three words that summed up how they wanted to be perceived: *HARD, DISCIPLINED, RELENTLESS*. Three powerful words. They had their trademark.

Hard: they wanted to be tough to play against, and never take a backward step. *Disciplined*: they vowed to maintain the highest standards, have a strong work ethic and no longer accept mediocrity. They would be accountable to each other, to make sure there was no slacking off. *Relentless*: on the field, they promised to be a team with a fighting spirit, a team who would keep running all day and never lie down, no matter how a game was unfolding.

Ray then asked the players to come up with a name for their trademark, to see if they could find one word that would encapsulate all it represented.

They tossed around ideas and then one player, I recall it was Heath James, mentioned 'the Bloods', the name the South Melbourne football club had once been known as.

Heath was a popular person, but one of the club's hard-luck stories. A talented junior, he was drafted at pick 28 in 1998 under the father–son rule, but his career was disrupted by repeated hamstring injuries. Heath knew something of the club's history because his father, Max, had played 54 games for South Melbourne/Sydney Swans between 1978 and 1982. Max had been part of the pioneering group of players who had relocated to Sydney.

Heath's suggestion was a winner. The players loved the idea of calling themselves the Bloods. Not only did that sound like a team that would do anything to win, they liked the fact it linked them to the club's heritage.

That link to the past was something we had already talked about before we came to Coffs Harbour. When I became coach, I was keen for the players to be educated about what happened when South Melbourne was transplanted to Sydney. I thought they should appreciate the struggles of the Swans who had gone before them, and reconnect with our history. They needed to be proud of the red and white jumper, and proud of their club.

We had already put together a video to outline a brief history of the club. When the team was first relocated to Sydney in 1982, the players had no gym, no proper training facilities, no welfare officers, no dieticians, no sports psychologists, no clubrooms. Even when I went to Sydney in late 1994 as a player, we trained on the Showgrounds next to the SCG and before some sessions we had to do a sweep of the ground to remove debris.

These players had a fantastic new facility at the SCG partly funded by our extraordinary club benefactor, Basil Sellers. I wanted them to realise how lucky they were and understand the plight of the pioneers before them, whether that be triple Brownlow Medallist Bobby Skilton in the 1960s and 1970s, or the players who were part of the last Swans premiership way back in 1933. The club's history should be honoured. It clicked with our guys. They understood the need to be respectful, and tried to think how they could link their behaviours with the past.

Then the Bloods connection was made at Coffs Harbour. It wasn't manufactured, it was a natural fit for the players as they set about forging their new identity – one that paid tribute to the past but looked to the future.

As well as deciding on the trademark, they also had to develop team rules and behaviours that everyone would adhere to – they would effectively be our way of life, our culture. The words came first, but the action and follow-through was all-important. How would a Blood behave on and off the field?

The players came up with various phrases that were their non-negotiable 'behaviours'.

They would always put the team first; they would be honest with each other; they wouldn't back away from any contest; they would always give 100 per cent effort and wouldn't wait for others to act. They would be united and accountable to each other. If one person did the wrong thing, then they pledged the group would have to pay.

It was plain to me this group was driven to get better, and would be prepared to push each other to get there. It was a fresh slate. There would be no more excuses, no more short-cuts, no more mediocrity.

The players were making good choices but there was still a big test to come. One of the features of Ray's program is that the players vote openly for a leadership group, not anonymously. The players had to publicly nominate those they believed best represented their new core values.

Each player was given a piece of paper, and on it they had to write the names of five teammates who lived the team's code and rules. They had to read the names out loud – a very confronting exercise.

Footy clubs are built on mateship and I half-expected players to nominate their own best friends, particularly as the vote was open. Or just nominate the team's best players. That didn't happen. They voted for the players who would best uphold our behaviours, the ones who already exhib-ited those characteristics. I realised how seriously the guys were taking their responsibilities. They wanted to change.

After the vote, we had a 10-man leadership group for the first time in the club's history. The group was a mix of experience and youth, of high-profile and lower-profile players – Michael O'Loughlin, Brad Seymour, Jason Ball,

Paul Williams, Andrew Schauble, Matthew Nicks, Stuart Maxfield, Jude Bolton, Leo Barry and Ben Mathews.

Several of the team's best players, including Barry Hall, Adam Goodes and Daryn Cresswell, weren't in the group. They were all highly respected, but others were considered better role models for the Bloods' trademark values.

Goodes in particular wanted to be seen as a leader, and was keen to understand what he was missing. The group discussed the reasons openly and the players gave him constructive feedback, so he had a roadmap to improve.

Those feedback sessions were the start of what became known as our peer reviews, where a player would stand in front of the group and be assessed by his teammates. There is no doubt these were tough, tense processes at times, but they ultimately made us stronger. And often the feedback was positive, which was also powerful.

The players had chosen their leaders, but the coaching staff now had to choose the captain. Like the players, we wanted to nominate the player who best epitomised our values, a player who was honest, disciplined and would bring the group along with him.

Stuart Maxfield, who was then 30, had received the most votes during the leadership ballot. Ray thought that was significant, and as a coaching group we did too.

He wasn't the team's most talented player, but that was no longer the main criterion for choosing a captain. Stuey was a standout role model in terms of his discipline and preparation. What mattered most was he would always put the team's interests first and set faultless standards. He was a hard nut who would ensure the players adhered to the rules they had all agreed to. He would challenge anyone who made excuses. A strong work ethic would be a given. It would be one-in-all-in under Stuey.

Outside the club, there was surprise when we announced he would be our captain for 2003. But inside the club, we knew he was the right person for a new era.

In the Swans' recent history, let's say since 2002, Stuart Maxfield's importance can't be overestimated. Without doubt, he was the most critical person at the club while I was coach. I honestly believe that without Stuey driving the standards and driving the behaviours, we wouldn't have won a premiership in 2005.

Stuart started his career with Richmond in 1990, and played 89 games there until he came to the Swans at the end of 1995. Never one for the limelight, he enjoyed the anonymity of being an AFL player in Sydney. He was a hard-running, super-quick wingman who played in our 1996 Grand Final team, and was second in the club's best and fairest in 2001.

When I took over as interim coach mid-season in 2002, he had a knee injury. We needed someone to fill the role I'd been doing, so Stuey took over as an assistant coach responsible for defence. For the final 10 games of 2002, he sat in the box on game day, and became part of the coaching group. Until that time, I believe Stuey was quite a blinkered player and didn't really see the broader picture of how each player fitted into the team as a whole.

That stint in the coaches' box helped him understand how important everyone's role was, how they were all part of the puzzle. It helped him see the game from the other side of the fence. That was pivotal. He grasped the concept that everyone had a job to do, and truly believed in what we were trying to achieve.

For me, as a new coach, it was incredibly helpful to have a captain who was so wedded to changing the culture and empowering the playing group.

Stuey already lived our trademark and our behaviours

and he was determined everyone else would too. He was a demon on the training track. The players liked and respected him, but that wasn't his chief concern. The most important thing was they trusted him to do the right thing for the club. He would never hesitate to look a player in the eye and tell them straight if they weren't pulling their weight, or were letting teammates down.

He was tough, but he also had empathy and knew if a player was struggling and needed extra attention or care. Stuey, along with the other leaders, made sure the players looked out for one another. He also embraced the mentoring system where the players in the leadership group all helped one or two young players develop their game and their training habits.

It was a critical period. Through Ray, we had a model for cultural change we wanted to adopt, and we had a coach and a captain both committed to it. Everything was coming together.

We'd made a good start. Ray was also adamant we had to continually talk about our behaviours, to set up a system to reinforce them and put a value on them long after we'd left Coffs Harbour.

Weekly meetings with the team leaders – one of the points on my 1998 list of coaching notes – were scheduled. We were putting our words into action.

When I go to corporate conferences, I see almost every company has a set of values they print in big letters and stick on the wall. They take them out at the conference, talk about them for two days, then roll them back up and put them in the drawer. They wonder why their culture is poor.

We pledged to regularly reinforce our desired behaviours. That was up to the coach, the captain and the leadership group. We would be the drivers.

Over the years, many teams would have come up with similar words and behaviours to those our players wrote down at Coffs Harbour. Player empowerment wasn't about the coach then giving over all responsibility and just letting the players do their thing. The crucial next step for me as coach was to help our players live the team rules and understand what they meant in the context of every day.

So it was back to my coaching notes: **A coach's job is to set strategies and give specific instructions to players.**

A good example of this in practice was the behaviour, 'When it's my turn to go, I go', one of the players' key team rules. It basically means that if the ball is there to be won, you must never back away, no matter how fierce the contest.

I talked about the example of Brett Kirk versus Tadhg Kennelly.

Brett is an inside midfielder who is going to go hard for the ball, hard at the contest, at least 50 times a game. Tadhg Kennelly is an outside running half-back flanker whose job is mostly to receive the ball in space, to run and carry and be creative, and send the ball into attack.

We had to carefully assist the players to interpret these behaviours. We didn't want Tadhg Kennelly playing like Brett Kirk, otherwise you don't end up with a balanced team that can win a premiership. We had to explain to Tadhg that he had to play to his own strengths, and play his particular role within the team. The players had to understand that Tadhg's tireless run and carry was valued as much as Brett's bravery to win the ball at the bottom of the packs.

For the coaches, it wasn't a completely literal reading of 'hard, disciplined, relentless'. The key for our players, and everyone in the footy club, would be those words in the context of 'know your role, play your role'.

We had to set the game plan and outline the expectations

for each individual player. I knew their strengths and what each of them was good at and could achieve. **Forty-two senior players – all different personalities, deal with each one individually to get the best out of him.** That would be done within the parameters of our Bloods behaviours.

We attacked the remainder of pre-season training with a strong sense of common purpose. Bring on season 2003. The Swannies had become the Bloods.

CHAPTER 6
The game plan

We had a heavy schedule when the players hit the training track at the start of November 2002. Two months earlier, we'd finished 11th on the ladder, our worst placing since 1995. Every moment of pre-season training had to be focused on overhauling our playing style and team culture.

I had made it clear I'd be disappointed if anyone came back from the break overweight or out of condition. I was determined to end the days when pre-season training was a time for shedding the kilos gained on the post-season beer fest.

We had to spend as much time as possible learning our new game plan and improving the players' skills. We had committed to lifting training standards and fostering a no-excuses culture, and now it was time for action rather than talk.

I have a pretty easygoing nature, but that doesn't mean I can't be hard. I don't have energy for people who are wasting their opportunity and wasting the coaching staff's time.

We set the tone early on. A week after we resumed training, Andrew Ireland and I had to tell one of our young ruckmen, Ricky Mott, that he was being cut from the list, effective immediately. (At that time, you could still delist players after pre-season training had started.)

Ricky was 21 and had rucked for the senior team in 17 games during 2002 while Jason Ball was out for the season due to a groin injury. But Ricky had been dropped for the last few games of the year and we'd thrown Adam Goodes into the ruck – where he tried his heart out even though he was under-sized for a ruckman.

At season's end, we'd told Ricky he had to make sure he came back after the nine-week break at his playing weight of around 104 kilograms. But when he turned up, he tipped the scales higher than that and had clearly been in a good paddock during his time off. Ricky lumbered around Centennial Park on the first run of the pre-season and struggled home last.

We called him into my office and told him we were sorry, but we didn't have time to wait for him to get his act together. He had not met the level we expected.

Ricky was a good kid, but he wasn't showing the commitment and professional attitude we were going to demand from our players – and more importantly, they were demanding from each other. Everyone got the message. We'd made it clear tough decisions would be taken when necessary.

As the pre-season went on, and through the years that followed, the leadership group took on the role of enforcing the team's rules and standards. There were numerous times the players called their own 'punishment' sessions and didn't even bother to tell the coaches. The squad of 40 or so would have to turn up at Bondi Beach at 6 am, each carrying two bricks from home.

These sessions were generally called for misdemeanours that some clubs might have considered minor. For example, if one player arrived late for a team meeting or training session, everyone would pay the price.

As Tadhg Kennelly said later that year, it was the sort of thing they would have let slide in previous years. Now there were no shortcuts, they wouldn't be doing anything by halves. It was one-in-all-in under the new Bloods code, and they handled it themselves. I joked that was the beauty of player empowerment – I didn't have to join them at 6 am.

The pieces were falling into place. We had a well-rounded coaching panel. John Longmire, who won the Coleman Medal when he was only 19 and was a premiership player with the Kangaroos in 1999, was forwards coach; Steve Malaxos, who won a best and fairest at the West Coast Eagles, was the midfield coach; and at the end of 2002 we had added Peter Jonas to the group. He'd played for North Melbourne and had coached SANFL club Central District to its inaugural premiership in 1998.

We had approval to employ an extra coach who would oversee development, as well as our reserves side, and we also had extra medical support.

Andrew Ireland's appointment as head of football was really significant. He and chairman Richard Colless had a very strong, trusting relationship, which meant all the board members were more at ease. Football club boards generally comprise people who are very successful in their business life. It can be challenging for them to take a more passive role in a football environment. Given the strong connection between Andrew and Richard, the board had a new-found trust in where the club was heading. Andrew, who helped create the premiership environment at the Brisbane Lions, went about the business of providing the resources we needed to implement our plans, and he gave everyone confidence the club was on the right track.

It was a much more positive environment than in the past few seasons. Everyone in the football department knew their role and we were united.

We also had a few talented new players. Nick Davis was our biggest recruit. An incredibly skilled half-forward, Nick had played 71 games for Collingwood but wanted to return to Sydney, where he'd grown up with his father Craig, who had played a season with the Swans in 1988.

We were also really pleased to recruit Craig Bolton from the Brisbane Lions in the pre-season draft. Craig had always been on the edge of the champion Brisbane team and was an emergency for the 2002 Grand Final side. Andrew Ireland knew him well and believed he could be a real asset for us in defence if we gave him game time and built his confidence.

In the draft, we had our first top 10 pick for several years and opted for Jarrad McVeigh, a local Sydney boy who had elite endurance and skills. We also picked up Sean Dempster under the father–son rule, and at pick 64 Nick Malceski, who was considered a very good decision-maker and ball user.

Paul Kelly, Andrew Dunkley and Wayne Schwass were gone, but our new recruits were a good blend of experience and youth.

Before Christmas, we made skill development a priority. We set up an intensive system where every player received individual attention. After Christmas, we concentrated on teaching our new game plan and doing drills specific to it. We were introducing game-related training.

I'd told the coaching sub-committee in my presentation in September that we'd be playing a one-on-one style of football, where I'd expect every player to be accountable for their opponent.

I'd explained we would need to improve our ball handling and work on our tackling technique, as these aspects of the game related directly to wins. We'd done an analysis and found that if we had fewer than 13 fumbles a game, we won 80 per cent of the time. Along with that, if 80 per cent of our tackles were effective in restraining the opposition player, then we also had an 80 per cent win rate.

These became our key indicators. Our number one team rule was based around these factors – win the ball, but if you don't win it, make the tackle. **Win the ball, make the tackle.** That was the non-negotiable expectation.

We never wanted to let the opposition get an easy possession. We would never rely on them turning over the ball and giving it back to us – we would try to get it back as soon as they had it. But you can't ask the players to do things they're not capable of. We had to make sure we were equipped to do that, so we devised drills to train for those skills.

We had to strip the game right back, break it down to simple components and hone those very basic skills of winning the ball and tackling, which had not really been practised often until then.

Picking a ball up off the ground – or ground balls as we called them – was actually about two skills. If we were going to minimise fumbling, there was the skill of securing the ball first, and the skill of giving it off cleanly to a teammate. Too many players thought it was just the one skill of handballing or kicking.

We trained with 'interference' to replicate what happens in a game. We would throw the ball up and have tacklers come at a player, and he had to secure the ball without fumbling and then pass it. We'd smash the player with tackle bags and repeatedly practise ground balls to teach the technicalities, the body positioning and the ball handling, so we got much better at them.

There were other drills crucial to our new game plan. To be a one-on-one team, every player had to be an attacker and a defender. They had to be able to negate their opponent in the open field as well as in congestion, which meant they had to run hard both ways.

Our most important drill was dubbed the 'basketball drill'.

I'd first seen it at the Australian Institute of Sport, where it was done on a court. We translated it to a full AFL field, which made for an incredibly taxing drill. We placed four players on four opponents in the main part of the field, then two forwards at each end, with one defender against them. So each side had four players in the midfield, two forwards and one defender.

It would start with me handballing to one of the midfielders. I'd blow the whistle and then the team with the ball had to run it towards their forwards while the others had to defend.

The drill required hard running and an extremely high work rate. One team would move the ball into attack, and then the defender would kick it straight back out again. His group of midfielders would then spread across the field, trying to get the ball and transition to their forward line. The first team of attackers had to very quickly become the defending group, and had to try to stop their opponents getting the ball forward.

I'd let it go and they might transition up and back a few times – a very tough drill with so few players on a full field.

It was also a great way to develop communication skills. Teams that play one-on-one football really need to talk to each other. If one player is getting blocked or screened, or is in space, they need to let each other know and help each other out. It honed their team-first mentality.

Players couldn't hide doing that drill, and the work required was brutal. With four on four, it was glaringly obvious straight away which players could handle the demands and those who struggled.

During that pre-season, it helped us find out which players were prepared to work really hard and commit themselves to running tirelessly. It became a staple drill for the next seven or eight years, and was especially challenging for the young guys who came into the club from the draft each year.

When we got very skilled defensively over the years, we switched the emphasis to make the players work harder offensively. It was a great drill to teach both sides of the ball, offence and defence, and to practise our game plan. And it also served the purpose of being fantastic for fitness.

It was the best drill we created, and it summed up everything we wanted to be. We were building a team of players who would work their backsides off to shut down their opponents as quickly as possible when they got the ball and try to stop them getting to their forward line.

At that stage, in my first pre-season as head coach, the defensive part of our plan was most important. I believe in training for all phases of the sport, but there is no doubt that defence is the first pillar, the absolute foundation of the game plan.

It's a philosophy I was criticised for numerous times during my coaching career, but one I'll never back away from. There's a simple reason for it: analysis shows that teams with the best defence win titles. Whether you look at world sport or local sport, the story is the same.

People don't want to believe it, because it's sexier to score freely. But take American sport – the gridiron teams with the best defence are generally in the NFL Superbowl; the basketball teams with the tightest defence fight for the NBA title. At American stadiums the basketball fans chant 'Dee-fence, dee-fence'. They love miserly defence because they know that's how games are won.

Late in 2002, John Longmire did a statistical analysis of AFL premiership teams. He found that, over a 20-year period, every premiership team bar one had been ranked in the top four in the competition for defence, with relatively few points scored against them.

When we looked at the Brisbane Lions 2001 flag team, they had an abundance of talent, but I can guarantee you they were also an unbelievably good defensive team. My former Fitzroy teammate and their key forward, Alastair Lynch, told me their coach Leigh Matthews put a big emphasis on hard tackling and thwarting the opposition.

We knew defence was a key to success, and we wanted to take it to the highest level possible.

It also related back to my view that not everyone in the team is a gifted superstar. We didn't have a squad of athletic freaks who could win games off their own boot. We had a few stars, and a big group of honest players who could all contribute.

When I'd rated all our players in my presentation to the Swans board, we had only one player – Paul Williams – given a nine out of 10 and one ranked eight, which was Michael O'Loughlin.

My view was that every player, no matter their talent level, can defend strongly. Everyone can tackle, everyone can chase, everyone can spoil and harass. Defence is mostly about effort and will, not talent, so anyone could master it if they had the right attitude.

Offence, on the other hand, is generally dictated by talent. Hawthorn's dynamo Cyril Rioli can kick goals few other players could dream of. Our star, Michael O'Loughlin, could turn on a coin and snap a goal from the pocket on an almost impossible angle.

There was no sense having a game plan that revolved solely around talent, because it was not something the coaches could control. But we could ask everyone to play their role, to contribute and put maximum effort into defensive acts. That's how we could forge a strong team where everyone played a part.

The players took to the new direction during that preseason. It gelled with their redefined values and culture.

They weren't going to flood the opposition backline and rely on opposition teams turning the ball over. They were going to work hard to win the footy and, if they didn't, they'd switch straight into defensive mode and get the ball back.

Several players started to shine. Brett Kirk was extremely good at the basketball drill. He was super-fit, but what stood out was his ability to read the play and make really quick decisions on offence and defence.

Kirky had been a bit-part player until that point. I'd rated him a six out of 10 in my presentation, and only an interchange player.

He was a hard worker from North Albury who had come off the rookie list, and had an amazing story of persistence. He'd been in and out of the team under Rodney Eade and it wasn't certain he'd make it as a long-term AFL player. He was then 26 years old and had been at the club for four years, but played a total of just 49 games.

During that pre-season, Brett was the standout, and we saw signs of how valuable he was to become to the team. His ability to impress in that drill translated into his game over the next eight years, when he went from fringe player to All-Australian in 2004, and best and fairest in our premiership year.

He was on the start line in every single match I coached at the Swans from the round 14 game in 2002 – he played 200 consecutive matches and didn't miss a game until we both left the club at the end of 2010.

He was not a quick runner, but an interesting facet of the drill was you didn't have to be super-fast. The quicker guys sometimes hesitated before they chased, because they thought they could run an opponent down.

But players like Kirky who were slower relied on acting quickly and making smart decisions. No one was going to get away from him easily. Our game plan was going to be based on that premise – every player needed a strong work ethic and they could not be lazy even for a second. They had to be right with their opponent all the time, limiting their ability to win the ball.

Ryan O'Keefe, then just 21, also stood out during that pre-season. He had only played nine matches in 2002, for a career total of 27, but he was emerging from the pack. Like Brett, he made sound choices on the field and had a strong character.

From our analysis of the latter part of 2002, we knew there was one more stat which would be important. If we could keep our opponents to fewer than 180 uncontested possessions per game, then we would give ourselves a strong chance to win.

But it wasn't all about desperate defence. We also trained to switch the ball across the field from defence and move through the centre corridor to hit our leading forwards. In the last half of 2002 when I took over, we had significantly lifted the number of times we went inside the forward 50-metre zone.

Everyone says I was a defensive coach, but when you look back, a lot of what we tried to do was offensive. But as I always say, the difference from training to games is that there is an opposition who do not always let you do what you'd like.

It illustrates how complicated it is and, no matter how much you train, you never get your ideal game plan going perfectly in one match.

I was fortunate that Rodney Eade had been a fantastic game day coach and the players were used to complicated midfield rotations and moves during games. He always tried to unsettle the opposition and outsmart them, so as far as game day went in the box, I couldn't have had a better coach to follow.

I wanted to build on that, but spend more time during

the week preparing players for what might happen on game day. We started to train for different scenarios, so that players would be more confident to make their own decisions and moves on the field.

For example, if Jared Crouch was playing on the West Coast Eagles' gun midfielder, Ben Cousins, and Cousins took him down to the goal square, I wanted to physically rehearse what we would do to counter it.

We started recording training. We didn't have $80 million to build an indoor facility with cameras like the American football clubs, so we did the next best thing – we rented a scissor lift and filmed from there so we could capture everyone practising. An economical alternative, you might say.

We became teachers or educators as much as coaches. We wanted to give players practical solutions they could implement during games, and not just point out problems all the time.

We wanted to make sure we put the concepts of player empowerment and leadership into action, so it wasn't just talk.

There was one day during the pre-season when our coaching group decided to test the players' independence and leadership skills. The assistant coaches and I didn't turn up for training, but instead went for a very nice breakfast at Bronte beach.

Meanwhile, the players turned up at the ground, wondering where we were. The only person who knew the plan was the head of fitness, Dave Misson, but he didn't let on. For the players, the only clue was the whiteboard in the change rooms, which always listed instructions for the upcoming training session. All it said was, 'Plenty of player involvement'.

After waiting around for a while, the players checked the whiteboard again, and a few of them twigged. The coaches weren't coming! They got together, decided what to do, and it turned out to be a fantastic training session.

We had filmed the session to see how the players would respond, and we were really impressed when we watched the vision later that day.

Without any input from the coaches, the players had got down to work, and most importantly, carried it out to a high standard. They didn't need us to spoonfeed them.

It was a great way of putting into practice the fact that on game day, the coach is not out on the field telling the players what to do. They have to take responsibility, and take the lead. It was player empowerment in action.

When I had written down my 25 coaching points in 1998, the things I never wanted to forget about being a player, they were mostly just concepts in my mind. The Coffs Harbour program with Ray McLean and Leading Teams had given us a structure for player empowerment, and thankfully I was finding out that I had a group who were ready to wholeheart-edly embrace the concept.

From Leo Barry, to Barry Hall, to Micky O'Loughlin, and our new captain Stuey Maxfield, it clicked. I was excited to see they were ready to take control of their footy club and they were ready to play for each other.

We lost our pre-season knockout game against Brisbane, but that wasn't a real concern. We were getting ready for round one.

In early March, we had the Guernsey Presentation, one of the biggest nights on the club calendar where the new players are formally presented with their red and white jumpers.

We were starting to re-form the links with South Melbourne, so Swans legend, triple Brownlow Medallist Bobby Skilton, addressed the crowd.

Bobby spoke about how the Melbourne-based fans were

returning to support the club. A former club captain, he also talked about leadership and emphasised that every player could contribute – he was on the same wavelength as us.

He told us about a letter his coach in 1970, Norm Smith, had given all the Swans players that year. It was from a US Olympic athlete, Clifton Cushman, whose message was that it was better to have tried and failed than not to have tried. Again, his message resonated with our new culture – all we were asking for was 100 per cent effort from every player.

In my speech, I described how we might quantify success in this new era. We would judge ourselves on how well we had taught and developed individual players and the team. I couldn't guarantee we'd win every game, but I guaranteed the players would give their all every week.

We were ready to be tested. Whenever the media asked about our prospects, I said we were in a rebuilding phase. To be honest, I didn't know what would unfold and what we were capable of achieving.

The media had a fairly uniform view of us, though. Virtually every pundit in the country had tipped us to finish on the bottom of the ladder, or only a rung or two above there.

CHAPTER 7

Staying the course

We were heading into the unknown. Our first game of the season was against Carlton, who also had a new coach. Denis Pagan had left the Kangaroos after 10 years and two premierships and was hoping to revive Carlton, who'd finished bottom in 2002. Even playing the wooden-spooners, not many tipsters picked us to win, but as a group we'd resolved not to care about outside opinions.

I had a set pre-game routine in the dressing rooms. Before the match I made sure I spoke to every player individually, to reinforce what we wanted him to do. It relied on me knowing and understanding what made every player tick. It was generally a short, positive message with clear and simple instructions.

Adam Schneider, a cheeky youngster from Osborne in southern NSW, was only 18 and we'd selected him to make his debut. He'd been drafted with pick 60 at the end of 2001 and his first year at the club had been hampered by injury and illness.

However, he'd excelled during the pre-season and we believed he could fill a role as a lively, crumbing forward. Before he ran out on the field, I looked him in the eye and tried to ease his nerves. I told him to enjoy the game. 'When you get your first touch, just kick it, don't worry about what happens.' Nothing more complicated than that.

I had a similar message for Craig Bolton, who had joined us from the Brisbane Lions, where he had struggled to break into their stellar team. Craig is an intelligent, humble person who judged himself harshly and lacked self-belief. We had named him to play at centre half-back and he was edgy before the game. I reminded him we'd recruited him because we had confidence he could do the job. A quick joke with Craig helped lighten the pressure he was feeling.

I was trying to act on one of the most important points on my coaching notes: **42 senior players – all different personalities, deal with each one individually to get the best out of him.**

Of course, there were non-negotiable team rules we'd drawn up in the pre-season – 'When it's my turn to go, I go', and '100 per cent effort every time'. Our prime on-field rule was, 'Win the ball or make the tackle'. These edicts applied to everyone, but when it came to motivation and the specific role we asked them to do on-field, there was a different message for every player.

I couldn't have asked for a better day. After a tight first quarter, we kicked eight goals in the second term and won the game by 12 goals. Our most talented midfielder, Paul Williams, was pivotal, but younger players such as Jude Bolton, Adam Goodes and Nic Fosdike had shone. And Adam Schneider had kicked two goals in his first AFL game, a real confidence booster.

But there's a golden rule in footy – best to never get ahead of yourself. By round five, the win was a distant memory and it was no dream start to my coaching career. We were 12th, with just one win.

We had lost consecutive games to Fremantle in Perth, Adelaide at home at the SCG, and Hawthorn at the MCG.

Hawthorn had doubled our tackle count and while we'd had more disposals than them, we'd wasted the ball. We lost by seven goals.

The mood was quiet and solemn when chairman Richard Colless appeared in the rooms after the game.

'Well, Roosy, you've inherited the worst playing list in AFL history,' Richard said to me. It was a big, bold statement from the chairman. On one hand it was pessimistic, to say the least. But on the other hand it could be read as a statement of support, acknowledgment that I was up against it in my first year as coach. I took it as a sign of his commitment to me, and evidence of the heady emotion, passion and personal investment in footy clubs.

Maybe Richard was right. At that stage, I genuinely didn't know which way our players would go. But there was one thing I was sure of – I wasn't going to change my plan to teach and develop the players on our list. I was sticking to the same path no matter how long it took to turn things around.

The next game, against Melbourne on Anzac Day at the SCG, was another big challenge. It was a showcase – we were playing Friday night footy on one of the most significant days on the Australian calendar.

We were in front at half time, but by three-quarter time the situation was dire. The Demons, who had played finals in 2002, had kicked five goals in the third term and were leading by 20 points at the last break. We also had two of our key defenders, Andrew Schauble and Craig Bolton, injured on the bench and they couldn't come back on.

My fledgling coaching career was flashing before my eyes. I remember walking down the stairs from the coaches' box to the ground thinking, *We're 20 points down, we play Collingwood and Brisbane in the next two weeks who are last year's grand finalists; we could be one win and six losses in two weeks time.*

But this was no time to dwell on the negative. I made a decision that, in hindsight, became pivotal to our season. When I reached the players, I took a deep breath, contained my emotion and stayed calm.

As I reached the huddle on the SCG, I laid it on the line and said, 'Look, guys, we're not going anywhere at the moment. Let's have a go. If we're going to lose, let's get belted, go down swinging. Just play the way we want to play, have faith and trust in what we're trying to do.'

In the next 30 minutes, the players ran tirelessly and threw away their fear of losing. We kicked 10 goals to run right over the top of the Demons and win by four goals. It had clicked. They had worked hard, above and beyond their normal limits. We had our second win on the board.

The task wasn't about to get any easier, facing top teams Collingwood and then Brisbane, but the win had given the players much-needed validation. They had evidence that our game plan and our emphasis on 22 players contributing every week was the right way forward. It was the catalyst to say, 'This might just work.'

As a group, they were mature enough to realise the power of unity. If everyone gave maximum effort and played the role we'd asked of them, we would win more games. During the next few weeks, we started to surprise the football world.

In round six we travelled to Melbourne to take on Collingwood, who had lost to Brisbane in the 2002 Grand Final. We wore a special commemorative team-of-the-century jumper that night and the players were really starting to embrace the history of our 130-year-old club.

We asked Brett Kirk to run with the Magpies' brilliant

captain, Nathan Buckley. Brett's amazing ability to concentrate on a task was coming to the fore and, even though Bucks got plenty of the ball, his impact was not as damaging as usual.

Adam Goodes was proving very hard for the opposition to match up on, due to his combination of height and athleticism. He continued his impressive start to the season, mostly playing forward. We got great impetus from Leo Barry, who took intercept marks and then ran the ball out of the backline. Tadhg Kennelly, our skilful, quick Irishman, was also creative off half-back.

We had all the momentum, but Collingwood wouldn't lie down in the last quarter. The match-sealing goal came from our recruit Nick Davis, playing against his old team.

As a coaching group, we were rapt with the players' work ethic, and their ability to spread the load. We had 11 goalkickers that day – half our team had kicked a goal. Goodesy and Michael O'Loughlin kicked three each, but our midfielders had also come to the party and even Tadhg had slotted one.

Goodesy had been so consistent over the first six rounds that people were already talking about him as a chance for the Brownlow Medal, the game's highest individual honour. Our veteran midfielder Daryn Cresswell told the media that Adam had always had potential and had now stepped up to become a superstar.

Adam wasn't in the 10-man leadership group at that stage. Missing out had stung him and he'd responded in the most positive way. Cressa predicted Goodesy would be captain in a few years.

I was content that Adam was simply able to worry for the moment about getting his footy right. He had a few flaws in his game and had lost his confidence under Rodney Eade, who was often hard on him.

Adam grew up playing soccer, and hadn't got into footy

until he was a teenager. He was incredibly athletic, but he didn't respond well to complicated instructions. He played on instinct.

Now his flaws were being ironed out and our new assistant coach, Peter Jonas, was playing a crucial part in his progress. Peter was amazed at Goodesy's endurance, strength and agility. Adam had only just turned 23 and Peter urged us to focus on all the things he was good at, rather than perceived weaknesses. It was a powerful message. We backed off and Adam bloomed.

Our belief as a team was getting stronger, but would it hold together against the best side in the competition? The following week we had to play the Lions, the team I had estimated were at least 15 per cent ahead of us when I presented my plan to the club board just a few months before.

The media was saying it would be a miracle if we won, but we went into the game with the attitude that we had nothing to lose. Our plan was about long-term development, so it was exciting to test ourselves against the reigning premiers, who were unbeaten in the first six rounds.

Our midfield match-ups were crucial. We asked Jared Crouch, our durable midfielder, to run with 2001 Brownlow Medallist Jason Akermanis, and Kirky got the job on Lions' captain Michael Voss.

Our mantra – win the ground balls, stick the tackle – was never more important. It had to be at the front of our minds against a team that never backed away from a contest. 'When it's my turn to go, I go' was definitely something the Lions lived by.

We jumped out of the gates, booting five goals in the first term. They came back at us in the second half, closing to within a few points, but we held our nerve and won by 19 points.

Goodesy had starred again, Micky O'Loughlin kicked five goals, and Leo Barry was going to another level across half-back. Adam Schneider was doing exactly what we asked, putting pressure on in the forward line and kicking a couple of goals. Jared Crouch had annoyed the hell out of Akermanis with his tight checking. Aka had four touches for the day, which said it all.

The team tipped to win the wooden spoon had upset the premiers. That doesn't happen every day. We had beaten our benchmark team and the self-belief switch was well and truly on.

I said in the media conference after the game that the key was our players' work rate and their even contribution. 'We can't have just four or five guys dominating and everyone else not doing anything, because we just don't have the top-end talent that can carry the rest of the team.'

New leaders were emerging to fill the void left by Kel and Andrew Dunkley. Players such as Jared Crouch, Jude Bolton, Leo Barry and Ben Mathews were taking it upon themselves to make things happen on the field. They weren't leaving it to someone else.

Stuey Maxfield was proving to be an exceptional leader. He was able to straddle the divide between player and coach – his stint as defensive coach in the latter part of 2002, when he was injured, had given him a perspective other players didn't have. He kept everyone honest.

Behind closed doors, our consistent message to the guys was 'Play your role'. It was a new term, but it was our way of saying we would give them specific tasks on game day and that was all we wanted them to do.

In devising roles for individual players, we thought about our game plan, how we wanted to move the ball and how we wanted to defend. We studied our personnel, and crafted accordingly.

For example, Micky O'Loughlin, then 26, could have been an unbelievable midfielder but he had shocking knee tendonitis. So we stationed him deep in attack, where he could use his special skills both in the air and at ground level. We had to make sure we had someone in the team like Schneider, whose job was to stick near Mick and run past for the handball.

Leo Barry was 184 centimetres tall, but he had a remarkable leap. We asked him to play as an under-sized defender, and taught him to use his body positioning and speed to beat bigger opponents. We didn't ask anyone to do a job we didn't think they were capable of.

We defined the game plan, explained the roles to players and made them understand they were all important cogs in the wheel. We fleshed it out during dozens of meetings in the pre-season.

There were no longer any fringe players. If Kirky did his job and Leo did his job and Jude did his job, it was easier for Micky O to do his job. We simplified footy. All they had to do was perform their own specific job as well as they could, and that was how they could best help their teammates.

For example, when we were playing Brisbane, we didn't want Crouch leaving Akermanis to chase kicks so his stats would look good at the end of the game. Too often in the past, players had worried about their disposal count and felt measured by that. Jared was capable of winning the ball and racking up numbers, but that wasn't how he could give most value to the team.

The coaching staff judged the players on how well they had carried out the job we asked them to do. For Crouch or Brett Kirk, if they had only a few disposals but limited the impact of Akermanis or Voss and helped us win, that's what mattered.

The job was different for every player and was tweaked according to our opponents each week. For someone like Tadhg, the emphasis might be on running hard to receive the ball, rebounding from defence and using his pace to break the lines. If he worked hard and used the ball well, he'd ticked the boxes.

Jude Bolton had to focus on hard-ball-gets, extracting the ball from the bottom of packs in his brave fashion. Schneider had to make sure he was at the feet of Micky or Barry Hall to swoop on the loose ball.

Hally was an interesting one. When he came to the club from St Kilda, he publicly stated his aim was to kick four goals every week. John Longmire, who was in charge of the forwards, corrected him. His first aim should be to run hard, tackle and chase, to lock the ball in our forward line. If he focused on that, then the goals would follow – and they did.

It was a different way of thinking for a lot of the players. They saw it was working and took to it.

The coaches continually reinforced what we valued under our new Bloods culture. During our post-match reviews with the players every Monday, we highlighted the selfless acts rather than the spectacular ones. If a player had broken a team rule, no matter who he was, we would point it out and move on. It had to be a fair process and this was a time when every player was treated the same. We always ended with positive vision so that the players went away with that mindset.

If the players thought they had performed according to the rules of 'Bloods' footy – playing their role, putting the team first and giving maximum effort – they would get up from their seat and move the magnet with their name on it across the whiteboard to place it under the Bloods heading.

As well, at the start of the first training session every week we had a quick, often light-hearted, ceremony on the

SCG where we'd gather together in a huddle and the coaches would award a football to the player who had best carried out his role for the team.

The win against the Lions placed us sixth on the ladder.

The group was gelling, and there was a lot of excitement around the club. The players understood we could be a good side if they stuck to the plan. Outside the club, we were earning respect and that had been one of the players' primary aims at our Coffs Harbour leadership camp.

But there was a long way to go, and I wasn't getting carried away. Our sights had to be firmly fixed on our long-term plans to reshape the team and the culture, rather than short-term results. When the media asked, I didn't sway from my assessment that we were 'rebuilding'. Playing finals was not on our minds.

I constantly referred to the 25 points on my coaching notes. They were my touchstone.

Motivate players by being positive.
Be specific at quarter time, half time, three-quarter time
by re-addressing strategies – don't just verbally abuse.

I'm naturally a fairly calm person, but my daily meditation practice also helped enormously. Tami and I had begun meditating four years before, and as a result I could generally keep my emotions on a fairly even keel. I talked to the squad about the practice, and Tami came in to teach meditation to about 20 players who were interested, including Brett Kirk, Craig Bolton and Adam Goodes.

There's a lot of anxiety in football clubs, even when you're winning. Players constantly worry about getting selected to play, getting a kick, stuffing up on the field, making mistakes, getting dropped. It can eat away at you. Meditation helped clear their minds and sharpened their focus. They could ride the emotional bumps more easily, and that meant they were better prepared to play.

We got on a roll. As the season went on, Kirky was one of the most improved players in the AFL. It was a great story, because in many ways he was lucky to still be at the club.

When I took over as interim coach after round 12, 2002, he wasn't in the team. In our match committee meeting ahead of round 15, Stuey Maxfield – there because he was injured and had stepped in to fill my role as defensive coach – urged us to give his mate another chance.

Kirky had done a few impressive jobs in those last few rounds of 2002, and our accountable game plan suited him. Over the pre-season, particularly during some of our more challenging one-on-one drills, we'd recognised his strengths. He had a fantastic defensive mindset, was smart and worked extremely hard.

We created a role for him in our new game plan and he fully embraced it. He had a great ability to win the ball himself while at the same time nullifying the opposition's best players. We called him a 'run-with' player, rather than a tagger. He was an incredible asset, and beat almost every A-grade midfielder in the AFL that year. It was all due to his concentration skills and strong-willed character.

Like Adam Goodes, he no longer had the fear of failure and it was a powerful tonic. Empowerment excited the players.

Our teaching focus remained strong and we revamped our weekly training schedule to suit our new methods. The science of post-game recovery was evolving and we were finding a lot of players weren't ready to train on Monday or even Tuesday. The first session of the week became somewhat irrelevant, so we had to look at how we continued our game plan development in-season.

So we changed the weekly set-up. It was another example where we looked at our needs and decided we didn't have to blindly do what had always been done.

On Monday and Tuesday we concentrated on skill development and individual and team reviews. Many players only did standing skills or off-legs work, as they were still recovering from the weekend's game, so demanding had the sport become.

Then we switched our main session to later in the week. It was scheduled on Thursday or Friday, always two days before our game, whether that was on a Saturday or Sunday (we only rarely played Friday games).

That way, we had almost everyone on the training track and we could train for our game plan and what we wanted to achieve in a particular match.

We started to close that last session to the media and public, as we began doing drills that simulated set plays or strategies we wanted to employ during that weekend's game. We wanted to keep out the opposition team's spies.

The 22 players selected to play senior footy were on one team, and we'd use reserves players to mock-up our opponents. One of the youngsters would put on a jumper and pretend to be Ben Cousins from the West Coast Eagles or Michael Voss from the Lions, complete with their number on his back.

We'd brief them to position themselves as those star players tended to do in games, and then we'd coach our midfielders on how they could counter them at the stoppages around the ground, or the centre bounce. To get a different perspective, I often watched from the grandstand and instructed via walkie-talkie.

The simulation took our game-related training to a new level. We also practised for pivotal moments in any game.

For example, what should we do if we're a goal down with a minute to play and the ball is thrown up in our forward line? How could we get a player free to collect the ball from the ruck tap and give him space to score? Where should the ruckman direct the ball? How should we try to bring the ball from defence into attack when we're behind in the last stages of the game?

We developed set plays which proved beneficial in tight contests over the next couple of years. We spent countless hours educating our players on every aspect of the game as we rebuilt the team, trying to fulfil our aim to improve every player on the list.

Between round five and round 17, we lost only two games. After round 17, we were sitting second on the ladder. Then we faltered, losing to the Adelaide Crows and Hawthorn in succession.

Next up? The daunting task of Brisbane again, this time at their home ground, the Gabba. The challenge forced our players to refocus on what they did best – working hard and playing for each other rather than as individuals.

We were down at half time but turned it on in the third quarter and came from behind to win by 14 points. Leo Barry, Andrew Schauble and Craig Bolton were rock solid in defence and Barry Hall was at his bullocking best, kicking five goals.

The following weekend was one of the most remarkable during my time in Sydney. We were playing Collingwood at Telstra Stadium, as it was then called, at Homebush. The build-up was incredible, and all of Sydney seemed to be excited by our surprise season.

On Saturday, 23 August, a crowd of 72,393 packed the stadium, as it was then called, to watch us take on the Magpies. Our young group had never played before a crowd like it. I'd been in Sydney since late 1994, and it felt as if the city had genuinely embraced us as its own. It's still the biggest crowd ever to watch an AFL game outside Melbourne.

Collingwood were too good for us that night, but the finals-type atmosphere turned out to be an invaluable experience for our players.

We finished the home and away season with a win over Melbourne. Port Adelaide were on top of the ladder, Collingwood second, Brisbane third, and we were fourth. We had earned the right to a double chance in the finals. We were playing Port Adelaide, in Adelaide, in a qualifying final. I had to say the 'f' word now.

Unfortunately, we weren't going to have all our best players available to take on Port, who had dominated the season and been on top for the past three months, three games clear of any other team.

Our number one ruckman, Jason Ball, very experienced and a real on-field leader, had suffered a shoulder injury a month before and he wasn't going to be fit. Michael O'Loughlin had sent a groan through the coaches' box when he tore his hamstring in the last game against Melbourne and there was no way he could play. Jason Saddington, a key part of our defence, had a knee injury and Ryan O'Keefe was out with a shoulder problem.

Time to turn to those dog-eared coaching notes again: **The coach's attitude will rub off on the players.** Every pundit in the country had written us off, but we kept the mood upbeat ahead of our trip to Adelaide.

By that stage of the season, the coaches and players had great confidence in each other, no matter how tough the task. The players were galvanised by the fact that everyone outside the club doubted them.

We flew over there genuinely thinking we could win. We

believed in our game plan and our reliance on teamwork and players carrying out roles, rather than relying on star individuals. We had faith that other players could step into those roles and do the job when there were injuries.

I said to them, 'Boys, don't think because it's a final you have to do anything differently or try harder. It will be faster and quicker because it's a final, so do it at speed but just play the way we know works for us. Play for each other.'

Port were raging favourites at home, but we kicked three goals in the first 15 minutes. Goodesy was in the ruck but running everywhere, driven, unstoppable. The fanatical Port fans were stunned and silenced, and at the end of the first quarter the Port players realised what they were up against.

Daryn Cresswell had a standout game. He was a brilliant offensive midfielder and when he kicked a goal prior to half time we were 40 points up. Barry Hall applied relentless pressure in our forward line and kicked six goals.

Brett Kirk got smashed by Port hard man Byron Pickett, but jumped up like a jack-in-the-box. His teammates were in awe. Leo Barry was fearless, almost to the point of being crazy. He went back with the flight of the ball, in a contest against Gavin Wanganeen. Wanganeen flinched and Leo didn't. Those acts epitomised our spirit and sent a message to Port that we could handle whatever they dished out.

There were so many inspirational moments. By the final quarter, Tadhg Kennelly, Stephen Doyle and Brad Seymour were injured and we had only 19 fully fit players. Port had so much talent and they kept coming at us. We kicked only one goal in the last quarter, but we hung on to win by 12 points.

The media dubbed it a miracle. But it was no miracle. The Bloods attitude had got us through – hard, disciplined, relentless footy. One in, all in. They had made a pledge to each other and stayed true to it. Stuey Maxfield said he was proud of his team of 'honest workers'.

We had earned a week off before a home preliminary final. In front of 71,019 spectators – just shy of our crowd against Collingwood – we played the Brisbane Lions, who were striving for their third consecutive premiership.

O'Loughlin, Ball and Brad Seymour were still out. We stayed with the Lions until three-quarter time, but had no more to give. We finally ran out of puff. We were simply not as far along the development path as the mighty Lions. In the last term, Brisbane had 12 scoring shots to our one and beat us by 44 points.

We had faltered, but won the admiration of the football world. Years later, I heard Swans star Kieren Jack recall how he was in the crowd that night, then a 16-year-old Sydney teenager, and how it had ignited his passion for the Swans and the sport.

The next week, Brisbane played Collingwood in the Grand Final and made history, winning their third flag in succession.

As I reflected on the year, I knew I had witnessed something extraordinary in that qualifying final win over Port Adelaide. It was the most courageous team performance I had been involved in. They might not have had the talent of other teams, but their spirit and bond helped them overcome significant odds.

They had a genuine love of the red and white jumper and a love of each other. You don't get that pride and passion and performance unless you really care for your teammates.

I knew the team had great leaders and a special character, something we could build on in the years to come.

We had climbed the ladder from 11th in 2002 to third in 2003. I was named the AFL Coaches Association Coach of the Year, a huge honour and a credit to all our coaches, fitness and medical staff.

There was another moment of enormous pride to come when Adam Goodes was awarded the 2003 Brownlow Medal, alongside two other very deserving winners, Nathan Buckley of Collingwood and Mark Ricciuto of Adelaide.

I had great pride in all the people I worked with. We were in it for the long haul, and we were in it together.

CHAPTER 8
Who says we're ugly?

In the years that followed, the foundation established in 2003 was the bed of granite. We'd tried the young guys, educated them and they had developed more quickly than we had hoped.

The benefits flowed off the field, too. The club had generated extra membership and marketing revenue, crowds had lifted by 16 per cent at the SCG and we'd averaged crowds of 50,000 for our three games at Homebush.

But your first year as a coach is almost like a free pass. No one had rated us in 2003 and we'd snuck up on a few teams. But the reality was we'd been towelled by Brisbane in the preliminary final and were still a fair way from where we wanted to be. How were we going to progress from there to reach our ultimate aim of a premiership?

Outsiders suggested our list might have been more talented than we'd realised – a year after most had judged us worthy of the wooden spoon. But internally, we knew that wasn't the case. The change in culture and spirit had made the difference in 2003. The team-first ethos was the key and the players believed it.

I told the media at the start of 2004 that I was determined not to waver from our accountable, one-on-one game plan.

My biggest concern was that, if we went through a losing streak, we must not be tempted to waver, jump around or suddenly dramatically change our ways.

The tendency among AFL coaches had been that if things weren't going well, they changed their plans in a bid to save their jobs. Most of those coaches ended up losing their jobs anyway, because the players were confused.

The only way forward was to stick with our long-term plan to rebuild and develop young players such as Lewis Roberts-Thomson and Adam Schneider – who had both impressed in 2003 – the emerging Luke Ablett, Jarrad McVeigh and hard-headed Paul Bevan, who had been elevated off the rookie list.

We had to teach them the right way to play. Hard work with a defensive mindset was the basis; we didn't want them to chase kicks and let their opponents get easy ball.

McVeigh was the perfect example of our approach to developing young players. A local boy from Sydney club Pennant Hills, he came to the Swans at the end of 2002, selected with our first pick (number five) in the national draft.

Obviously he was highly talented, one of the best juniors in the country. He had great skills and superior endurance. A midfielder, he was used to gathering possessions at will each week at the under-age level. Like most highly touted juniors, he was a great attacking player but had never had to worry much about curbing his opponents. They were usually chasing him.

But that way of playing wouldn't cut it at the highest level, not under our system anyway.

Jarrad expected to play senior footy fairly quickly, but we made him wait. He spent the entire 2003 season in our reserves side while we taught him our ways. He was a great ball winner and knew what to do when he got it, but in the

Sydney system the emphasis was firstly on tackling, chasing, smothering and sticking with your opponent.

We had to iron out any bad habits. Pressuring the opposition was a pillar of our game and he wouldn't be ready to play in the seniors until he did that consistently. He had to start with a defence-first attitude and the rest would flow.

Jarrad didn't always like it, but it helped him develop into one of the best two-way running midfielders in the AFL.

We stuck with that patient way of developing players during my entire time at Sydney. No one got a game just because they were a high draft pick.

Luke Ablett, nephew of the great Gary Ablett and cousin of Gary Ablett Jnr, was another example. He was a second-round draft pick but spent the best part of three years in the reserves before he established himself as a run-with player during 2004.

Luke now says that he believes giving players senior games before they deserve it is a reason why some other teams are chronic under-performers. Those players have never been taught to eradicate their weaknesses.

In 2016, just after I finished as coach of Melbourne, Jarrad McVeigh sent me a message. He was then captain of the Swans and about to play in his fourth Grand Final in 10 years (2006, 2012, 2014, 2016). 'Roosy, thanks for teaching me the right way to play,' his message read. It was one of the most powerful messages of support I received during my coaching career.

People often ask me who are the best players I've coached, and even after that first year as coach of the Swans I believed Leo Barry and Brett Kirk could be absolute champions of the game. I couldn't think of two players better able to maximise the talent they had, to work to their strengths.

How could Leo Barry play as a key defender when he

stood 184 centimetres tall and weighed 88 kilos, often against opponents much taller and heavier? He worked with what he had – his amazing agility, high leap, and his closing speed. He didn't try to wrestle the big forwards he played on, but beat them because he was quicker and smarter than them.

And then there was Brett Kirk, who had been knocked back repeatedly but had conquered every star midfielder in the competition in 2003 through a combination of physical and mental toughness.

It reinforced my belief that we should concentrate more on helping players maximise their strengths, rather than focusing on their weaknesses.

Jared Crouch was another good example. He was never the most skilful player, but his discipline, mental strength and physical endurance were out of the ordinary. He used those strengths to do much-needed jobs for us and blanket opponents.

In round one of 2004, we were scheduled to meet Brisbane again. In the lead-up, Crouchy had to deal with being called a cheat by Jason Akermanis – a sign of how much he had got under Aka's skin.

We lost in a close one to Brisbane, and it was the start of a genuine roller-coaster of a season. We won three in a row and then fell into a month-long slump.

Forwards Michael O'Loughlin, Adam Schneider and Nick Davis had injuries and our key defender, Andrew Schauble, had a long-term hamstring injury. These things happen to all clubs.

We'd been able to cover for injuries before. The real problem was a drop-off in our defensive efforts, particularly in the midfield, where our core group of players were below their best. Against Essendon in round six, we'd lost the clearances 51 to 30.

It was a real test of our system, which was based on the players taking responsibility. After four losses on the trot and several soul-searching meetings, the Bloods identified what was going wrong.

Jude Bolton, who had led the team in hard-ball-gets and clearances in 2003, articulated it. He said their work rate and ability to create a contest had dropped off. He vowed to lift his pressure skills, to chase, tackle and harass the opposition into mistakes.

It was harder for the players that year. We couldn't slip under the radar after 2003, and Jude and other players were paid a lot more attention by the opposition.

But we also loved the challenge of studying other teams and working out the best ways to counter their strengths.

From my study of overseas sporting teams, I believed good teams had two traits – they had their own firm identity and style, but they also had the ability to take away the opposition's identity and stop them doing what they liked. There were generally two or three things the other team did well. As a coaching group, we worked out what they were, and devised ways to stop them.

In round 11, we faced St Kilda, and they were having an incredible season. They had won the first 10 games of the season and boasted a gang of monster marking forwards led by Fraser Gehrig, who had kicked nine goals the previous week.

Our biggest defender, Andrew Schauble, was still out with injury, so it was over to Leo Barry.

Leo did the job, as always. Gehrig was 10 centimetres taller than Leo and 13 kilograms heavier. At the end of the day, Gehrig had not kicked a goal for the first time in a match that year. His sole disposal tally was two handballs. Leo's was 23 disposals and five marks.

Leo was playing as well as any defender I'd ever seen. He was strong, quick, courageous to a fault. Craig Bolton curtailed the brilliant Nick Riewoldt and Paul Williams was pivotal in the midfield. Crouchy kept Stephen Milne to a single kick and that was a clanger. Barry Hall kicked five goals, as we upset the Saints by 36 points.

This was the sort of against-the-odds challenge that brought out our best traits, the type of win we had made our trademark in 2003.

It was a highlight of our season, along with a fantastic win over the Lions in round 18 that was one of the most disciplined team displays I'd seen. Hall kicked just one goal but competed ferociously, laying tackles and barging his way through to help teammates.

Brisbane Lions coach Leigh Matthews said our defence was stifling, and lamented how hard they had found it to score. We had controlled the pace and the tempo of the game, slowing it down at times to hold on to the ball and stop the Lions gaining momentum. That tempo football had become an important tactic for us.

We were developing a reputation as a team who made it hard for our opponents to win the ball, restricting other teams to low possession counts. We copped some criticism in the media for our style, but my response was simple: isn't the aim of the game to stop your opponents getting the ball, to make it hard for them?

We were sixth at the end of the home and away season and had to play the West Coast Eagles in an elimination final at Homebush.

We were worried about their goal sneak, Phillip Matera, who had kicked five goals against us earlier in the year. We turned to 29-year-old Matthew Nicks, whose career was nearing its end. He'd played mostly at half-forward, so it was a big ask. I told him we were giving him a big job, but believed he could do it. He just had to focus and come ready to play.

I always tried to bring a sense of calm and purpose when I spoke to the players before games.

Our plan for Matera worked so well that Nicks restricted him to three handballs for the match, and two of them were ineffective. It was one more example of the power of putting ego aside and reaping the rewards.

But it wasn't all shutdown football. We'd gone on the offensive against the Eagles' best ball winner, Chris Judd, giving the job to our veteran midfielder Paul Williams. The move had paid off as Paul gathered 31 touches and restricted Judd – who was to go on to win the Brownlow that season – to well below his average with 19.

As thunder, lightning and rain pounded the ground, we beat the Eagles by 41 points. It was the first final the Swans ever played against the West Coast Eagles, but it certainly was not going to be the last.

We had showed grit and played hard, contested football. I told the media we could never fault the players' effort levels. The crucial thing was they never got their ambitions mixed up with their capabilities.

Overall in 2004 we didn't perform as consistently as we needed to and injuries didn't help, though they had forced us to blood the young guys throughout the season.

The following week in a semifinal at the MCG, St Kilda turned the tables on us. They ran rampant, we couldn't shut them down and they won by eight goals.

St Kilda didn't make the Grand Final, though. It was a contest between Port Adelaide and Brisbane, with the Power thwarting the Lions' bid to win four consecutive flags.

We had finished fifth and had valuable finals experience, but we had to find ways to progress again.

My view has always been that you spend all year developing your current playing list as best you can, then at the end of the season you bring in as much new talent as possible.

The conventional approach was to do some horse-trading in the trade period just after the season, and then use the national draft to select the best youngsters in the country and wait for them to develop. You used a combination of trade and draft to boost your list, but the draft was considered the primary focus.

That year our first pick in the draft was number 15, a valuable commodity. At that time, most clubs wouldn't dream of giving away a first-round pick. But one Sunday night Tami and I did an analysis of the long-term outcomes for high draft picks across all clubs. A high proportion didn't make the grade. At the age of 17 or 18, they were too much of an unknown quantity.

At the end of 2003, we'd brought in four players through the draft, and re-drafted Amon Buchanan. Only one of those five – Amon – ended up playing more than a handful of games.

I began to seriously doubt the draft was all it was cracked up to be. My thoughts also harked back to my coaching presentation to the board at the end of 2002. I had said we should try to identify under-achieving players with potential at other clubs, those who might fill a need for us.

That philosophy had worked when we'd recruited Craig Bolton from Brisbane. He'd gone from a fringe player at the Lions to a key cog in our defence, flourishing with the opportunity. Craig felt needed at the Swans and responded to the faith we'd shown in him.

There had to be more players like that at other clubs who could help us improve.

During 2004, we had decided our key priority was another ruckman, as we'd been hampered by injuries to our big men for a couple of years. Our game style relied on doing well at the stoppages and we needed more depth in our ruck stocks. We had put too much pressure on Jason Ball and Adam Goodes, who was too small and valuable elsewhere to be a permanent ruckman.

I told our national recruiting manager, Rick Barham, that we should give up pick 15 if we could get a ruckman from Melbourne, Darren Jolly. Rick nearly fell off the chair.

Rick is an extremely good recruiter and talent spotter, but I wanted to bring in a player who was a known quantity, rather than gamble on a teenage draft pick I had no real idea about.

Jolly was then 23, and a 200 centimetre giant who had played 48 games for the Demons. He was talented, but at Melbourne he played second fiddle to their star number one ruckman, Jeff White. He was exactly what we wanted – a player craving more game time and more responsibility. If we could pull off a targeted recruitment of Jolly, our list would be better overnight, an injection of talent in the position we needed.

We did the deal. Melbourne were happy with pick 15, which they used to draft Lynden Dunn, and we were happy with Jolly. That wasn't a common outcome during the trade period at that time. A few clubs had a reputation for really trying to screw other clubs in trades and it annoyed me. It was better to make a realistic, fair offer and both clubs could benefit.

That philosophy of strategic, targeted recruiting became the basis for all our trading while I was coach of the Swans and it paid off.

The 2005 season was about to start. We had developed some great kids, recruited well and our older players were at their peak. We had finals experience and played a hard, tough brand of contested football. We should be in the mix.

Our new players, including Jolly, had gone through an induction, as all new players to the club had done since our Leading Teams leadership and team-building program at the end of 2002.

The players ran the inductions. One of the more experienced guys, like Stuart Maxfield or Leo Barry, would outline a brief history of the club and its famous players, the original Bloods. They explained what it meant to be a current-day Bloods player, the behaviour and discipline expected on and off the field. It had been over two years since we reset our culture and the players were passionate about maintaining the standards and passing on the legacy.

Stuey spoke at the annual Guernsey Presentation just before the season began and gave the audience and the media an amazing insight into the Bloods culture. 'From the player's perspective, our new culture is evident from the moment a newcomer walks through the door. Those who make excuses are challenged, those who are honest with themselves are encouraged, a strong work ethic is non-negotiable, courage and discipline are rewarded,' he said.

When the season began, we hit the ground running in a high-scoring win over Hawthorn. In round three, we came from behind to beat Brisbane. But over the next few weeks our momentum halted. We played badly and had disappointing losses at home to Adelaide and Melbourne. Then we suffered a seven-goal thrashing at the hands of West Coast over at Subiaco. We had dropped to 12th on the ladder.

Our commitment to contested, dogged, team-oriented footy was faltering. I'd always said it would be hard to maintain, so demanding was our style. But it wasn't that the players were physically or mentally exhausted. It was worse. The players fully understood the system, but had stopped playing for each other and were more worried about individual glory.

The Eagles were a fantastic team, make no mistake, but we had let them run all over us. Our players hadn't been accountable. We had midfielders flying for marks in the forward line, we had guys getting cheap kicks, the players hadn't run hard or helped each other out. It was a disastrous loss, a complete mess.

After that game, I absolutely blew up – I went nuts, to put it bluntly. It wasn't something I often did, and it went against my rule of not flying off the handle after a game. But the time was right. I'd had enough.

I actually said to the players, 'I'll leave, I'll go to Richard Colless and tell him I'm finishing up.' I told them they had stopped valuing our system, stopped caring about playing their role for the team.

'Guys, I'm wasting my time. Deep down, you don't really value what we're trying to do. Deep down, you don't believe that if you play your role we're a better team and that's the way we can win a premiership. So let's just forget it,' I told them.

I was serious. I could have walked away then and there. I had always said I wasn't a career coach, hanging around just for the pay packet. I wasn't interested in the job if we weren't going about it the correct way and sticking to our values.

I told them they were no longer living by the creed and behaviours that had made us successful in 2003 and 2004. In particular, they weren't living it on game day, the most important day of the week.

'We're living it during the week, we're a good bunch of guys. We train hard, but we can't have players playing like this. If we do, we are kidding ourselves.'

I threw my arms in the air and walked out of the room.

It was a pivotal day for the club, and not just because I had blown up.

That same day, the chief executive of the AFL, Andrew Demetriou, had been interviewed on Melbourne radio station Triple M. Asked about playing styles, Andrew made the extraordinary comment that he didn't like the way we played, and that we wouldn't win many games. These were the words of the AFL boss on Triple M, on the weekend of round six, Saturday, 30 April 2005:

> I would like to see the Sydney Swans winning more games because it's a very important market for us. I don't like at all the way that they're playing football, but that's just a personal view. I think it would be fair to say in the early part of the season we saw some games that weren't attractive, and I think they've been described as ugly. And probably there would be a brand of football played on the other side of the border which is not particularly attractive.

Demetriou went on:

> Unless the Swans change that style of play, they won't win many football matches. I don't think there's anything we can do because we wouldn't intervene. But I think unless there's a change in the manner and style in which they play, they will lose more games than they win.

Over in Perth, I was unaware of the comments until after the game, but the media had called Richard Colless. Richard responded that he was 'stunned' and almost in total disbelief.

I had a similar reaction when I was told what Demetriou had said – though I held my tongue in public. Why was he trying to tell a football team how they should play? I couldn't run the AFL, and Andrew couldn't coach an AFL team, so we should each stick to our own jobs.

As my assistant coach Ross Lyon used to say, let the cobblers do the cobbling.

Andrew was a controversial person who had strong views on many subjects. In terms of the corporate side, television rights for the AFL, membership and sponsorships, he did a very good job.

But he was off the mark with those comments. Imagine if the CEO of Coca-Cola said he or she wouldn't buy Coca-Cola in New South Wales, because the Coca-Cola on the other side of the border was terrible. The repercussions of trashing their own brand would be enormous. From a corporate point of view, to have the CEO of the AFL criticise the brand was not smart.

I've often been asked if I was angry about Andrew's comments. I wasn't angry, but I definitely found the comments unnecessary.

What I learnt about Andrew was that he had a very different leadership style to me. Andrew didn't appear to value creating relationships. As our chairman Richard Colless said at the time, Andrew had not been to a game in Sydney that year, or rung him about anything.

I've since met Andrew Demetriou many times at official functions. People often ask me if the incident had an effect on our relationship. It didn't, because we never had much to do with each other anyway. I was like many people in the football industry – Andrew was the CEO, and I was the coach of the Sydney Swans, and there wasn't a lot of meaningful interaction. If I had any disappointment, it was directed at the AFL Commission, which made no public response to his comments.

My belief was that the Commission had been set up to hold everyone accountable for their actions, and to always put the interests of the game first.

I was concerned, from a leadership point of view, that the Commission had not come out and supported one of its clubs in the face of Andrew's comments.

Interestingly, Bill Kelty, the long-time leader of the Australian Council of Trade Unions (ACTU), who at that time was an AFL commissioner, revealed in 2016 that he had strongly disagreed with Demetriou's comments, and had told him so behind closed doors.

I believe if the AFL's corporate governance had been working as it should, then Bill Kelty, or the chairman, or another senior commissioner, would have come out publicly at the time, and held Andrew accountable for his comments.

The following week, I was scheduled to speak to staff at the AFL about football in NSW. But I spoke to Richard Colless and Andrew Ireland and decided to cancel. Why would I go and do that for the AFL when the CEO of the organisation is effectively telling everyone how bad we are, and that he doesn't rate us?

During that period in 2005, there were plenty of commentators having a crack at what they called our shutdown, stifling game style – most of them ill-informed – but that was their job. It was a different thing when the CEO of the competition did it.

As a club, we were solid and united in our response. I was willing to put my hand up and say we weren't playing well and needed to play better. There was no question about that.

But all clubs play poorly at times. We also had several of our key players missing, including ruckmen Jason Ball and Darren Jolly, and midfielders Paul Williams and Ben Mathews, so our ability to move the ball and score wasn't as potent as usual.

There is a difference between playing poorly and being accused of having a game style that is tarnishing the game and never going to be successful.

There was so much misinformation and misunderstanding about the way we played. The criticism was basically that we strangled other teams by sending extra players to our backline. But we had never been a team that flooded our defence.

We played one-on-one football, which is the opposite of a flooding team that lets its opponents run loose and then corrals them in defence and tries to win the ball back there. It is an indictment on the industry that so few people recognised that.

We wanted our players to run hard, stay with their man, get up the ground and get back to help each other out. If the other team put extra men back, we matched up on them.

Why would we let Jason Akermanis get the ball his usual 30 times, when Crouchy could play tight on him and keep him to 10 disposals? Why would we allow Gary Ablett to roam loose and damage us with 35 touches when we knew Ben Mathews could stick with him and curb his influence?

We had other strategies that resulted in extra numbers around the ball at different times – part of our plan to help us score and not let the opposition get easy take-away ball.

The role of our half-forwards, such as Ryan O'Keefe and Amon Buchanan, was to come up to the stoppages, and try to drag their defenders with them. We called it playing 'three-quarter ground', and it also meant we'd have a more open forward line, and less congestion for our key forwards Barry Hall and Michael O'Loughlin.

If the opposition's defenders dropped off our half-forwards, then we'd have extra numbers at the stoppage. At training, we worked a lot on improving our handball out of stoppages, so if we used the ball well we could get it into space and down into attack to Hally and Mick.

The biggest myths about the Swans were that we flooded, and that we were hell-bent on creating stoppages. Both were wrong.

Our basic philosophy was to either get the footy, or if they had it, get it back as quickly as possible. What's the quickest way to get it back? By tackling. But if they didn't get rid of the ball and we didn't get a free kick for the tackle, there was a stoppage and a ball up.

We didn't want stoppages – we just wanted the ball, wanted to thwart the opposition, and score ourselves.

If Eagles star midfielder Ben Cousins got the ball at a stoppage, my expectation was that one of our guys would tackle him straight away. That wasn't because we wanted to create another stoppage, but because we wanted to get the ball or at least make it a 50-50 situation. Every contest mattered to us.

We didn't really care what people thought and in some ways it worked in our favour that few people really understood the way we played. We were surprised that hardly any opposition club scouts came to watch us train, and few people in the media analysed our game plan closely. One person wrote or said something in the football media and then it became gospel.

But it was also frustrating at times. The misinformation had an impact because so many people, including I believe the umpires, wrongly thought we were deliberately trying to congest the game and play 'negative' football – whatever that is.

Demetriou's comments were causing a stir, though it wasn't nearly as big a deal in Sydney as it was in Melbourne.

Either way, I had more immediate issues to deal with. Back in Sydney a few days after the loss to West Coast, Stuey Maxfield came to see me, as he regularly did. He was upset with my criticism of the players after the game and he had a real crack at me. Stuey said he thought I'd got carried away and been too hard.

It wasn't always a bed of roses between Stuey and me, or between Brett Kirk – who was now a key member of the leadership group – and me. They had firm opinions and were both strong, vocal leaders.

I explained to Stuey that I still believed my view was justified. It was a vigorous discussion but that day, as always, when we walked out of our weekly meeting we were in agreement about where we were heading.

The players took it on board. At our review meeting, I could see they were grappling with it – were they happy just being a group of individuals who made finals, did well enough and got a couple of pats on the back? Or were they really serious about trying to be the best possible team, playing to their Bloods values?

That was their wake-up call – the week the players decided they were on board. Looking back, it was probably the biggest moment of the home and away season for us, a real turning point.

We made several changes for our game the following week against Essendon. Jarred Moore made his debut, and Luke Vogels was elevated off the rookie list. We sent a message to the players that they had to play our way to earn a game.

Stuey had to pull out of the team at the last minute due to a chronic knee injury. The following week, he announced he was stepping down as captain for family reasons, as he needed to spend several days each week in Melbourne with his children. Sadly, he wasn't able to play again. The match against West Coast in round six was his final game of football, though his influence on the playing group remained profound.

We decided to appoint a group of six players as joint captains, to be rotated every two weeks during the rest of the season – Jude Bolton, Ben Mathews, Barry Hall, Leo Barry, Brett Kirk and Adam Goodes. Kirky said at a media conference that sharing the role was a fantastic concept, and showed the depth of leadership we'd created at the club over the past couple of years.

It was back to business. During the next few weeks, we turned our form around, got back to our core values and started to play much better footy. Andrew Demetriou had done us a favour in a roundabout way. While we didn't waste too much time talking about his comments, they did galvanise us.

I got pretty passionate at a team meeting a couple of weeks later, after some free kicks had gone against us in a game. After round seven, we didn't win the free kick count in any of the following 19 games we played that season. I felt all the commentary about our game style might have been having a subconscious impact.

I could sense the players felt there was a lot stacked against us, so I addressed it at the team meeting. 'Guys, if we're going to win, it's just us, just the people in this room. We have to stick together, because it's us against them.

'We're going to do this by ourselves. We can do it, we're up for it. Don't worry, there is enough courage and strength in this room to achieve what we want even if things don't always go our way.'

The message resonated with our players. A number of them had a similar personal story. Kirky had nearly got the arse and now he was one of our captains. He loved proving people wrong, and he wasn't alone. Amon Buchanan, Luke Ablett, Paul Bevan, Sean Dempster, Ben Mathews – they all knew people didn't really rate them, and they had worked their backsides off for their success.

The players developed an even stronger bond. They had pride in their club and their team, and they didn't like what was being said about us. They bottled the feeling and took it out with them on the field. It gave them a steely resolve.

The Bloods were on a mission.

CHAPTER 9
Here it is!

At our annual Guernsey Presentation night at the start of the 2005 season, I'd spoken from the heart: 'I will acknowledge there are more talented teams in the competition. But I won't acknowledge there is a better team in the competition.' As the season reached its climax, those words would be tested to the core.

In round 21, we beat the fifth-placed Kangaroos by 37 points and moved into third place on the ladder. We had locked in a top four finish. After hiccups earlier in the season, the players were living up to their team-first ethos on the eve of the finals. I refused to get caught up in speculation about our premiership chances, but there was a fantastic mood around the club.

Our first quarter against the Kangaroos had been super-impressive. We'd stunned them with a seven-goal term and, for a change, everyone was talking about our potent forward line rather than our shutdown defence. When we'd lost to the Kangaroos in round two, we'd managed seven goals for the entire game.

Our forward line was dubbed a multi-headed monster, boasting Barry Hall, Michael O'Loughlin and Nick Davis, as well as the strong-marking and mobile Ryan O'Keefe, and the crumbing forwards, Amon Buchanan and Adam Schneider. Adam Goodes also sneaked into attack to add height and firepower.

That day Davo kicked five goals, Hally kicked three and Mick kicked two. If one forward was tied down, another would bob up. They knew each other's moves inside out.

But Hally had been our standout forward over the whole season. As we went into the final home and away game, against Hawthorn at the MCG, he was a good chance to win one of the AFL's most coveted individual honours, the John Coleman Medal, awarded to the league's highest goal-kicker after the regular season.

He was in a two-way battle for the medal with St Kilda's Fraser Gehrig. Ahead of round 22, Gehrig had 74 goals, and Hall had 69. Then Gehrig was ruled out of the Saints game against Brisbane due to a groin injury. If Barry kicked five or more goals against Hawthorn – a feat he'd already achieved in six games that season – he'd at least share the honour.

He was on fire. He had six goal assists in the first half of the game, which was then an AFL record, according to Champion Data statistics. He led hard, took 13 marks and had 19 disposals. He kicked three goals and had easy chances to kick at least three more. Instead, he repeatedly dished off the ball to his teammates.

He was our best player as we won by nine goals. But what we admired most was his selflessness. On a day when he could have been excused for being a bit selfish in a bid to win the Coleman Medal, he gave the goals away to others. In the coaches' box I was saying, 'Mate, have a shot at goal, for God's sake!'

But his attitude typified where we had got to as a footy team.

Hally made it clear team glory mattered far more than individual honours and he was leading by example.

It wasn't surprising. He had come to the club from St Kilda at the end of the 2001 season with a stated aim to kick four goals a game, along with a reputation as a hothead. He wasn't dubbed 'Big Bad' for nothing. But at the Swans he had seen the benefit of applying pressure first, and then worrying about kicking goals after that.

Hally had matured enormously and was a role model. They were traits Stuey Maxfield had highlighted during his captain's speech at that same Guernsey Presentation in March 2005.

'He has shown a lot of personal growth and is now one of the most influential leaders in the team,' Stuey said. 'When he came from Victoria he had a bad boy image. He has embraced the new culture. People don't know him, but he is an intelligent, sharp guy and his input into team discussions is really valuable.'

As we prepared for our third consecutive finals series, Hally was living up to that praise. As well, his form was incredible. During the season, he had grabbed the most contested marks inside the forward 50 metres of any player in the comp. He had the second-most score assists in the AFL and most others on that list were midfielders who fed the ball to the forwards. He had hit the target with his kicks 88.8 per cent of the time – the best percentage of any of our players.

We decided to name just one captain for the finals. Barry Hall was the man for the job.

Adelaide had finished on top of the ladder, West Coast Eagles were second, we were third and St Kilda was fourth. That meant we had to fly to Perth to play the Eagles on their home ground, Subiaco, in the first week of the finals.

Qualifying final
West Coast Eagles v Sydney Swans

Friday, 2 September 2005
Subiaco Oval

We had played West Coast twice during the year, and it was one win apiece, but we were definitely the underdogs as we travelled across the Nullarbor.

We went over three days before the game, which was 48 hours earlier than normal. We'd had little success over the years at Subiaco Oval, the biggest ground in the competition and about 30 metres longer than our home ground, the SCG. That equated to an extra short kick to goal and I wanted to make sure we had a full training run on Subi and adjusted our plans before the final. There's also a two-hour time difference from Sydney to Perth and we didn't want to leave anything to chance.

The Eagles were a much better side than a year before, when we'd beaten them in an elimination final. They had been on top of the table most of the year.

Their midfield was brilliant. Ben Cousins was a powerhouse who could run all day; Chris Judd was so quick and athletic and could explode into space from the stoppages; Daniel Kerr was a ball of muscle, very fit and very hard to stop. It didn't end there. Andrew Embley was a classy outside running player, Chad Fletcher won plenty of the ball and Tyson Stenglein was a tough-nut tagger.

But, as usual, we had faith in our midfielders to do the job. Benny Mathews was an unsung hero outside the club, but inside we loved his consistency, discipline and commitment to carry out whatever role we asked.

He was also very fit and generally played on Daniel Kerr, and I reassured him we had faith in him to do the job. Footy can get complicated and players can worry about every little thing, so I always tried to simplify it for the players before any game, but especially on an occasion like this.

It was the same message to Luke Ablett, who had the job on Judd, and young Sean Dempster, who had made his debut in round three. He was a quiet kid, but had a defensive mindset and was a great runner, so he often shadowed Cousins.

The game was played at red-hot pace from the opening bounce. Kerr was off the chain in the first quarter and the Eagles kicked the first two goals. Our players trusted each other and regrouped. We were on top in defence and kept them to just a single goal over the second and third quarters, even though their midfielders were playing really well and repeatedly banging the ball into their forward line. At the last break, we were leading by 14 points and the Eagles had kicked only five goals so far.

In the last term, they swung defender Adam Hunter into attack and he hauled in two strong marks – one from a turnover kick from our young defender Lewis Roberts-Thomson – and kicked two goals.

At the other end of the ground, Eagles full-back Darren Glass was containing Hally, but Nick Davis and Mick O'Loughlin were doing all they could to keep the scoreboard ticking over.

It was down to the wire. We were nine points up when umpire Shane McInerney made an incorrect decision that hurt us.

Kirky, who had busted his guts for the team as always, was awarded a free kick in the Eagles' forward half. Leo Barry was running past when Stenglein, who was manning the mark, stepped into his path and they collided. McInerney took the ball from Kirk and handed it to Stenglein, who went back and kicked a long goal.

Most commentators were mystified by the decision, as we were in the coaches' box. As it turned out, a few days later umpires boss Jeff Gieschen admitted McInerney's decision was wrong. Stenglein had moved off the mark and initiated the contact. Leo had not been at fault and the ball should never have been taken from Kirk.

The last minutes of the match were frenzied and the Eagles came over the top of us to win by four points, **10.9 (69) to 10.5 (65)**.

It had been a matter of centimetres, a couple of silly mistakes by us and a few controversial free kicks in a long and grinding contest. Their star midfielders had all played well, but we had still come so close to winning.

The mood in the rooms after the match was like a funeral. The players were shattered. All that bruising effort and we'd lost in a way that was hard to take. I had to act quickly to lift the players out of the gloom. One of a coach's most important skills is reading the mood of the group and deciding how to respond to it.

When I spoke, my aim was to keep them positive: 'Guys, we're still in the competition. Don't feel sorry for yourselves, we're playing next week. That's over, that's done, we've finished with it. There's nothing we can do about it now except focus on next week and win that one.'

I caught the midnight flight home to Sydney so I could watch my sons Dylan and Tyler play footy the next morning. The red-eye from Perth to Sydney is always a horror flight, but it was a special form of torture after that loss.

Figures released a few days later, in the lead-up to our semifinal against Geelong back home at the SCG, were interesting. They showed we'd had more free kicks paid against us than any other team that year. Leo, who was named in the All-Australian side that week, had given away 26 free kicks in our defensive 50-metre zone – double any other player in the AFL.

A poll of 2100 readers in the *Herald Sun* found that 79 per cent believed McInerney's incorrect free against Leo had robbed us of victory in Perth.

The then Premier of NSW, Morris Iemma, who had played Australian Rules footy in the local competition, joked there was a conspiracy against us.

We weren't happy and there was only one place to focus that energy. 'There's nothing wrong with being disappointed and angry and we have to come out and play angry tomorrow night against Geelong,' I told the media. 'The guys are pretty keen to get back out there.'

We made one change to our team, the only selection change in the last eight weeks of the season. Tall forward Luke Vogels, who had been elevated off the rookie list and played 11 games in his debut season, was the hard-luck story. He was out for 20-year-old Paul Bevan, a fearless local Sydney boy. Bevo hadn't been in the side since round 13, but he was more versatile and could slot into attack, defence or midfield.

I expected the team that could sustain its hardness and attack on the ball for the longest time would prevail. It would be a fight to the death. How true that turned out to be.

Second semifinal
Sydney Swans v Geelong

Friday, 9 September 2005
Sydney Cricket Ground
It was a strange night in many ways. It was perfect weather in Sydney, but when we arrived at the ground, the SCG surface was wet and boggy, as if it had been pouring with

rain. We wondered whether the ground staff had left the sprinklers on.

We were flatter than we'd been for months and couldn't get our game going at all. There's a fine line when it comes to harnessing emotion. It had been a tough week and maybe the anger had taken too much out of them.

We found it hard to move the ball and tough to score. We had two goals to half time, and scored only one more in the third term. At three-quarter time, we were down by 17 points, 3.12 (30) to the Cats 6.11 (47). We were playing badly, being pressured by the Cats and blanketed in attack, but they hadn't got too far away from us. Ben Mathews had kept their star player, Gary Ablett, quiet. We hadn't given up hope, but it would take all our never-say-die spirit to win this one.

Then, at the start of the last quarter, with our season on the line, Geelong defender David Johnson ran into the Cats' forward line and kicked a goal. They were four goals ahead, and so far we'd still kicked only three goals all night.

Johnson was Nick Davis's opponent. I saw Brett Kirk run to Davo and look him straight in the eye. We didn't know it then, but later Davo revealed what Kirky had shouted at him: 'Davo, you owe us!'

It was one of the team's strengths. If someone made a mistake or let their teammates down, the coaches didn't drag them off the field. They were answerable to each other.

A few minutes later, Davo kick-started the best quarter of finals football I've seen from any player.

He snapped his first goal from the forward pocket. A few minutes later, he ran back towards goal, out-bodied two opponents and took a strong mark. His set shot sailed through the goalposts. Then his third goal came, a brilliant kick around his body from nearly 40 metres out. There were only a few minutes to go and we were still three points down.

With about 40 seconds to go, I thought we were gone. Then Leo Barry came to the fore, as he so often did. He was the third man up at a stoppage, and hit the ball out of the contest and away into space. We had often spoken about doing that in a tight situation if we were behind.

The ball bounced along our half-forward flank, close to the boundary line. Luke Ablett and Hally did exactly the right thing, keeping the ball in play and then sending it towards our goal square. Almost every player on the field was scrambling around the contest. Ryan O'Keefe tried to kick the ball and it was smothered. The umpire called a ball up. There were 10 seconds to go.

In the coaches' box we watched the players set up in our forward pocket. The game-related training we had introduced in 2003 was about to be put to the ultimate test. We'd trained so many times for this exact scenario – a few points down, a few seconds to go. We knew what to do, but would we be able to pull off our set play?

Jason Ball, our experienced ruckman, showed true leadership. He made things happen under pressure in a game situation. He waved players out of the area and let the midfielders know where he'd tap it. Adam Schneider stepped to the side and put a perfect block on Davo's opponent, and other players had managed to clear out a small space in front of the ruckmen.

The ball was tapped down, Davo ran through the narrow channel of space, the ball juggled in his hands, he whacked it onto his left boot.

I actually thought it was a point until the goal umpire raised two fingers and the SCG crowd of 39,000 roared the house down. The other coaches were going off their heads and

I was telling them to shut up until the realisation came – it was a goal and there were only a couple of seconds to go.

We'd won by three points, **7.14 (56)** to **7.11 (53)**. We had fought and struggled and got over the line with the last kick of the night.

All four goals kicked by Davo were different and illustrated his incredible talent. He could do things few other players were capable of. At times he lacked discipline and was lazy, but he was as smart as any footballer I'd played with or seen. He had beautiful technique and was a great kick. He picked things up more quickly than anyone at the club, whether that was our structure at a forward stoppage or the best way to use his body in a marking contest.

We saw his full repertoire on display during that last quarter. His third goal, the one he kicked across his body running away from the stoppage 30 or 40 metres out, was a goal that only one per cent of players could have kicked.

It was a night I'll never forget, and brought back memories of the preliminary final I'd played at the SCG in 1996, when Tony Lockett's point after the final siren sent us into the Grand Final.

I was thinking about that as I raced down to the ground, where the players were euphoric. When we'd won that prelim final nine years earlier, we had gone crazy and spent so much energy that I felt we'd lost focus ahead of the Grand Final. I didn't want that to happen this time. I wanted to put the proverbial lid on it.

I called the players into a huddle in the middle of the SCG and calmed them down. It was an amazing win and we could celebrate, but it was important not to get carried away or lose sight of what we still had to do. We weren't finished yet. We had to use the momentum and take it to the preliminary final.

The week before, after the loss to the Eagles, I'd been trying to lift them up; now I was trying to contain their emotions. You definitely need to be a part-time psychologist to be a coach. It's all about balance.

Preliminary final
St Kilda v Sydney Swans

Friday, 16 September 2005
MCG

Once again, we were the underdogs as we arrived in Melbourne to take on the Saints. They'd had a much easier run to the preliminary final. They had beaten Adelaide in a qualifying final two weeks earlier and earned a week's break while we were slogging it out against Geelong in the semi-final. Everyone expected we'd run out of steam after two incredibly taxing finals games.

We started well but the Saints, stacked with top-end talent in their forward line including Nick Riewoldt and Gehrig, kept coming back. At three-quarter time, we were seven points behind, but as I addressed the players I could sense we weren't done yet.

We blitzed the Saints in the last 30 minutes. We were expected to tire, but instead we ran harder than before on the wide, open spaces of the MCG. We kicked seven goals and held St Kilda goal-less. Our livewire forward Schneider had one of his best games, nabbing three goals for the quarter as we ran away to win **15.6 (96)** to **9.11 (65)**.

It had been a three-year journey with the players and we were going to the 2005 Grand Final.

Grand Final
West Coast Eagles v Sydney Swans

Saturday, 24 September 2005
MCG

When I played in the 1996 Grand Final, I'd made a conscious effort to enjoy it, as for most footballers playing in a Grand Final is a rare event. In 2005, I wanted to put everything in place so the players could soak it up and appreciate Grand Final week as much as possible.

There is a danger the few days leading up to the game can be overwhelming. I had seen that happen in 1996 to our full-back, Andrew Dunkley. After the preliminary final he was charged with striking Essendon's James Hird and the club went to the Supreme Court to have his ban put on hold. He'd been allowed to play, but the controversy had drained Dunks and it showed when we played North Melbourne in that Grand Final.

On Monday, a couple of days after our win over St Kilda, we found out we were going to have a tribunal drama of our own. There had been media comment over the weekend that Barry Hall might be in trouble with the AFL's Match Review Panel for an incident involving St Kilda's Matt Maguire.

Hally had gone into the preliminary final pretty fired up. After all the build-up at the start of September, he hadn't played his best football in our finals against West Coast or Geelong. He wasn't worried what the public thought, but he felt he had let his teammates down.

He had taken to the field against St Kilda desperate to make amends. Other teams loved to harass and niggle him, to try to get under his skin, and the Saints had been no different.

In the first quarter, he had a run-in with Maguire. Trying to get space and lead for the ball, he had swung his arm into Maguire's stomach and the Saints player had doubled over.

On Monday, the AFL announced that the Match Review Panel had assessed the incident and decided that Hall deserved a two-week suspension. It ruled that Hall's strike was 'behind play', which carried a higher penalty. If we didn't challenge the ruling, our captain wouldn't be playing in the Grand Final.

Our head of football, Andrew Ireland, swung into action and we announced the club would challenge the panel's decision at the AFL tribunal. A hearing was set for the following night. The club hired a QC, Terry Forrest, and they began poring over the television footage of Hall's hit.

We couldn't argue he was innocent. The vision proved there had been contact. We had to argue the incident was 'in play' rather than 'behind play', and hope to have the charge downgraded so it wouldn't attract a match suspension.

Hally flew down to Melbourne with Andrew in a private jet and was there at the tribunal as Terry Forrest argued that the incident met the AFL's own definition of 'in play'. The tribunal took only four minutes to agree. The charge was downgraded from level two to level one. Barry received a reduced points sanction and accepted a reprimand. He was clear to play. I'd been very nervous back in Sydney waiting to hear the result. It was a huge relief.

While it had been a nerve-racking few days, as a coaching group we had done all we could to maintain a sense of calm around the club. Grand Final week becomes almost like a mini-season. It's so exciting and you have to be careful everyone doesn't mentally play the game over and over too early in the week.

On Monday and Tuesday, we made sure the players had tickets sorted for the countless family and friends all clamouring to be at the Grand Final. Being in Sydney, there was plenty of attention, but it wasn't suffocating.

We were able to get training out of the way and keep everything as routine as we could. By that stage of the season, we had such a set way to play and a very clear process to follow. We knew what the match-ups would be and didn't make any selection changes for the Grand Final. We'd made only one in the last eight weeks. Our team was incredibly stable and match-hardened.

We flew down to Melbourne for the Grand Final Parade and I'll never forget the incredible sea of red and white and the feeling that so many old South Melbourne supporters were behind us.

As a group, we didn't talk about the Swans' 72-year premiership drought. We didn't need to. We were well aware the club hadn't won a flag since 1933. But right now we couldn't get caught up in the past. We wanted to make our own history.

Once again, we weren't the favourites to win, but I felt we were ready to win the premiership. I'd spent time thinking what I should say to the players at our most important meeting of the week, the night before the Grand Final.

It had come to me that day. It often happened just after I'd meditated, or while I was meditating. I had the strong feeling this was the right message. That Friday night, just after the team, coaches and support staff had dinner at the Crowne Plaza on the Yarra River, I called the players together for our meeting.

It was time to get down to the nitty-gritty. My message was simple but clear. For the first time since I began coaching, I gave the players an iron-clad promise. 'If you stick to our plans, play our way for 120 minutes and give maximum effort, then I guarantee you will win.'

I didn't have to go into too much detail. By that stage, they knew exactly how we won football games. No matter who the opposition was, the fundamentals were the same. Play the role you've been assigned, do the things that help us win. Win the ball or stick the tackle. Be selfless. Run hard. Be disciplined, relentless.

Our key indicators hadn't changed. If our tackles were effective, if we didn't fumble the ball, if we stopped them having too much easy, uncontested possession, we would win. Our defenders had to stick with the forwards and not trail in behind them when the ball came into attack. It had to be contest after contest after contest, and every single contest would have a bearing. That was our way.

A lot of the talk in the lead-up to the game was about the stellar talent in the West Coast line-up. I was concerned our guys might start to question whether they were good enough to beat the superstar Eagles. Or start to think they had to do more than normal. It is the Grand Final, but the ball is the same, the ground is the same shape, the goalposts are in the same position. It's the team that stays composed, that plays to the game plan and does it for longer, that generally wins.

That meeting was much more about mind games than tactics. The players knew the stakes. I wanted them to understand my expectations were no different from any other game. Do what we've been doing all year.

I didn't want anyone to leave that room with any doubt that I believed we would win. It wasn't a long meeting, only 20 minutes or so, but my aim was to send the guys to bed on Grand Final eve knowing everything was in place.

As a coach, the night before the game was my time, the players were looking to me. I had to lead the way. I'd let them know how confident I was in them. Now it was over to them. It was game time . . .

We arrived at the MCG a couple of hours before the bounce, as we always did. My pre-game routine was the same as every other game. In the rooms, I went to every player and had a quiet chat with him about his responsibilities.

Luke Ablett was going to play on Chris Judd, who'd won the Brownlow Medal the year before. 'Don't get frustrated if he gets away at a couple of stoppages, that's fine. Just make sure the defensive cover is in place and force him into that area, corral him.'

We had three really inexperienced players in the side – Paul Bevan, Lewis Roberts-Thomson and Sean Dempster, who had all played fewer than 50 games.

LRT, as we called him, had been a pet project that year as we taught him how to play as a key defender. We'd brought in Steve Silvagni, the former champion Carlton full-back, to do one-on-one tutoring and fast-track his development. Lewis had grown up playing rugby union and there had been some hairy moments as he learned our game. But we had faith in him. He was going to line up on Eagles forward Ashley Hansen.

Bevo was a tough nut who would come on and off the bench. Sean, who made his debut earlier in the year and had played only 21 AFL games, was given the task of negating Eagles captain Ben Cousins.

I pulled them aside and did what I could to calm their nerves. I told them to soak up the atmosphere and tried to ease the pressure. 'You're an important part of the 22 players out there, you have a role to do and if you carry it out, we'll have success.' It's fair to say they still looked a bit edgy, but they knew we trusted them.

I tried to have a laugh or a joke with players, to be conversational. For a coach, being in the rooms before the game is the worst possible time. I was mindful that some players have headphones on and some are sitting quietly, others are kicking the footy or getting a massage. Everyone has their own way of preparing and their own superstitions. As a coach, you're just trying to fit in.

We had a great group of coaches. Ross Lyon, John Longmire and Peter Jonas were my main assistants, and there were others too, such as our long-time ruck coach, Steve Taubert, and one of the best development coaches in the AFL, George Stone. We all got on well, so we stood around and chatted, passed the time. You're trying to stay alert but relaxed before the game, because you don't want the players to see you anxious.

The team meeting before the game was short. I reiterated the message about match-ups, discipline and how we wanted to cover the Eagles' exits at the stoppages. We had to make sure we had players set up as defensive cover and corridor cover so they couldn't run away with the ball. To be honest, at that stage the players weren't taking in a lot of information. I was only trying to emphasise three or four key points. Finally, I told them again they would definitely win if they gave 100 per cent effort for the entire game.

There were players with injuries, so there were a few in and out of the medical room. Jude Bolton, our hard-headed midfielder, had dislocated his AC joint a few weeks before the Grand Final, so he needed treatment. Leo Barry had three fractures in his cheekbone, which he'd suffered against the Eagles at Subiaco. I knew Leo was going to be okay, because he was as mentally tough as anyone who'd played the game. You don't worry about players like Jude or Leo, you know they'll play through pain.

Adam Schneider also had a fractured cheekbone and ruckman Darren Jolly had been playing with a broken hand. It was all normal. By the time you get to a Grand Final, both teams have players carrying injuries. There are bruises, strains, fractures. You're hoping your team's injuries are going to be levelled out by their injuries.

Our medical staff, led by Nathan Gibbs and Matt Cameron, and our fitness staff, headed by Dave Misson, had done a brilliant job getting our best team on the field. We'd had fewer injuries and played fewer players than any other club that season, and we were primed, physically and mentally.

The Eagles kicked the first two goals of the game, but we hit back to lead by two points at quarter time. They didn't kick a goal in the second term and we kicked three. In the third quarter, it was our turn to go goalless as they added three. We led by two points at the last break.

Here we go again. It was so close, but the truth is I always felt comfortable because we had been in front, or right there with them, for the whole match. They had never skipped away from us.

Before the game, you can never predict what will happen but one of the aims is to be close enough towards the end of the game that you can win it. So to get to three-quarter time and be two points ahead was exactly what we wanted. The players were carrying out their roles and the game was being played the way we liked it.

I ran onto the MCG at three-quarter time and the players came into the huddle. 'This is what we spoke about last night,' I said. 'We've played our way and see what's happened – we're in front.' It had given us validation. 'We've done it for 90 minutes. Only 30 minutes to go – just keep doing what you're doing.'

As I moved away, Kirky grabbed them and spoke in his intense, passionate way. The players were in it together, ready to play Bloods footy for one more quarter.

I've never watched the entire 2005 Grand Final on replay, only the last quarter. As I think back now, I recall the game as

ving the SCG after my last game,
emifinal loss to the Crows in 1998.
as often on the bench that season,
I learned so much about coaching and
yer psychology.

irfax/Dallas Kilponen)

My first game as Swans caretaker coach, 30 June 2002, after Rodney Eade had resigned. I vowed to empower the players and never drag them for making a mistake. *(Getty Images/Nick Wilson)*

At the end of season 2002, I had no guarantee I would remain coach. Supporters started a 'Choose Roos' campaign, and in early September they presented a petition to the Swans board. *(Newspix/Mark McCormack)*

n 19 September 2002 I was announced as Sydney Swans coach for three seasons, and was
ined by two former Swans coaches, Ricky Quade and Ron Barassi. My message was for
ns to be excited, but patient. *(Newspix/Phil Hillyard)*

A new era begins. With his teammates by his side, Stuart Maxfield is announced as our new captain in February 2003. He was the most critical person at the club while I was coach. Without Stuart driving the standards and the Bloods' behaviours, we wouldn't have won a premiership in 2005. *(Newspix/Renee Nowytarger; Newspix/Bret Costello)*

May 2005, Stuart Maxfield played his last game, due to a chronic knee injury. We pointed six players to share the captaincy – Adam Goodes, Barry Hall, Brett Kirk, Leo rry, Jude Bolton and Ben Mathews. It was a football tragedy that Stuey wasn't able to y in the 2005 premiership. *(AFL Media/GSP Images)*

2005, Nick Davis played the best quarter of finals football I've ever seen, kicking four ls in the final term of the semi against Geelong. He is embraced by Michael O'Loughlin er kicking the match-winner with only seconds left to play. *(AFL Media/GSP Images)*

Relaxing with Tami, Tyler and Dylan on the eve of the 2005 Grand Final. I made sure my family was always part of the club and part of the job. *(Fairfax/Dallas Kilponen)*

Our banner on Grand Final Day 2005 could not have been more fitting. The premiership united the old South Melbourne people and the Sydney fans. *(Getty Images/Mark Dadswell)*

structing Luke Ablett during the 2005 Grand Final. My best and worst moment involved
ıke – in the last quarter his errant kick was marked by Ben Cousins, who goaled to put
e Eagles in front. But Adam Goodes and Tadhg Kennelly ran to Luke to lift his spirits,
hich gave me great confidence in the group. *(AFL Media/Mark Dadswell)*

the final term, Barry Hall kicked a captain's goal to regain the momentum. He flexed his
cep and roared. The players got strength from that moment and I felt we couldn't lose.
Getty Images/Ryan Pierse)

It all came down to Leo Barry. As the ball flew towards the Eagles' attack, he launched himself and took the most incredible mark. We had been almost dead and buried, but this Swans team would never lie down. *(Getty Images/Hamish Blair)*

For the people who've waited 72 years to see South Melbourne, slash Sydney Swans, win the premiership, HERE IT IS!' It was by far the best day of my long career in football. (*Newspix/George Salpigtidis*)

Jason Ball showed true leadership, making things happen when we needed them to. His ruck taps to Nick Davis in the semifinal, and then Amon Buchanan in the Grand Final, created match-winning goals. He went out a champion, retiring after the premiership. *(Getty Images/Ryan Pierse)*

ABOVE: With assistant coaches and key staff. So many people had contributed to the premiership and so much planning had gone into it. We had delivered it together. *(Getty Images/Adam Pretty)*

LEFT: I sat by myself for a few minutes, reflecting on how hard it had been to make it to that Grand Final, and how amazing it was to have won. *(Newspix/Colleen Petch)*

n the 2006 qualifying final in Perth, we hit the lead when Michael O'Loughlin goaled. He kept running, screaming at the Eagles cheer squad members. It symbolised the raw passion of our intense rivalry. *(Newspix/Phil Hillyard)*

t was devastating to lose the 2006 Grand Final against the Eagles by a point. Ironically, think we got more credit after that loss than we did when we'd won a year earlier. *Fairfax/Sebastian Costanzo)*

LEFT: All Swans players were put through the same development system, whether they were a top draft pick like Jarrad McVeigh or a rookie pick. In 2016, when Jarrad was Swans captain and about to play in his fourth Grand Final, he sent me a message: 'Roosy, thanks for teaching me the right way to play.' *(Getty Images/Mark Nolan)*

BELOW: With Barry Hall, walking to the media conference where he announced he was leaving the club, on 7 July 2009. Barry's on-field behaviour was the most difficult problem during my time as Swans coach and I didn't manage the situation as well as I should have. *(Getty Images/Mark Nolan)*

Brett Kirk was the heart and soul of the Bloods. This was after a five-point elimination final win against Carlton on 5 September 2010, at ANZ Stadium. The following week we lost and, for both of us, our time at the Swans had come to an end.
(Newspix/Phil Hillyard)

On 6 September 2013 I was appointed Melbourne coach. The announcement was made at the MCG, alongside CEO Peter Jackson (centre), who had convinced me to coach again, and newly appointed Demons chairman Glen Bartlett. *(Getty Images/Michael Dodge)*

At Melbourne training with assistant coaches George Stone (left) and Ben Mathews. I wouldn't have taken the job if I hadn't been able to bring in people I knew well. We had to hit the ground running. *(AFL Media/Michael Willson)*

My first win as coach of Melbourne, in round four, 2014. Cameron Pedersen, Dean Kent, Rohan Bail, Jack Watts (left to right) and I belt out the club song.
(Getty Images/Michael Dodge)

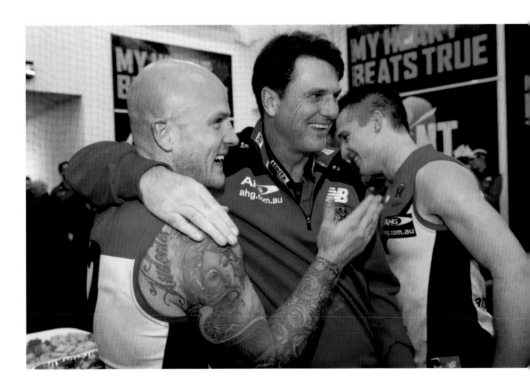

We appointed Nathan Jones co-captain in 2014, and I came to have huge respect and affection for him. This was taken after a one-point win over Essendon in round 13, 2014. *(AFL Media/Michael Willson)*

imon Goodwin's appointment as my uccessor was one of the most critical ecisions during my time at Melbourne. By '016 he had a broad, hands-on role to make ure there was a smooth changeover at eason's end. *(AFL Media/Michael Willson)*

Jack Watts had been unfairly maligned, so when I arrived we set about building his confidence. It took time to overcome the mental scars but in 2016 he blossomed. *(AFL Media/Sean Garnsworthy)*

he banner for my last game as coach, against Geelong, on 27 August 2016. When success omes for the Melbourne Football Club – as I know it will – I'll be as happy as anyone. *Getty Images/Darrian Traynor)*

Tami, Dylan, Tyler and I loved being intimately involved with two AFL clubs. We will be forever grateful for the experiences we had at both the Sydney Swans and Melbourne.

Tami and I have set up a business, the Roos Synergy, centred around leadership, work/life balance, meditation, and the power of the mind. We're very excited about this next phase of our lives.

a series of moments etched in my mind, some great and some not so good, and most of them in that brutal final quarter.

My best and worst moment of the match came early in the last term. Luke Ablett, who'd had a tough day trying to curb Judd, took a brave mark in defence. He attempted to kick across the face of the goals to Leo Barry in the opposite back pocket, but he hadn't noticed Ben Cousins lurking nearby. Cousins drifted in and marked at the top of the Eagles' goal square. He went back and kicked the goal to put the Eagles in front.

But that disaster also became my favourite moment of the game. I watched as Adam Goodes and Tadhg Kennelly both went straight to Luke to console him and lift him up. That moment reinforced the team culture, the mateship and belief in each other we'd all worked so hard to create. It's amazing that one moment in the game can be both the best and the worst.

It had been a roller-coaster week for Barry Hall. In the final term, he kicked what can only be called a captain's goal. From outside 50 metres, he went back, loaded up and kicked it through the middle. That goal got us back to within six points.

Talk about cometh the moment, cometh the man. As the ball soared through the posts, Hall flexed his formidable biceps and roared. It was so strong and powerful, a sign of real intent. There are certain subliminal messages players send to their teammates, and that was one of them. He nailed the goal at a pivotal time. With him at centre half-forward, I felt we couldn't lose and the players got a lot of strength from that moment. Before that, the Eagles had kicked two goals in a row. It's a game of momentum and Hally's goal got us right back in it.

We'd talked so much about staying in the moment and simply doing what we needed to do at any particular time.

He was at his peak as a player, a true power forward, and he'd done the job. He was 100 per cent committed to the cause.

Then there were the phenomenal efforts of Amon Buchanan in the last quarter. He got us back into the lead with a goal from a textbook set play, and it turned out to be the last goal of the game. It was a carbon copy of the goal Nick Davis scored two weeks earlier to snatch the win over Geelong.

A ball up near our goal square, with Jason Ball in the ruck. Bally's deft tap into the space in front. This time, Amon ran onto it and squeezed his kick inside the left goalpost. It was the match-winning goal.

It wasn't something that happened by accident or good luck. That was why we'd had all those leadership meetings and done countless hours of game-related training over the past three years. It was for these pressure moments, so the players had the head and the heart to put our plans into action.

But Amon wasn't finished there. He was playing one of the most difficult roles in the team, as a high half-forward who was expected to get to all the stoppages. His job was to provide cover to stop Judd running from the defensive side of the stoppage into space, or stop Cousins getting away into the centre corridor. Beating the Eagles midfielders was a group task.

In the last frantic minutes, Amon didn't stop. He spoiled a kick on one wing as the Eagles attempted to move the ball clear, then laid a brilliant tackle in the open field and gathered a couple of clearances.

He had been a star at junior level, and had kicked a bag of goals in an under-18 TAC Cup Grand Final on the MCG five years earlier. We were asking him to concentrate on tackling and chasing. He was incredible. Talk about playing your role within the team – he performed thankless tasks, but they were highly valued in our system.

He was a stocky, dogged kid, another in our team with a battler's story. He'd been drafted in 2000, then delisted at the end of 2003. But we'd re-drafted him and he'd grabbed his chance. Everything he did in the Grand Final was selfless.

So many players gave their all that day. LRT had learned his lessons well. He was faultless in defence against Hansen, probably our best player to half time.

Nic Fosdike was also a standout. He had been a high national draft pick, number three in 1998, and it had taken him time to understand we didn't want him to be a free-wheeling midfield superstar, we just wanted him to play our way. He'd been in my sights that year for his tendency to forget his opponent and chase cheap kicks.

On Grand Final day, he understood his strengths and his value to the team. He did his job to perfection, as an outside midfielder cutting down the influence of Eagles Chad Fletcher and Michael Braun on the wings. Fos had developed belief in our system and ended up being close to best on ground in the Grand Final.

There was another heart-in-mouth moment in the last few minutes. We were a few points up after Amon's goal, and Jude went third man up at a stoppage – that ploy was only supposed to be pulled out when we were behind on the score-board in the last minutes, not when we were in front. We'd trained to keep the ball in close in that situation, not whack it into space, but Jude got over-excited. Perhaps it wasn't surprising given he had a large gash on his head and was wearing a helmet to contain the bleeding.

But Jude's hit meant the ball was swept down into the Eagles attack in the last minute of the game, where luckily

Tadhg rushed it through for a behind. We were now four points ahead, 58 to 54.

And then it all came down to Leo Barry. He had started at the club in 1995 as a high-flying half-forward, but often seemed to get lost in the game. He could easily have gone by the wayside. Around 2002, he had been moved into the backline and now he was our best defender purely because of his athleticism and determination. His story was a lesson for all players – he understood what his strengths were.

Leo had stopped the Eagles giant forward, Michael Gardiner, from scoring at all in the Grand Final. But he had also used his flair to provide rebound from defence. Leo was unbelievable at getting the ball out of the backline when we looked trapped. He'd step around three players, do a blind turn and suddenly the ball was on the wing and then he'd jog back to position. As a defender, his stock in trade was punching the ball away from forwards. But, given his leap and his flair, we had also always encouraged him to go for a mark if the ball was there to be grabbed . . .

The quarter seemed never-ending. After the rushed behind, Tadhg kicked out to Leo, who in turn kicked long down the line to Darren Jolly and the Eagles ruckman Dean Cox. The quarter had been going for 32 minutes and 35 seconds when Cox grabbed the mark, and then kicked the ball straight back to where it had come from. I looked away towards the other end of the ground. My attitude was, *Whatever is meant to be, will be. If we're meant to win, we will and if we're not meant to, I guess we'll have to cop it on the chin.* There was nothing I could do.

So I didn't see Leo come rushing in from the side, running at full pace for 20 metres. I didn't see him launch himself across the front of a pack of seven other players, and stick his long arms up in the air to take the most incredible mark. Peter

Jonas yelled out, 'Leo has marked it.' Four seconds after Leo's mark, as he walked back to take his kick, the siren sounded.

I turned around and everyone was screaming, going crazy. The game was over. It had come down to the last moment and we had won **8.10 (58) to 7.12 (54)**. They had been almost dead and buried, but this Swans team would never lie down. Elation. It was a fine line between winning and losing, but a gulf when it came to the emotion.

I didn't want to race straight down onto the MCG. I wanted to spend a minute or two celebrating in the box with the other coaches. We had worked so hard together.

I was deliberately mindful and aware. I took my time to walk slowly down to the ground and to embrace the moment – the Swans fans, the euphoria, the energy in the arena after 72 years without a premiership.

Then to walk on the field and see my wife and my kids . . . it was just amazing. To see players who had given so much to the Swans over the past decades but never won a flag – Bobby Skilton, Barry Round, Paul Kelly and Ricky Quade, guys who had bled for the footy club. And people who had kept the club afloat, such as Peter Weinert, Mike Willesee and Basil Sellers. Every single one of those people contributed to that premiership.

If I had let myself get overwhelmed or over-excited, I would have missed soaking up what was happening. My memories are still so vivid of what we created together and the absolute joy that football brings to people.

Seeing all those people made me realise what an enormous effort it was, not just for the players and coaches that day, but for the football club as a whole. Our pre-match banner had read, 'Two cities, one team, together living the dream.'

Now we'd won and the old South Melbourne people and the Sydney fans were united. The day was about healing the pain and the wounds and bringing the two parts of the club back together.

Earlier in the day, I had rehearsed a short speech, but as I stood on the stage with the 2005 Premiership Cup in my hand, other words came to me and I went off my script.

'For the people who've waited 72 years to see South Melbourne, slash Sydney Swans, win the premiership, HERE IT IS!'

It was three years, almost to the day, since I'd presented my plan to the board with the final PowerPoint slide: 'I will inspire, teach and lead the Sydney Swans to be winners and ultimately deliver a Premiership.'

It shows you the power of a strong plan and a vision. But it was 'we' who had delivered a premiership. So many people had contributed to that victory and so much planning had gone into it.

I told the players we were forever indebted to them. The only sad note was that Stuey Maxfield, who had unflinchingly driven our new culture, had not been able to play. It was a football tragedy.

After the game, as we mingled in the dressing rooms with the players' families and all the staff, I felt an incredible sense of satisfaction. At one stage I sat by myself for a few minutes, reflecting how hard it had been to make it to that Grand Final, and how amazing it was to have won.

Around two hours after the game, Andrew Ireland suggested that the team, key staff and the coaches should take the Premiership Cup out to the middle of the MCG. Under dim lights, before empty grandstands, we stood in a circle and belted out our club song. 'Cheer, cheer the red and the white' had never sounded so good. We were a team in the true sense of the word. We had worked so hard, and it was all worth it.

There were about two thousand people at the club dinner in Melbourne that night. I told the gathering that the premiership had been won because of the characteristics of the Bloods.

'That is the ethos they espouse. Lesser teams and lesser people and lesser characters would have fallen away, would have given it away. Would have given it away against Geelong two weeks ago, would have given it away against West Coast three weeks ago, would have given it away at three-quarter time against St Kilda last week and would have given it away today when they were 10 points down. But that is not the group of players we have, or the people around this footy club.'

It was by far the best day of my long career in football.

For the first time in nearly 25 years, since I began playing for Fitzroy in 1982, I felt that the season had actually come to a close. There was an end point to what I had been doing since I was 17 years old. I'd watched so many Grand Finals. Now I knew what if felt like to win one.

The NSW Government decided to put on a ticker-tape parade for us. As I hopped into the open-top car at Circular Quay, beside captain Barry Hall, I was a bit worried that not many people would turn up. After all, Sydney is primarily a rugby league and rugby union town. How wrong I was. I'll never forget the sight of the thousands of Sydneysiders who turned out to welcome us as we travelled down George Street to the Sydney Town Hall.

A few weeks later, I was sitting on a beach in Maui wearing my 2005 premiership hat, thinking how proud I was of everyone at the Swans.

An Irish guy saw the hat, came up to me, and asked, 'Do you follow them?' I told him I coached them. So we had a great chat about the game, and about his fellow Irishman,

Tadhg Kennelly, who had done his Irish jig on the podium when he received his premiership medallion.

Our win had touched so many people, far and wide, and for the first time ever in my football life, I felt completely satisfied. Now we could start afresh.

Part Three

2006–2010
Scaling the
Mountain Again

CHAPTER 10
The rivalry resumes

Everything had changed and nothing had changed at the start of the 2006 season.

For the first time in 72 years, we had a Premiership Cup proudly on display at the Sydney Swans headquarters at the SCG. I had received hundreds of letters and messages since the Grand Final and knew how much our win meant to so many people.

But what never changes in football is that when a new season begins every club starts on zero. You don't get any points for winning the previous premiership. In fact, the only certainty is that every other club is coming to get you.

I kept thinking back to when I played at Fitzroy in the 1980s and early 1990s. During that time, we did our pre-season training at the same venue as Hawthorn, who were the dominant team for nearly a decade. They won premierships in 1983, 1986, 1988, 1989 and 1991.

Each year, they would turn up for pre-season training weeks after we had started slogging it out in the heat of summer. The Hawks players would be so relaxed, but excited to be back at training. I often wondered how they kept driving themselves to come back motivated to win another premiership, and then another one.

Now that I had been there and been part of a winning club, I knew the answer.

At the start of 2006, I looked back and realised what had made those Hawthorn players work harder than ever, year after year. The feeling you get from winning a premiership is so good, it drives you to do it again. Once you've won a flag, you don't want to miss out. You want that feeling again, and again, and that pushes you on.

I wasn't resting on my laurels. I wanted to climb the mountain once more.

But every year, you've got to be mindful of the bigger picture and how the trends of the game and the technology might be changing. You don't want to get caught behind, but you've also got to stick with what has worked for you.

Late in 2005, at one of our first meetings after the post-premiership break, one of the coaches asked what we should do differently in 2006. But we all decided the right way forward was to make sure we did the same things – but even better than we had last year.

We were motivated, but the greatest fear of the coaching group heading into the 2006 season was that the players would be happy with what they'd achieved in 2005 and would start to worry more about their individual performances. We had won the premiership because we played as a team and we didn't want that to change.

If I had to name a character trait I really don't like, it would be an out-of-control ego. It's the greatest impediment to success in any organisation, be it a football club or a business corporation.

Of course everyone has an ego, and a footballer needs confidence. The problem arises when your ego starts taking over and you think you're more important than anyone else.

I'd seen it before in footy clubs and if that happens, ego can destroy organisations.

I saw a few signs that concerned me during the pre-season competition. In a match against Richmond, several players tried some show-off, selfish moves. We had lost the game by 40 points, but the score line didn't matter.

I'd never worried about results from pre-season games. Our preparation was often several weeks behind other teams because we'd played in finals until late in September. The pre-season was a chance to test out younger players, get the required amount of game time into the more experienced guys and work on our plans.

But when we saw players going outside our team rules, our job as coaches was to stamp that out as quickly as we could.

We showed them vision of the pre-season Richmond game. As always, we didn't discriminate and that had a powerful effect. It didn't matter if it was Brownlow Medallist Adam Goodes or a rookie-listed player such as Kieren Jack, if a player did something wrong, it would be shown. They were all equal and we pulled no punches.

Fortunately, our concerns were nipped in the bud. The players responded quickly and beat St Kilda in our final practice game.

Stuey Maxfield had retired and we had new leaders driving our standards. As was now our tradition, the players had elected the 10-man leadership group and the coaches had chosen the captains.

For the first time in the club's history, we'd appointed three co-captains – Leo Barry, Barry Hall and Brett Kirk. They were a fantastic combination and complemented each other. All strong leaders in their own ways, they believed in our system and were driven to continually improve.

Leo and Brett were both NSW boys – Leo from Deniliquin and Brett from Albury – and had forged their careers the hard way, while Hally had evolved to become a team-oriented player and leader.

Ray McLean, from Leading Teams, who was still regularly working with us, was big on sharing the captaincy role. The idea to have co-captains was a result of the successful experiment in 2005, when we'd rotated the captaincy among six players after Stuey stepped down.

We'd seen a number of benefits. Having multiple captains spread the load when it came to corporate and media commitments and meant none of them ever felt over-burdened by the role.

We hadn't taken a back seat in the trade period either. Even though our defence had been brilliant in 2005, we wanted to bolster our depth, so again we'd scouted players starved of opportunities at other clubs.

We liked the look of Ted Richards, who had played just 33 games for Essendon since making his debut in 2002. He'd be in the team for a game or two, make some mistakes and then be out of favour again with coach Kevin Sheedy.

But we saw his potential. Ted was 193 centimetres tall and athletic, and we believed he could bolster our versatile but relatively short defence. We'd gone to visit him and explained how we saw him fitting into our team. That gave Ted, who was lacking confidence, a clear sense of purpose – which was important, because several other clubs including the Bulldogs were also interested in him.

Our first pick in that year's national draft was number 19, so we put that on the table as part of the deal to recruit Ted. After some to-ing and fro-ing, and adding a swap of later picks, the Bombers agreed.

For the second year in a row, we had traded away our

first-round pick in the national draft, but we were confident the move was worthwhile. Ted was only 22 and Darren Jolly, who'd been recruited from Melbourne in exchange for pick 15 the previous year, was 24 and now a premiership player.

They were still young and had a lot of football ahead of them, so I didn't believe we were compromising our future in a bid for short-term success. We had simply moved to cover weaknesses, and the evidence showed me it was often a more reliable method than using the draft.

We started the season with two losses but got back on track and had six wins in a row until mid-season, when I sensed complacency and a lack of appetite for the contest.

In round 12 we lost to Collingwood and our ability to win the 50-50 balls was poor. In round 14 we played Adelaide, who were then on top of the ladder, and always a team that gave us trouble. We really struggled to score and lost by 39 points at home. It had been a great opportunity to test ourselves against the competition's in-form team and we'd hardly fired a shot. We were sixth, with eight wins and six losses.

After that terrible performance, I didn't hold back in my post-match media conference. I said my main worry was our players' lack of hunger. 'You've got a hungry team in Adelaide against a team that won the premiership last year that has lost the hunger.'

We had lost the qualities that had given us an edge. Our intensity and attack on the ball had dropped off. If we kept playing like that, winning the premiership again was beyond us. It was more evidence that we were a working-class team, and we had to play at maximum effort every single week to succeed. That was a tough ask.

But I knew the players wanted to succeed as much as ever.

I was confident they would eyeball each other, challenge each other, and address the problems.

'If we can improve, then we'll get that opportunity back, but as we sit here now, we are clearly incapable of winning the premiership.'

It's notoriously difficult for teams to go back-to-back. The Lions had defied the odds, but for most teams it's hard to maintain the super-human standard required. Even if they have the motivation, as I believed the Swans did, circumstances change each year and can make it tough. I knew our players were still driven, but we had obstacles to overcome.

Paul Williams, our classy midfielder who had pace and was a great ball user, was 33 and his body was breaking down. After the Adelaide game, he retired. It was a big loss.

As well, our warhorse Jared Crouch had finally succumbed to injury. Crouchy made his debut in 1998 and did not miss a game until round 13 of 2006 – an extraordinary 194 consecutive games, a credit to his discipline and physical and mental toughness. It was as if the armour he had built for himself was starting to crack.

But one player in particular was causing me headaches. Nick Davis, the hero of our 2005 semifinal against Geelong, was lacking discipline and falling into some old, bad habits.

Nick had always been mercurial and his attitude waxed and waned. He had a well-known appetite for fast food and tended to put on weight. He had the hunger, but not the right kind . . . and that obviously made it harder for him to maintain his work rate during games.

He was as talented a player as I'd seen, but the sad part was he could have been so much better. In the end, your talent can take you only so far. If your work ethic doesn't exceed your talent, then you're going to get caught out eventually.

After the loss to Adelaide, the match committee decided we should drop Nick from the team because he wasn't showing the required discipline. He needed a stint in the reserves and to have a good think about his commitment level.

Since 2002, when we'd decided on our set of non-negotiable behaviours, we always said that players acted their way into the system and the team, and they acted their way out of them. It wasn't subjective and the players knew where the limits were.

Nick pushed those boundaries harder than many other players and at times I got the impression the game wasn't really that important to him. But until that point he had stayed within the confines of our culture. There were people at the centre and people at the edges but still inside the square of acceptable behaviour. The hardest thing for Davo at the Swans was we had so many guys who always did the right thing, but we weren't so inflexible that we couldn't accommodate more laid-back, larrikin personalities.

But after he was dropped, Nick did a media interview and lashed out at our decision. He said he'd been made a 'scapegoat' for the loss to Adelaide and that being sent back to the reserves was a slap in the face and not fair.

I was not happy, in fact I practically had steam coming out of my ears. The players' leadership group was also not amused. Speaking to the media without authority and publicly criticising his club and coaches was a breach of our team rules.

We had strict guidelines on contact with the media and keeping any problems in-house. Media leaks had been a big problem in 2002. I'd seen how much damage could be caused if internal issues were aired in public.

Nick's behaviour was a test of our culture and our code. At other clubs, he might have got away with his antics because he was one of our best players, but we had made a pledge to apply the rules equally no matter who the player was.

We decided Nick wouldn't be considered for senior selection again until he had convinced the coaches and his teammates that he really wanted to be part of the team. Nick had put his own interests ahead of the team and I described it as 'very un-Sydney-like'. I spoke to Davo and said in no uncertain terms that it was his fault he had been dropped, no one else's.

Our next match was against the West Coast Eagles, the first time we had played them since the 2005 Grand Final. While we went to Perth intent on reviving our season, Nick went to Wagga Wagga in country NSW to play with our reserves, who were being coached by Stuey Maxfield – just the right person to bring Nick into line.

We hit the ground running against the Eagles, showing real desire for the first time in several weeks. We were 32 points up at half time.

In the second half, we were hampered by injuries and the Eagles came back to win by two points. It was another chapter in our intense rivalry with the Eagles. Another fierce contest decided by less than a goal, the third in succession.

Despite the loss, I thought it was our best performance of the season. The players' effort and spirit had returned. Kirky could also see the positives and said the team had found the intensity lacking over the previous month. Most importantly, they had got back to playing for each other.

There were seven games left in the home and away season and our destiny was in our hands.

The following week, I had a meeting with Nick Davis and he apologised for his outburst. But I couldn't guarantee when Nick would play again – he had to show remorse and commitment with his actions, not just words. Davo spent six weeks in the reserves, and didn't rejoin the senior team until round 21, the second-last game of the home and away season.

To give ourselves a real shot at another premiership, we needed to finish in the top four. It was touch and go, and we only secured fourth spot in the last round when we posted a big win over Carlton.

The Eagles had been the standout team all year and finished on top of the ladder. That gave them the right to host a home final in the first week of September. We had to travel to Perth to play a qualifying final against the Eagles, a repeat of 2005. *Déjà vu.*

The 2006 qualifying was one of the most intense games I'd been involved in. We were a couple of goals up at half time but the Eagles had a great third term and our lead was cut to three points at three-quarter time. Another absolute heart-stopper was on the cards.

In the last quarter, the lead changed six times. We were behind with three minutes to go when we took possession of the ball deep in our defence.

Luke Ablett started a chain that ended up involving 10 of our players. It went to Amon Buchanan and eventually to Nick Malceski in the corridor. Nick was playing his 20th senior game and first final. A beautiful left-foot kick of the ball, he sent it long to the goal square, where it was contested by Ryan O'Keefe and then bounced into the hands of Mick O'Loughlin.

He gathered the ball, booted it through for a goal and then kept running right to the fence, roaring at the Eagles cheer squad members. It was an amazing piece of football theatre, and it symbolised the raw passion and competitive zeal when we played the Eagles.

We knew we'd need effort from every player and the last goal of the night, the winning goal, typified that. It was another set play we had practised at training, to transfer the ball from deep in defence, through the corridor and over the top to our forwards, and again we saw the benefit in a big game.

We won by a solitary point, **13.7 (85) to 12.12 (84)**. It was hard to believe how close every game was against the Eagles – they were such a struggle – but we had prevailed. It's fair to say it was a much more pleasant flight home than 12 months previously.

We had earned a much-needed week's rest and met Fremantle two weeks later, at home in Sydney. In the preliminary final at Telstra Stadium, we ran away from them in the second half to win by 35 points. Barry Hall was unstoppable, with six goals.

The following night, West Coast beat the Adelaide Crows by 10 points in the other preliminary final. For the second year in a row, we'd be taking on the Eagles in the Grand Final – this time no longer burdened by the pressure of a 72-year premiership drought.

Everyone was talking about our rivalry, and Kirky had dubbed himself and Jude Bolton a couple of old Ford Cortinas chugging along against the slick 'Lamborghinis' – Ben Cousins and Chris Judd – of West Coast.

Of course it underplayed our talent level, but it was important we still viewed ourselves as honest workers who had to get down in the trenches and fight till the end.

Chris Judd has said we constantly undersold our team as part of the Bloods mandate of being a team of battlers. He's right. But it worked for us; we needed that mindset.

To be fair to the Eagles, while everyone focused on their star-studded line-up, we had enormous respect for their team. They also worked extremely hard and were incredibly driven to succeed.

The 2006 Grand Final began very differently from the previous year. The Eagles jumped us at the start and we couldn't contain them. By half time, they were leading by four goals and the game wasn't being played the way we liked. We'd never been arrogant enough to think we could take the Eagles on at their own fast-paced game.

Over the two seasons, we had tried a few different tactics. We'd excited football fans when we sent Adam Goodes, the 2003 Brownlow Medallist, to run with Chris Judd, the 2004 Brownlow winner, in our round 15 game and then again in the 2006 qualifying final. But Goodesy was the exception in our team and it was rare for us to go head-to-head offensively with them.

That certainly wasn't our plan in the 2006 Grand Final, but subconsciously I think the players got a bit ahead of themselves and tried to do that in the first half. It clearly wasn't working.

At half time I walked to the dressing rooms, stewing on the fact we were 25 points down against one of the best teams of all time. I feared we could get beaten by 100 points. I spoke to the other coaches: 'What are we going to do?'

And one responded: 'Well, we're not doing the things we do well. Why don't we try those first?'

We had created an environment where the players knew what it took to win games. Our key indicators hadn't changed for the past four seasons. We needed hard running, to give maximum effort, to handle the ball cleanly, and to chase and tackle and apply pressure. We had to play our way.

In the second half, we staged an incredible fightback, led by Goodesy and Brett Kirk.

The contest became more familiar. Everyone at the MCG could sense it was going to be another down-to-the-wire tussle. The Grand Final was not going to blow out into a one-sided affair and they would have to wait until the last moments for a result.

That's what happened. We made a couple of mistakes, our players including Hally and Jude missed easy goals. The Eagles produced inspirational acts. Daniel Chick's smother on Ryan O'Keefe led to a goal to Adam Hunter. They called it their Leo Barry moment. With the ball on our half-forward line, the siren sounded. We had lost by one point.

Remarkably the points tallies were the same as in the qualifying final, but reversed, the Eagles winning **12.13 (85)** to **12.12 (84)**.

It was bitterly disappointing, devastating. But after the game, in the media conference, I said we had great admiration for the Eagles and it was probably fair that we had one premiership apiece. It was hard to say, but I meant it, and still believe that.

As we knew well from the 2005 Grand Final, there is a very fine line between winning and losing. We don't have a Grand Final series in AFL like they do in some other sports – it is one game, winner takes all.

If Leo Barry had dropped the mark in 2005, we probably would have lost. In 2006, if Sean Dempster hadn't bombed the ball in long to our forward line, where Eagles player Andrew Embley was waiting, we might have won.

In the 2010 Grand Final, if the ball had bounced towards St Kilda's Stephen Milne, rather than away, the Saints probably would have won and my very good friend Ross Lyon (and my Swans assistant coach in 2005 and 2006) would be a premiership coach. Or in the 2009 Grand Final, if Geelong's Matthew Scarlett had missed his toe poke on the ball in the centre of the ground, the Saints would probably have claimed victory.

I get disappointed when the media don't recognise what a

fine line it is, and when Ross gets criticised for not winning a premiership. I've said to him many times that the only difference between him and me is that Leo marked a ball, and Stephen Milne missed a bounce of the ball.

Logically, there is no difference in the skill and hard work that went into the coaching and the performance.

The line that separated the Eagles and us was finer than most. We had played five games during 2005 and 2006, and the biggest margin was four points. Five contests in succession decided by less than a goal. Four points in a qualifying final; four points in a Grand Final; two points in a home and away game; one point in a qualifying final; one point in a Grand Final. Over two seasons, we were separated by a total of 12 points.

If you add in the first home and away game of 2007 at Homebush in Sydney, when the Eagles also beat us by a point, there has never been a run of six games decided by such small margins in AFL history. And never before, or since, have three games in a row between two teams been decided by one point.

What made our rivalry with the Eagles so extraordinary? We had different game styles, different talent levels and different cultures, but we knew each other so well. We knew how they wanted to play, and they knew how we liked to play. The match-ups stayed almost the same.

Both teams had enormous respect for each other. Every time we met, players found extra reserves. Every game was contested to the last ball and at the highest level of intensity. Every game was physical but never nasty or spiteful. For 120 minutes, the contests were one-on-one, each player striving to outdo their opponent. No one gave an inch.

As Swans coaches and players, we looked at any game against the Eagles during that period as the ultimate challenge.

We put so much time, thought and energy into how we could counter their great midfield group that had so much sheer talent.

We spent time strategising and working on ways to nullify their strengths as best we could. That's why we sent Jarrad McVeigh to Ben Cousins in the 2006 Grand Final, and Ben Mathews to Daniel Kerr, and Jude Bolton to Chad Fletcher.

We made sure it was a team effort. We always had other players come up to the stoppages to cover the exits. If Judd or Cousins or Kerr got into space, they were almost impossible to stop. We had to take away that strength.

We set up ways to use our own strengths. Our midfielders, apart from Goodesy, weren't as gifted but they were fit, disciplined, accountable and had an extraordinary ability to concentrate on a task.

Our forward line with Barry Hall and Mick O'Loughlin, Ryan O'Keefe and Davo, was better than the Eagles' attack. We pushed our half-forwards up to the stoppages to leave our forward line more open for Hally and Mick, to give them more chance of being one-out with their defender near goal. If we got the ball out of a stoppage quickly with a releasing handball, we gave our forwards a strong opportunity to score.

Both teams had good defenders – the Eagles led by Darren Glass, who generally did well on Hall. We had Leo Barry, Craig Bolton and Tadhg Kennelly.

As coaches, it required a very conscious plan to take on the West Coast Eagles. We loved trying to scale the highest mountain. The players didn't fear it and the coaches didn't fear it. We were up for it.

It was credit to the Swans players that they were committed to being a great team, and I was lucky to coach a group like that. When we had team meetings before Eagles games, you knew the players were energised and excited by what was ahead.

There was always a bit of nervousness in the coaches' box about one of their midfielders getting away from us. If Cousins got on top of McVeigh or Judd got away from Luke Ablett, what would we do then? Their midfielders were so explosive they could quickly turn the game.

There were times when we'd have to say, 'Let him go.' Andrew Ireland, our head of football who was down on the boundary line during games, was a fantastic influence. Andrew would say you don't want to fix one problem and create three headaches.

We held our breath and trusted the players to fight through. We'd weather the storm and back our guys to play the style of footy that would stop the Eagles from getting too much of a run on.

While they had a more free-running attacking style and we were more defensive, their backmen did play one-on-one, tough, accountable football. Like us, the Eagles rarely dropped an extra man back in defence and their defenders stuck with our forwards.

I always thought Eagles coach John Worsfold was more content than me to sit back and let the game play out, to trust his stars to prevail, and I was happy to work my match-ups. Every game was like an arm wrestle, and we were all proud to be part of one of football's great modern rivalries.

Ironically, I think we got more credit after our 2006 loss than we did when we won a year earlier. By getting to the Grand Final again, and coming so close, it legitimised the '05 victory. It proved it was no fluke and we were a good team. The players finally got the recognition they deserved.

The enormous interest in those games across the nation and in the non-traditional NSW market played a big part in driving television audiences and boosting AFL television rights revenue by millions of dollars.

In more recent times, I've been saddened by the stories of drug use at the Eagles during the period from the early 2000s to 2007.

There is no more upsetting a story in football than the downfall of Ben Cousins.

The revelations about the Eagles' culture, which were contained in a report commissioned by the AFL, also surprised me. Basically it seemed that if the club was successful on the field, then how the players behaved off the field, especially if they were good players, didn't matter enough.

Tadhg Kennelly, who was in the Swans leadership group and a member of both Grand Final teams, said he felt sorry for the players who succumbed to drugs and that the Eagles' management of the issue was of concern.

Tadhg put it perfectly when he said the players' health should have been the main priority and it was a worry to have 18-year-olds walking into a drug culture that wasn't being addressed.

Imagine a kid, just drafted, arriving wide-eyed at the club. He has to be pretty strong-minded to walk into a bad culture and buck the trend. Conversely, it's hard for him to walk into a good culture and not follow the lead being set for him. Young men want to fit in. Richmond legend Kevin Bartlett said he was putting a black line through the Eagles' flag. Tadhg says he wouldn't want a premiership medallion from 2006, because it wouldn't mean anything. Barry Hall has said the same thing.

I'm often asked if I think we were cheated out of the 2006 premiership, given we lost the Grand Final by one point.

Despite everything that has happened, I don't think of it like that.

There is no evidence, and there are too many unknowns,

to say we were hard done by. I still prefer to think of our contests with the Eagles as a great footy rivalry, first and foremost.

I'm disappointed to learn their culture was not what it should have been. That's not to say we were perfect – far from it. But staying true to our values and behaviours was an overriding principle. As I had discussed with the Swans board many times, success is not only defined by the number of games you win, or by premierships.

CHAPTER 11
Changing of the guard

In 2005 and 2006, Barry Hall was at his peak. He was formidable. He was one of the league's leading goal-kickers, but also one of our most team-oriented players. He tackled and chased 'with intent', as he liked to say. He intimidated opponents and made his teammates walk taller.

But after our one-point loss in the 2006 Grand Final, Hally went through a challenging period. He had kicked six goals in the preliminary final win over Fremantle, then remarked after the game that it didn't matter to him because 'next week is the one where you've got to play well'.

It didn't work out that way. In the Grand Final at the MCG, he had what can only be described as a rotten day. It wasn't for lack of effort, but his nightmare began in the first quarter. He received a rare free kick directly in front of goal, only 15 metres out, but shanked the kick. His frustration mounted as the game went on and he repeatedly fumbled the ball, something he didn't often do. In the third quarter, he again missed an easy goal from 20 metres out.

After the loss, he was very emotional in the rooms. He had taken the one-point loss to heart, as we all had, and he refused to come out and do any media interviews.

The journalists weren't happy with that and were pretty harsh on his performance.

Barry was far from the only one who had made blunders that day, but he took it harder than most. He bottled up his feelings. The performance haunted him for a long time and his career was on a slow spiral from there.

We never looked at that 2006 Grand Final as a group and I didn't address it individually with Barry. It's hard, as everyone heads off in their own directions a few days after the season ends. In hindsight, I should have made a point of helping Barry come to grips with the devastating one-point loss, knowing how tough he was on himself.

The following season, the team could not get back to the level we had played at during 2005 and 2006. Injuries played a significant part, with Tadhg Kennelly, Leo Barry, Jared Crouch and Lewis Roberts-Thomson all missing significant chunks of the season.

Hall was also troubled by a serious groin injury. He was tough and soldiered on, but he was forced to miss a few games. When he did play, his explosive power and running was limited. He remained our leading goal-kicker, but his output dropped from 78 goals in 2006 to 44 in 2007.

As a team, we were unable to find consistency and, while we still played finals, we bombed out in the first week, losing an elimination final to Collingwood.

The pundits concluded we were on the way down, and predicted our era of success was over, with our players ageing and too slow.

It was true we needed more speed, but we would never concede our time was up. I have always strongly rejected the idea that teams have a premiership window and once that closes, the wise move is to sink to the bottom of the ladder, get high draft picks and reshape the list.

The idea of bottoming out and rebuilding from there is garbage, and the evidence shows that teams who have taken that approach don't usually win premierships anyway. There's no formula to winning a premiership. If going to the bottom of the ladder was a proven solution, everyone would do it, which would be disastrous for the competition.

That was never our way. For a start, it would not have been good for the national AFL competition to have the only team in NSW (as we were then) languishing and losing support.

I firmly believe teams can rebuild while remaining competitive.

Some years that might mean taking early draft picks and some years it might mean bringing in more mature players from other clubs, as we had done with Craig Bolton, Darren Jolly and Ted Richards.

If I could point to one thing that made the Swans ultra-consistent during my time as coach, it was that we identified under-achieving players who had limited opportunities at other clubs and gave them a new home. Our attitude to trades became a clear advantage for us over many other clubs.

We missed the finals only once while I was coach, and had only two top-10 draft picks in that time (Jarrad McVeigh and Gary Rohan). But we regularly fielded six or seven players who had come to us through trades, and another five or six who'd climbed their way up via the rookie list.

At the end of 2007, before the players went on their break, I met with the leadership group including co-captains Brett Kirk, Leo Barry and Barry Hall. I asked them: 'Do you want to improve our list or do you want to battle on with the group of players we have here already?'

They agreed we needed to get better. So I told them every player in the room, and every player on our list, was potentially on the trade table if we could get a good player to the club in exchange.

'I'm laying this on the table because it might be one of you guys,' I told them. 'Make sure your managers have all your details before you go away.'

During our list management meetings, the coaching and recruiting staff had identified our shortcomings. We were still a hard and physical team but we needed players with more speed and outside run, players who could break the lines and use the ball well.

A couple of clubs asked if we'd trade Jude Bolton, but there was never any realistic trade offered for one of our favourite sons.

We had identified an Adelaide Crows player, Marty Mattner, as being the type of running half-back we needed. The catalyst for Marty's arrival was a game he played for Adelaide at the SCG when he dominated on a wing and at half-back. He'd played 19 games for the Crows in 2007, but they'd left him out of their finals side. He was quick, kicked the ball long and was an effective tackler.

I had a good relationship with Adelaide's recruitment manager, Matt Rendell, and I'd played with him at Fitzroy. I spoke to Matt and he said they wanted a second-round draft pick. The deal was done and Marty came to us on a three-year deal.

But we then had salary cap issues. We had to lose a couple of players, as I'd warned the group. So two of our premiership players, Adam Schneider and Sean Dempster, were traded to St Kilda to join Ross Lyon, who had left us to coach the Saints. Giving up Schneids and Sean was tough, but in the end we all benefited, as they went on to play in Grand Finals for the Saints.

It was a significant period of change and renewal. While difficult in some aspects, it also laid the seeds for future success. In the two years that followed, we took the same strategic, hard-nosed approach to improving our list.

At the end of 2008, when we had finished fifth, we brought in speedster Rhyce Shaw from Collingwood and delisted Nick Davis, who had only managed three senior games that year due to poor form and injury.

Dan Hannebery was a great pick-up in the 2008 draft – we knew he had talent and we were lucky to get him with a second-round selection, number 30.

There were also creative gambles, such as the decision to list Canadian rugby player Mike Pyke as an international rookie. We made him no promises, but he was an extraordinary athlete and his determination and intelligence were assets. His rapid progress under the tutelage of ruck coach Steve Taubert was amazing and he played eight senior games in 2009.

But at the end of 2009, we dropped off to finish 12th. It was the first time we had missed playing in the finals since I'd become coach, so we were even more aggressive in both the trading period and the draft.

We traded for midfielder Josh Kennedy, who wasn't being given much opportunity at Hawthorn, as well as powerhouse ruckman Shane Mumford, who had been left out of Geelong's 2009 premiership side. Josh was only 21 and Mummy was 23. They fitted our mould. In the draft, we snared some young talent – speedsters Lewis Jetta and Gary Rohan, and young key position player Sam Reid was a bargain at pick 38.

It was a major rejuvenation of our list as we looked to both the short- and long-term future, determined to remain competitive. We were rebuilding the Swans way.

As it turned out, all four of those players traded in – Mattner, Shaw, Mumford and Kennedy – would go on to play significant roles in the Swans' 2012 premiership, as did Jetta and Reid. So would Ted Richards, who was picked up from Essendon in 2006, and Mike Pyke, who in four years developed from an international rugby player to a premiership ruckman, one of the best players on the field in that 2012 Grand Final.

At the back end of the 2007 season, the core of the group that had taken us to the 2005 premiership was scattering and we were attempting to climb the peak again.

The 2008 season started with promise but, four rounds in, everything was upended in the most dramatic fashion. Barry Hall's frustrations boiled over and he imploded in a way that would have serious repercussions for him and the club.

We were playing our old foe, the West Coast Eagles, in Sydney, and Hally was grappling with his opponent, Brent Staker. He was clearly annoyed because Staker was retarding his lead. Barry thought he should have been given a free kick, but that was nothing out of the ordinary – it had been happening to him for years. This time, Barry responded in a way that shocked us. Suddenly, he swung his arm and let fly with a left hook that felled Staker and left him concussed.

We could hardly believe our eyes as we watched the TV replay in the coaches' box. Barry had come to the Swans from St Kilda with a reputation as a hothead, but he'd transformed. He hadn't seriously lost his cool for years.

It was a terrible night. Later in the game, Barry crashed into the fence and broke his wrist. But that was the least of his worries.

After the match, he was full of remorse and apologised to Staker. He had shocked himself as much as anyone. A few days later at the tribunal hearing, he pleaded guilty and was asked why he'd punched Staker. He could only say it was a brain snap and out of character with the person he'd become since joining the Swans in 2002.

'I think through frustration, a mind-snap, a bit of a lapse, something came out that looked really bad that I didn't intend in terms of the impact. I think it happens to everyone at stages of their lives – you do things which are out of character and you cannot explain. I certainly can't explain it,' he said to the tribunal.

'The incident was unacceptable. I will now try and better myself so it doesn't happen again.'

He was given a seven-game suspension. It was out of character and we were hopeful it was an aberration. That was not the Barry we knew. Outside the club, he often got a bad rap, but the truth was he had matured into a different man. On the field, he was formidable but played the ball, and off it he was laid-back, popular with his teammates and a natural with kids.

He had been a junior boxing champion in Victoria and his father, who was a boxing trainer, had desperately wanted him to make a living from that sport before he'd turned to football. He was aggressive, but over time it had been channelled in the right direction. He was honest, hardworking, humble and never one for making excuses.

After his suspension, he resumed playing in round 12, 2008. Then, in just his third game back, he tried to hit Collingwood player Shane Wakelin. He was charged and suspended again. We also imposed our own club sanction and stood him down from the team for a week until we felt he could handle his emotions on the field.

In 2009, his demons came to the surface again. In round 13, against Adelaide, he whacked their defender Ben Rutten and received another two-week suspension.

At a club where discipline and putting the team first were non-negotiable, his actions were outside our boundaries.

Barry's behaviour in 2008 and 2009 was the most difficult problem I had to deal with during my time as coach of the Swans. In a bygone era, when fists were more acceptable on the football field, it might not have mattered so much. But times had changed. These were the rules the players had set for themselves at the Swans and his repeated flouting was not acceptable.

It was especially hard to manage because Barry Hall was a good person.

Fundamentally, I've always found players want direction, they want discipline, want to know what the parameters are. Barry had come to the Swans in 2002 with a reputation after numerous tribunal suspensions. But for six years we had no problems.

We loved Barry as a teammate and as a person. He was easy to get on with and had developed into a great leader who cared for his mates. He had helped create our Bloods system and he was a giver.

His nickname outside the club was still 'Big, Bad, Bustling' but he had always hated that nickname. Leo Barry said that Hally was really a teddy bear and a sensitive new-age guy.

I had to think this through and tried to put myself in the player's shoes. I could see he was frustrated and angry. But when he punched Ben Rutten, it was his third offence in two seasons. There was disbelief – how could he do this again? I normally don't get too annoyed, but I just didn't know where to go from there.

Barry had already been given chances. We weren't so rigid that we couldn't accept people made mistakes.

The first incident, when he punched Staker in 2008, had

not been difficult to deal with because Barry handled that exceptionally well. He put his hand up in the air, he knew he'd done wrong, he apologised and took his punishment.

But then came the Wakelin incident, and finally the Rutten punch. We were an action-based footy club and his actions spoke loudest to me. It appeared to me that he didn't want to be part of the team anymore.

After that game in Adelaide, I spoke with Andrew Ireland and we decided not to rush into a decision about Barry's future. It was definitely the biggest test we had faced of the Swans culture and it needed careful consideration.

But unfortunately events spun out of control and over the next few days I didn't manage the situation as well as I should have. Barry and I hadn't spoken directly after the Adelaide game, but he called me the next day, and I didn't return his call. That was a mistake.

I have empathy for the players, but if I feel someone has let me down, I can be tough. Of course I was going to talk to him, but I needed a bit of time. In hindsight, it was the wrong way to respond. I should have grabbed him after the game and spoken to him, or at least returned his call. I had broken one of my golden rules. I prided myself on communicating with the players, but my frustration had got the better of me.

Three days later, Andrew Ireland and I met with Barry at the club. Barry was upset. He felt we'd turned our backs on him and hadn't supported him when he needed it. We talked it out, but left with no resolution. I still wanted time to think through the best way to deal with the situation. Given Barry had been dealt a two-week suspension for hitting Rutten, I didn't feel we had to rush into any decision.

But there was a media frenzy and, the following day, Brett Kirk spoke to journalists. We were trying to be open and face the controversy head-on rather than shutting down and potentially making things worse – a lesson we had learned after the 2006 Grand Final when we allowed Barry Hall to avoid the media.

Kirky said he'd trust Barry with his kids, but he no longer knew if he could trust him on the field. It was an honest statement, but it affected Barry. He felt publicly shamed by his club.

A few days later, Hally made his own decision. He announced he was leaving the club and having a break from footy because he could no longer trust himself and didn't want to do more damage to his reputation.

By the time he actually decided he was going to leave, I had apologised and told him that I had let him down – I should have taken more responsibility. But he said, no, it had been his responsibility.

We didn't push Barry. It was his decision. He told the media he was taking into account the club, his teammates and his family. 'Ultimately they have suffered grief over some of my wrongdoings and I have to take them into consideration.'

After the drama of the previous week, I felt my last meeting with him before his announcement had gone okay. We had come to grips with an unfortunate situation and had no hard feelings. He handled his press conference unbelievably well and clearly articulated why he was resigning.

It was a sad day for the Swans. I had stood on the dais with Barry in 2005, holding the Cup aloft together when we broke the club's 72-year premiership drought. He had played 162 games for the Swans and kicked 467 goals. His legacy was enormous, despite how his time ended. His buy-in was crucial when we established our new culture. I had nothing but admiration for Hally and the way he handled himself 99 per cent of the time.

At the end of the year, we traded him to the Western Bulldogs, where he continued his career, eventually retiring in 2011. He then released a book in which he had a dig at me for not communicating with him. I thought we had cleared it up before he left, but he obviously had some lingering anger. I was sorry to hear that was how he felt, but I didn't take it too personally. People see things differently and it had been a very trying time.

We've since crossed paths many times and are colleagues at Fox Sports. We both could have handled things better, but the positive thing is we have a good relationship now.

When I look back, what matters is that for six years he was wedded to the club and focused on being a brilliant team player. How, and why, it went off the rails in 2008 and 2009 is something we may never fully understand.

At the end of the day, I think the reason he left the club of his own accord was because he had faith in our system. He didn't believe he could follow the team rules anymore, so he walked away. The culture had been upheld. As the mantra went – you acted your way into the Bloods and you acted your way out. Barry had stepped outside.

That year, 2009, was disappointing and challenging in many ways. We won only eight games and finished 12th.

It was definitely the end of an era. Our premiership captain Barry Hall was gone, and seven other premiership players departed that year. Leo Barry, Luke Ablett, Jared Crouch, Nic Fosdike and Michael O'Loughlin retired, while Amon Buchanan was traded to Brisbane, and Darren Jolly, who had requested a trade home, went to Collingwood. We had also missed Tadhg Kennelly, who had returned to Ireland to pursue his dream of winning an All-Ireland final with County Kerry, as his father had done before him.

In the last game of the season, when Leo, Luke, Jared and

Mick were playing their last game, we lost to the Brisbane Lions by eight points. I was bitterly disappointed. I didn't often get upset with the group, but I did that night. Those champions of the club deserved to be sent off with a victory, and their teammates hadn't done enough to make that happen.

During that era, it had become folklore that we had a 'no dickheads' policy at the Swans, a line attributed a few years earlier to our recruiter, Rick Barham. That was never strictly true – there was never a policy as such – but in a sense Rick was right because we put a high mark on character.

But we had never claimed everyone at the Swans was the class goody-goody. As I'd written in my coaching notes 11 years before: **42 senior players – all different personalities, deal with each one individually to get the best out of him.**

What didn't change was the expectation that they all followed the team rules. We could accommodate players who arrived with reputations, such as Barry or Peter 'Spida' Everitt, because they knew where the boundaries were.

We didn't treat the stars differently and, most importantly, they didn't expect to be treated differently. Rick Barham and Kinnear Beatson, who took over as manager of player acquisition, did a lot of background checks on prospective players. We valued the character of the players we brought into our club because we believed it was just as important as ability and talent – if not more so.

One day, we had done some specific research on the draft. On a whiteboard, we put up all our draft picks from the previous few years and marked the players on character as well as their 20-metre sprint test, three-kilometre time trial and so on.

There were two traits that stood out with the guys who had been most successful at the Swans – they had a good three-kilometre time trial result and, overwhelmingly, they scored well on character.

What did we mean by character? To us, character was displayed in their work ethic, their competitiveness, their ability to listen, their preparedness to work on their game and help others. They weren't all the same, but what they had in common was that they were high-quality individuals with the right attitude.

Those players who left in 2009, and the others before them who had helped created the Bloods ethos, epitomised those traits. They were good people and they left a legacy handed on every year to new recruits.

But in football clubs, we're all passing through. There was a changing of the guard, and I was part of the change.

I had signed a new three-year contract at the end of 2008, but at the time I told Andrew Ireland and Richard Colless I couldn't promise I would serve to the end. I had been head coach for six years to that point, and I had not forgotten my view that a coach's lifespan at a club was around seven or eight years. After that, it was time for a fresh voice.

They understood and had no issue. Andrew had a great attitude towards contracts, and we had a deep trust, so we'd chatted casually about when the time might be right to hand over to a new coach.

Then, in 2009, I spoke to my family and we decided I would step down as coach at the end of 2010. We wanted to do other things in life, to travel and have more flexibility. I felt fortunate to have been given the job in the first place and to have won a premiership. The club was on a solid foundation and successful. We had played in finals six out of seven years and I felt we'd achieved the objectives set out at the start of my tenure.

I was contemplating when to tell Andrew and Richard when a few things affected the timing.

My senior assistant coach, John Longmire, was in the running for other coaching jobs including the Kangaroos, the club where he'd been a premiership player in 1999. Kangaroos coach Dean Laidley had resigned mid-season, and they were interviewing candidates.

That prompted me to decide I should let them know about my decision sooner rather than later. I wanted to give the club the opportunity, if they saw John as the appropriate person to take over from me, to make sure they could hang on to him.

A few weeks earlier, Collingwood had announced that Nathan Buckley was going to take over from Mick Malthouse in two years time, at the end of the 2011 season.

I told the media I thought succession plans were the way of the future for AFL coaches. I didn't believe it undermined Mick's position, and said the days of looking over your shoulder and worrying about assistant coaches were finished. If Mick did his job and Nathan did his job, the plan would work. That was the key.

In August, we announced our own version of the succession plan, with John appointed to take over from me at the end of the 2010 season. I didn't appoint John Longmire, but I was certainly 100 per cent supportive of the idea, and wanted to make sure the club didn't lose him and get left without an obvious successor.

I had always said I wasn't going to be a career coach and I stayed true to my word. I didn't hate the job . . . It was more a case that I had said I'd coach for no longer than eight years, and that would take me to the end of 2010. I had to hold myself accountable to my own beliefs.

I was really happy our next coach was coming from within

our club. John played a big part in developing our system and would be able to carry on our culture. I had found it strange that every time an AFL coach was sacked, which happened too often, there would be 10 people interviewed and none of them came from his club.

That meant prospective new coaches had no idea about the internal workings of the club, and didn't know the players. The administration of those clubs was effectively saying our culture is no good, and everyone already at our club is no good, so we have to get someone from outside.

A number of clubs approached me after I left the Swans, inquiring how to implement a succession plan. But the idea has not become widespread in the industry, which I think is a shame.

A lot of coaches don't want to step down – they are career coaches. The thought of grooming someone else for their position is difficult for them. That makes a smooth succession impossible. For a succession to work, the coach has to be willing to help the next person in line, and has to step down willingly.

The career path for AFL coaches is a thorny issue, and the AFL has acknowledged it needs to do a better job in developing pathways for coaches. Alastair Clarkson has been very active on the issue through the Coaches Association, and there is now a two-year, Level Four coaching course along the lines of what is needed.

After seven years in the job, I knew very well that there was a world of difference between an assistant coach's role and a senior coach, who knows his job is basically on the line every single week.

The assistant has influence but no real pressure, so there is a massive jump to senior coaching. It worries me that clubs are still appointing coaches with limited experience as an assistant. They really need to do a proper apprenticeship and have great people management skills.

I wanted John Longmire to be as prepared as possible when he took over from me at the end of 2010, so the transition would be seamless for the players. During that season, John went to board meetings, established relationships with people in all parts of the club and was exposed to many aspects of the senior coaching role.

But I was still in charge and naturally I wanted to go out on a high. It was a familiar start to season 2010, with most of the experts writing us off again as they had seven years earlier.

To be fair, the situation was similar as we dealt with the departure of senior players with hundreds of games of experience. But our regeneration plans allowed us to stay in contention once again. The players we had recruited, in particular Shane Mumford and Josh Kennedy, hit the ground running.

Our development program was also reaping benefits. Kieren Jack, the son of NSW rugby league legend Garry Jack, had been elevated from the rookie list in 2007 and was one of the most improved players in the competition. Like Jarrad McVeigh, we had initially taught him to be a run-with player and then he had evolved into one of the best two-way, offensive/defensive midfielders in the AFL.

McVeigh won our best and fairest in 2008, and Kieren was our club champion in 2010.

Dan Hannebery, recruited to the club when he was still a 17-year-old Melbourne schoolboy, was the standout young player in the league and won the NAB AFL Rising Star Award. The signs were bright.

There were ups and downs, as happens when the team is rebuilding and the group is getting used to playing together. We'd string a few wins together, then drop our bundle for a few weeks. Our losses included a dismal performance against Richmond at the MCG where we gave up a 33-point lead and lost by four points. The competitive beast in me was unleashed and I wasn't happy.

As the end approached, it wasn't always easy to stay completely true to my coaching creed. It's an emotional, demanding, cut-throat game. It was rare that I blew my gasket, but I can assure you it did happen. However, there was generally a point to it. I'd be annoyed they were not following our behaviours, strategies and plans; it wasn't personal. When I met with the leadership group, as we still did every week, we always talked it through, and left the room united.

We had another horrible 73-point loss to Melbourne in round 17, which sent us to eighth on the ladder. As they had done so many times before, the players responded. Led by our co-captains Brett Kirk, Adam Goodes and Craig Bolton, they were brutally honest with each other during the week, and got back to the basics of how we wanted to play.

Kirky, the heart and soul of the team for years, had announced he was bowing out too. It's difficult to do justice to his value. His story was so compelling – rejected and sent back to Albury once, then almost dropped off the list again. He had overcome deficiencies and worked on his strengths to become one of the club's greatest ever players, a captain, and best and fairest in our premiership year. He was in the top three in the club champion award from 2003 to 2009. Brett came to epitomise the resilient spirit of the Bloods.

He was a great role model, and the young players looked up to him. But they could also see that he wasn't quick, he wasn't tall, he was not especially strong. He couldn't kick very well and he had a strange running style. But he had the determination, drive and courage to make up for any weaknesses.

He led the way and made them realise that heart, and will, and work ethic were more important than physical traits.

Brett played 200 consecutive matches from mid-2002 to the end of 2010, for a total of 241 games for the Swans. He didn't play in the first two games when I took over as interim coach, but his mate Stuey Maxfield had urged us to select him for round 15, 2002. We took Stuey's advice, and Brett did not miss a game from then until we both retired. What an effort – quite extraordinary.

Our time was nigh. We finished the home and away season with four wins on the trot and were placed fifth as the finals started. We'd defied the critics again. We earned a home elimination final, and lined up against Carlton at ANZ Stadium. It was a tense day and we got up by five points.

The following Friday, we played the Western Bulldogs in a semifinal at the MCG. We were evenly matched and it was another thriller. We missed a few easy goals, the defenders made a few errors and we lost by five points. There weren't too many relaxing days at the office during my time as coach.

It was not the end I craved, but perhaps a heart-stopper was fitting. I walked away satisfied that I had achieved all I promised to do when I presented my coaching vision to the Swans board eight years earlier.

We had won a premiership, been runners-up, and played in the finals seven out of eight years. We had proved you could rebuild and stay competitive at the same time. We had created a lasting culture admired throughout the football industry. We had won respect, and developed a succession of leaders who will be forever remembered in Swans history.

I'd been in charge for 202 games, including 16 finals, and we'd won 116 times.

It had been the right club for me to coach, and it was the right time to leave. I had an emotional connection at the

Swans, and had absolutely no interest in coaching another club. They say you should never say never, but I was certain my AFL coaching days were over.

I'd enjoyed the job, but it was time for a break from the intensity of coaching, and time to do other things.

Part Four

2011–2013
Moving On

CHAPTER 12
Coaching kids

When the Sydney Swans Academy was set up during my last year as coach in 2010, it was the most significant development for the club since the move from Melbourne in 1982. That's a big call, but not overstating it.

Establishing the academy was a watershed moment for the Swans and for the sport. It was an opportunity we'd been waiting for. It had the potential to create significant change that would strengthen the club and, just as importantly, the AFL, for decades to come.

It was the saviour for junior football in Sydney and NSW. In turn, that would create a bigger pool of potential draft picks for all clubs at the elite level, while also developing a generation of good local players who would in turn become junior coaches and passionate advocates for footy in NSW.

While it was incredibly exciting, it was also frustrating it had taken so long to convince the AFL this was the way to go if they wanted to deepen the code's roots in the highly competitive NSW sporting market.

The AFL had tried several schemes in the early 2000s to boost the number of players drafted from NSW. There was an expensive NSW scholarship program, where any club could sign a teenager and work with him until draft age, but in nearly 10 years that resulted in only a few youngsters being picked up, such as Will Langford (Hawthorn), Taylor Walker (Adelaide) and Craig Bird (Swans).

The AFL poured money into footy clinics in schools across NSW and boasted that junior numbers were booming. But the reality was many of those kids had fleeting contact with the sport and didn't seriously pursue it.

The youngsters who did have passion for the sport and dreamed of being drafted ran into obstacles.

Australian football was not offered as a sport in secondary schools in Sydney or most of NSW, apart from the Riverina, which was a traditional stronghold. So kids would be playing rugby league or union on Saturday morning and then trying to back up for an Aussie Rules game on Saturday afternoon or Sunday.

Many people in NSW tried to convey the widespread problems to the Victoria-centric AFL so that they would realise the sport hardly made a dent in the biggest state in the country, and real change was needed.

I gave a talk to the AFL's community staff in Melbourne where I tried to give an insight into the NSW situation. There was plenty of passion, but the kids weren't getting the standard of coaching and competition that could prepare them to play at the highest level. I explained that some coaches in the junior competitions I'd been involved with through my sons didn't know all the positions on the field, let alone the finer points of the rules. They were shocked.

The AFL was trying, but there was so much wasted opportunity. The evidence for that, and also the solution, was obvious in the history of draft picks from NSW.

I always pointed back to 1998, when there had been five boys drafted from NSW/ACT – Mark McVeigh to Essendon at pick nine, Lenny Hayes to St Kilda at pick 11, Nick Davis to Collingwood at pick 19 under the father–son rule, Craig Bolton to Brisbane at pick 33 and Ray Hall to Richmond at pick 79.

In 1998, the best boys were part of an intensive elite program where they lived and trained together in Canberra. They played as the NSW/ACT Rams in Victoria's TAC Cup under-18 competition, the main recruitment pathway to the AFL. They had a high-quality, ongoing training program and played in the best under-age competition in the country. The benefits flowed, and all five of those players went on to have successful AFL careers.

At the end of 1998, the AFL decided to disband the Rams program, saying the travel made it too expensive and that it wasn't fair to ask 17-year-olds to relocate. They reverted to a system where the best players came together for just a few weeks a year, to play in the second division of the under-18 National AFL Championships.

There was a dramatic drop in draft numbers. In 1999 and 2000, not one NSW player was drafted onto the primary list of any AFL club. In 2001 and 2002, a few boys made it through, including Mark McVeigh's brother, Jarrad, taken by the Swans at pick three, Lewis Roberts-Thomson and Adam Schneider. But most years it was a sorry tale. Over seven drafts from 2003 to 2009, a total of nine NSW/ACT players were drafted onto primary lists.

At the Swans, we argued the answer was an ongoing intensive program with expert coaching, and a high level of competition week-in and week-out. That was the only way local boys were going to reach the required standard, and the only way the AFL could meet its target that 10 per cent of players drafted should come from NSW/ACT.

Andrew Ireland, who was elevated to the Swans' chief executive role in 2009, had been putting the case to the AFL for years, outlining an academy-style system where we could develop our own talent.

Finally, the commission listened and agreed to the establishment of club academies for teams in the northern states from 2010, partly because they had decided to create a second team in Sydney, the Greater Western Sydney Giants.

With the Gold Coast Suns also entering the AFL competition, there was an urgent need for an extra 80 players to stock their lists and they had to come from somewhere.

The idea was that the northern academies – at the Suns, the Brisbane Lions, GWS and the Swans – would identify and nurture talent from their own designated state zones. If the players turned out to be good enough, the club would have first call in the draft on their services.

During 2010, I had agreed that when I stepped down as coach of the Swans at the end of the season, I would take up the position of academy head coach.

Some people might have thought it strange I would go from coaching a top AFL team to overseeing a bunch of young boys and teenagers, but I was really looking forward to it.

I'd been involved in junior footy in Sydney for years with my own sons, Dylan and Tyler, and really wanted to make a difference for the thousands of kids in NSW who loved the game. As well, the academy was a chance for the Swans to control their own destiny, and I wanted to be part of that.

During 2010, Andrew and I worked closely on the academy program and structure with Chris Smith, who had been appointed to run the operations day-to-day. Chris grew up on a farm in the Riverina, and had been on Richmond's playing list. He had been on the Swans' recruiting team for several years and had a very good eye for spotting talented youngsters, even at primary school level. Smithy had a fantastic vision for the academy.

A working paper from the AFL suggested clubs should have around 10 kids at each age group from under-14 to under-18, so probably no more than 50 kids in each academy. At the Swans, we turned that idea on its head. We said the academy had to be on a mass scale and start from the age of 11, so we could instil technically sound skills and good habits.

A small-scale academy would have been another waste of time. As an industry, we had enough trouble picking the 10 best kids at under-18 level, let alone the 10 best kids at under-11 level in NSW.

QBE, the Swans' corporate partner for more than two decades, got behind it and became the principal partner of the academy, which gave us a solid foundation and the means to widen the scope.

We decided our academy would have around 600 young members, from the under-11 age group to under-20. It was to be structured like a pyramid, with hundreds given an opportunity in the youngest age groups and then smaller numbers at the pointy end, as players neared the senior level and draft age.

In 2010, the try-outs started. It was quite a scene and quite a production. At the first trials, held in the school holidays, around 400 boys turned up at the Lakeside Oval opposite the SCG, vying to be part of the first under-11 intake of the Swans Academy.

Of course, only a small fraction of boys would make it to the Swans, but the huge numbers given expert coaching and a sense of belonging ensured there would be a flow-on effect for other AFL clubs and for local football.

Andrew Ireland predicted it would take a few years before the advantages became apparent, but there would be a quantum change in the numbers drafted.

He was right. Four years later, at the end of 2014, four boys I had watched come through the ranks of junior football and coached at the academy from age 14 were drafted to the Swans in the national and rookie drafts – Isaac Heeney as the club's first selection, as well as Jordan Foote, Abaina Davis and Jack Hiscox. Daniel Robinson, another academy member from Sydney's north shore, was elevated from the club's rookie list to the senior list.

In 2015, Callum Mills, who had been in the academy since he was 13, was taken by the Swans with pick three in the draft – the first time ever a boy from metropolitan Sydney had been taken as one of the top 10 young players in Australia. In 2016, the Adelaide Crows recruited Ben Davis, a Maroubra boy who had been in the Swans Academy from age 12, showing the academy also benefited other clubs.

Callum and Isaac have both said on many occasions they would have stopped playing Australian football if they hadn't been part of the Swans Academy program. The academy gave them a clear roadmap and guidance to play at the highest level and both slotted seamlessly into the Swans' line-up.

It was proof the academy system we created was on the right track. A further nine players from NSW/ACT and Queensland were drafted to other AFL clubs in 2014.

The Giants Academy has always had it easier than the Swans, as their zone includes the Riverina, where there was already a strong football culture and plenty of expertise.

At the start of 2017, the AFL announced it was restricting the GWS Academy zone, so they could no longer have first pick on players from Albury, or the northern side of the Murray River along the Victoria/NSW border. That was fair, and really should have happened earlier. The GWS Academy wasn't doing enough to develop young players, especially in Sydney's west, and were picking the eyes out of the southern NSW region where football is already the number one sport.

For the Swans Academy, draft numbers were only one measure of success. We employed up to 50 part-time coaches at the academy, to take training at hubs in our zone, which stretched from the northern NSW coast to Wollongong, south of Sydney. Coaches were being developed as well as players.

From the start, our coaching and training philosophy was very simple – a lot of skill development at an early age. We focused on teaching kids how to kick, handball and mark properly. We emphasised how important it was to hit targets and use the ball well. The coaching was very technical and our skills acquisition specialist at the Swans, Ben Moore, did a fantastic job developing targeted drills suitable for young footballers.

The other important aspect of the program was the Academy Series, where the best boys played against each other every week. This was on top of their club football, so the boys were getting more high-level game experience.

There was a strong education focus during the series, and once they got to under-14s we taught them how to play AFL-style football, not junior football.

I often umpired, and would blow the whistle if a player tried to do something he would not get away with at AFL level. On one occasion in the under-16s, Isaac Heeney broke through three tackles and got clear. His club coach back on the Central Coast would have loved that, and it showed how far above most of the other players he was. But I awarded a free kick against him. He was incredulous, but we wanted to rub out any habits that wouldn't stand up to scrutiny in senior football.

In the lead-up to the under-16 national AFL carnival, the Swans Academy played a series against the GWS Academy, as players vied for selection in the NSW/ACT team. Isaac was close to the best kid in the country, but he played poorly in the first game. So in the next match we sent him to tag one of the Giants' stars, Liam Griffiths. 'I want you to learn to play on someone who is going to take you to the ball, and you have to learn how to beat him to the ball,' I told him.

The AFL staff frowned upon tagging at under-age tournaments, but that was an edict I didn't agree with – our aim was to develop players capable of playing AFL-style football.

Whenever we had a game, we would regularly stop it to make a point. There would be free kicks paid against kids if they didn't handball as soon as they were tackled, or if they played selfishly and didn't try to share the ball with teammates.

We taught them to hit targets and look inside the corridor for a better option rather than just banging the ball down the line. We showed them the team-first play valued at an AFL club like the Swans.

The boys were expected to have a positive attitude. They had to turn up to training on time, and if a kid didn't listen or he wasn't respectful, there was no place for him in the academy, no matter how talented he was. We owed it to the players to teach them about discipline and teamwork so they had a valuable experience at the academy, whether they continued with football or not.

During my time as Swans coach, we had several young players arrive from Victoria, South Australia and Western Australia with big raps on them. They'd been stars in those states, knowing from a young age they were likely to be drafted. It had come easily to them and I often found their attitude wasn't great. They just expected things would happen for them, and didn't understand that the hard work was just starting. We had more success with players who fought their way off the rookie list into the senior team, such as Brett Kirk, Heath Grundy, Kieren Jack, Nick Smith and Paul Bevan.

I took that knowledge with me to the academy. It didn't matter if you were Isaac Heeney or Callum Mills, you had to be a good team player, hard-working, disciplined and not arrogant. The 'no dickheads' policy was at work at the academy too, as I heard a father joke one day when he watched how attentive the squad of teenagers were at training.

At the academy, we put all the groups from under-14 to under-18 through a modified pre-season training program in November and December. They did three-kilometre time trials, three-minute runs, intense skills training. We didn't thrash them, but gave them a taste of what it would take, mentally and physically.

The benefits of the Swans Academy program were reinforced to me after I left the job in late 2013. We moved to Melbourne and I went and watched teams train for the under-18 TAC Cup competition, where my son Tyler was playing.

The standard of development was not what we had implemented at the academy, but it wasn't the coaches' fault. They had 100 kids aged 17 and 18 in their pre-season squads in November, which was not manageable.

From my perspective, the TAC Cup competition, considered the best junior pathway in Australia, relies simply on natural talent rising to the top. It is purely a talent league, not a development league, so there are too many good kids who fall through the cracks.

The coaches of the TAC Cup teams are paid virtually nothing, even though they're training some of the most promising kids in the country. I believe the system is flawed. When you're living in Sydney, you think the training and development is better in Victoria, because that's what the industry tells you, but I was surprised to find that wasn't the case.

The TAC Cup games themselves are high-quality, because there are so many good athletes who've been playing since they could walk. But the tactics, the AFL-modified rules and the training standards don't do the players justice.

The AFL has ruled that coaches have to use a zone system, with a certain number of players in each area of the field at certain times, and no tagging. I believe the restricted rules don't allow some of the less obviously talented kids to show they could be competent AFL players. And they don't do the really talented kids any favours either.

Take the example of a player like Western Bulldogs' forward/ruckman, Tom Boyd, a 201-centimetre giant. Boyd played for the Eastern Ranges in the TAC Cup and he was the competition's leading goal-kicker in 2012.

In 2013, he was the number one AFL draft pick but did not make an impact when he debuted for GWS in 2014. He was traded to the Bulldogs at the end of the year for big money, but couldn't find any consistency and it wasn't until late 2016 that he started to realise his potential.

I believe Tom's struggles were at least partly the consequence of the TAC Cup rules, which are designed to show off a player's skills unimpeded by pressure. There was Tom in the TAC Cup, 201 centimetres tall and in most matches he was playing on a defender who was 10 centimetres shorter than him. But the game style played by all teams in the TAC Cup means Tom has mostly one-on-one contests every week, and naturally he wins the majority of them against a much smaller opponent.

Then he gets drafted with big promise, and the first AFL game he plays, he's got the opposition ruckman standing in front of him, he's got two defenders on him, there are midfielders all around him. No wonder it took him time to find his feet.

I don't believe the TAC Cup rules advance the development of young players. All they do is show off the players who are already good, and make it harder for them – especially the tall players – when they do play AFL football.

I have very strong views on junior development, because I want to see more young players get a chance to play AFL footy, and be better prepared so they can make a real success of it.

My other concern is that the draft age of 18 is too young, an opinion also expressed by former Fremantle Dockers captain, Matthew Pavlich.

Pavlich was drafted at 18 and says he would have been much better equipped to handle it if he'd had another year or two of life experiences outside the AFL. Pavlich, now retired but still president of the AFL Players' Association, believes 19 or 20 is the right age, because too many young players enter the AFL ranks not mature enough to handle it and fall by the wayside.

Not only are too many young players failing to make an impact when they do get drafted, too many others are passed over because they're late developers.

I believe we need to raise the draft age and introduce an elite under-20 national competition. We need to find ways to keep promising kids aged 19 and 20 in the system, to allow them to keep improving and stay on the recruitment pathway.

With the draft age at 18, I also worry it has a detrimental effect on the education of many boys, who are trying to do year 12 at the same time as they're trying to play their best footy and get drafted.

It's too hard on young men to ask them to play national under-18 championships, do year 12, play TAC Cup footy and play school footy. Too often schoolwork gets put on the backburner while they pursue footy goals. The fact most are doing year 12 in their draft year should be a red flag to the AFL. If the draft age is at least a year older, it will solve that problem.

I loved coaching the Swans Academy and being so involved in junior football for three years. The only disappointment is I would have liked to see more kids drafted, and I believe more should have been. I could name 20 kids from the academy and the TAC Cup who I believe should be on AFL lists now but didn't get picked up.

We need to stop discarding boys from the system at 18, especially if we want to see more players like Swans defender Dane Rampe.

His story illustrates the folly of passing over boys when they're still developing. Dane grew up in Clovelly, just a few kilometres from the SCG, but didn't start playing footy until he was 17. He'd found his passion, so he moved to Melbourne when he finished school, to improve his game and see what he could achieve. He did a pre-season with the Bulldogs and played for Williamstown in the VFL. After a couple of seasons there was no interest from AFL clubs, so he moved home to Sydney, giving up his dream.

In 2012, he was playing in the Sydney Football League for the University of NSW/Eastern Suburbs Bulldogs, when I saw him, as my son Dylan was also in the team. Dane, who was 22, dominated the competition.

I recommended he should be given a chance to play as a top-up player for the Swans reserves (the Swans can include players from the local Sydney competition to make up the numbers in their reserves side).

Dane played for the Swans seconds against the Giants at the Showgrounds in Sydney. The Giants reserves team had a lot of their best youngsters playing, who had been high AFL draft picks.

Dane was easily the best player on the ground, but there

was reluctance from clubs to look seriously at him because he was now 22. And from my experience, as an industry we tend to focus too much on flaws rather than strengths.

There was scepticism about his kicking prowess, but I liked the fact he could get the ball, he was tough, big and athletic. Occasionally he turned the ball over but, really, there wasn't a lot not to like about him. Why should it matter that he was 22? He could play.

The Swans, to their credit, decided to put him on the rookie list at the end of 2012. He played senior football in 2013 and has gone from strength to strength. In 2016, he was named an All-Australian player.

Dane is typical of many young players, but sadly not many end up having his eventual success. They're late developers, or there might be a flaw in their skills, or something else that we could fix. They have great character, great work ethic, great endurance, great passion, great love for the game, and they really want to play. But another kid, sometimes not as good but slightly taller or stronger, gets taken above them.

We spend too much time looking for weaknesses, and too much time crystal-balling about how a player might develop. As an industry, we should focus more on the talent right in front of our eyes.

Part Five

2013–2016
Back into the Fray

CHAPTER 13
Peter comes knocking

When the Swans won the 2012 premiership, I was as pleased as anyone. It was two years since I'd coached the team, but not for one moment did I feel a sense of loss. I was in the rooms after the game, working for Fox Footy, and got enormous pleasure seeing the players and coach John Longmire celebrating.

I had no regrets, there was no part of me that wished I had stayed on. There were a few things I occasionally missed about coaching – the feeling of a good win and the camaraderie of the team environment – but they weren't enough to lure me back.

When you're a coach, you effectively have 44 sons you care about and have a deep interest in, and that takes a huge amount of energy and emotional attachment – as anyone who has even one child would know.

I'd been asked so many times when I would coach again. At the time, I genuinely thought I wouldn't do it again. As much as I had loved it, you have to be ready to give it everything, to have an open door, communicate and be prepared to work hard on relationships. As the 2013 season approached, I was still content with coaching the kids at the Swans Academy and working in the media. It was a perfect combination, developing juniors but still involved as a commentator and analyst at the AFL level, without the stress of coaching.

It turned out to be a tumultuous year for the AFL competition. In February, a month before the season began, the Essendon supplements scandal exploded, when the Bombers asked the AFL and the Australian Sports Anti-Doping Authority (ASADA) to investigate the supplements program it had in place during 2011 and 2012. It was disturbing, and while it was impossible to know the full story, it upset me to think players might have been given harmful substances.

There was a raft of other issues rolling along. I was down in Melbourne on Mondays during the season, to appear on the Fox Footy program, *On The Couch*. It was a program I really enjoyed doing, casting an eye over all the clubs and trying to help the public understand the intricacies of footy, the trends in the game, and why teams won and lost.

When we'd finished the show, my colleagues Gerard Healy, Mike Sheahan, Alastair Lynch, Fox's Billy Cannon and I would head to a pub nearby in South Melbourne, Lamaro's. Gill McLachlan, then deputy chief executive of the AFL, would often join us after he had played basketball. Over a few drinks, there would be vigorous debate and banter about the state of the game and the AFL.

Towards the middle of the year, I was often the focus of the banter and they'd all get stuck into me. Several clubs were struggling on and off the field and, as usual, it was the coaches taking the hits. Melbourne and the Brisbane Lions were especially under the pump, and whenever that happened, the speculation would start about when I'd coach again. I laughed it off, and would give it straight back to Gill, saying I didn't think the AFL had done a great job supporting and developing coaches within the industry.

The AFL had realised how challenging it would be to get 88 new players for the GWS Giants and the Gold Coast Suns, but I don't think they foresaw how hard it would be to find the extra ancillary staff, including coaches. There was a shortage of experienced people across the competition. So we'd discuss all the burning issues, but the running joke was that I had better get back into coaching.

During the years I'd been out of coaching, half a dozen clubs had approached me, either directly or indirectly. Some wanted advice on culture change and transformation, or succession planning, while others were interested in me coaching. But, it has to be emphasised, I didn't get approaches from any club that still had a coach under contract.

As the midway point of the season approached, Melbourne was the AFL's primary concern. The Demons were regularly suffering huge losses. In round two, Essendon beat them by 148 points and in round three they went down by 94 points to West Coast. It didn't get much better from there. In round 10, Hawthorn trounced Melbourne by 95 points, and then came a humiliating loss to Collingwood on the Queen's Birthday holiday – the Demons kicked only five goals and went down by 83 points in the showcase game at the MCG.

As well, there were troubles off the field. The club was losing money and the AFL was concerned it was a financial drag on the competition.

In April, the Melbourne chief executive Cameron Schwab had resigned. AFL chief executive Andrew Demetriou had approached experienced administrator Peter Jackson to take the role, with a brief to restructure the club from top to bottom and get it back on solid footing.

Peter had been CEO of Essendon from 1996 to 2009 and was a business executive highly respected in the industry.

He had played amateur football, and been chairman of AFL Victoria.

He spent two months reviewing the club's operations, and the performance of the team under coach Mark Neeld. At a Melbourne board meeting in mid-June, a few days after the round 11 loss to Collingwood, they decided to sack Mark.

Mark had been coach since the end of 2011, so he'd had less than two seasons in charge. He'd previously been an assistant coach at Collingwood and had come to Melbourne vowing to be a hard taskmaster and to make the players tougher.

For whatever reasons, it hadn't worked, and the team had won only five of the 33 games he had coached – four in 2012 and just one to that point in 2013.

Like most of the football industry, I took an interest in the media conference held at the Melbourne footy club on Monday, 17 June to announce the board's decision. Mark was there, alongside Peter Jackson, which must have been very hard for him to do. I admired how honest both he and Peter were.

Jackson said Mark wasn't being made a scapegoat, but the huge losses were unacceptable. Mark spoke bravely when he said the whole club had to be shaken up. 'There's going to be changes across all parts of it, and I'm one. I take responsibility for my component, no doubt.'

Former Adelaide coach Neil Craig, who was the club's director of sports performance, was appointed caretaker coach for the rest of the season.

Not long after Mark had left, Peter Jackson came to visit me at home in Sydney, to gauge if I had any interest in coaching Melbourne. I enjoyed hearing his thoughts and we had a frank discussion, but I still wasn't tempted.

Around the same time, I got a visit from Brisbane Lions

chairman, Angus Johnson. Michael Voss, one of the greatest midfielders of all time and a club legend, was coaching, but there were internal divisions. Johnson didn't ask me to coach, but was seeking advice on the best way forward for the Lions.

But a month or so later, in early August, Voss was sacked with three rounds to go in the season, even though the Lions' form had improved after the bye. It was sad to watch. Voss had been one of the game's greatest players and had been coach since 2009.

As an industry, we still don't have a proper understanding of what makes a good coach. Clubs get caught up in the emotion of appointing a legendary player as coach, and the fans love it. The emotion often outweighs logic and it's unfair on the inexperienced coach.

Vossy's situation reinforced my view that we shouldn't assume a champion player and club captain is going to easily make the transition to coach. The requirements of the two roles are vastly different.

Even the most selfless players, like those I'd coached at the Swans – Ben Mathews, Luke Ablett, Paul Bevan or Sean Dempster – only had to worry about preparing themselves to play every week. Their job was to train hard, eat well, understand their specific role and execute that. First and foremost, it was about them.

The coach must have a completely different mentality. A coach is looking after 40 or more players and the job is to make every one of them think they're the most important person in the club. On top of that, the coach has to manage medical and fitness staff, assistant coaches, recruiters, marketing, sponsorship and the media.

Would you take the best miner at BHP and make him the CEO without management training? That's effectively what happened to champion-players-turned-coaches, but emotion dictated the appointment.

So, by August, Mark Neeld and Michael Voss had been sacked, and at Essendon coach James Hird had been given a 12-month suspension for his role in the supplements scandal.

I had historic links to the Lions, because my old club Fitzroy had merged with them in the 1990s, but I didn't want to move to Brisbane.

I was repeatedly asked about the Melbourne job by the media. In July, during *On The Couch*, I had said I wasn't entertaining the idea, but had told Peter Jackson that, if anything changed, I'd let him know.

Then suddenly, in August, the landscape did dramatically change. Swans CEO Andrew Ireland said he wanted to see me about my contract at the academy.

When I went to that meeting, I knew there might be changes afoot and expected Andrew might tell me my next contract would involve a pay cut. I had put a lot of time, effort and passion into the academy, and I was getting well paid.

I had guessed it might be in the line of a 20 per cent cut, but Andrew said they had to reduce the next contract by 60 per cent. That was a shock.

Andrew and I had a strong relationship and he had been a great support when I started out as coach in 2002, and throughout my career. When he was delivering the message to me, I'm sure Andrew knew I wouldn't accept a reduction of that size and that I'd leave. In a roundabout way, that was see-you-later.

It was an uncomfortable meeting, but I could never be critical of the Swans. They had looked after me incredibly well as a player, coach and then at the academy. But I'm the type of person who looks for signs. I walked out feeling pretty clear this meant my time at the Swans was over.

I've never closely questioned why that happened. Some people have suggested that the AFL, which had intervened to revamp Melbourne, had a hand in it, but I'm not sure, although a comment from Andrew Demetriou a month or so earlier had pricked my ears.

'We don't recruit players and we don't recruit coaches, but Paul Roos, as a general comment, is an incredibly gifted and talented coach and as an industry we are the lesser for not having a person of Paul Roos' talent coaching in the AFL ranks,' Demetriou had said.

To be honest, it didn't matter why and there was no point dwelling on it. I'd had an amazing experience at the Swans and made great friends. I had no bitterness, but it was time to sit down and talk with my family and think about our next chapter.

A few days later, I was sitting in my hotel room in Melbourne before heading to Fox Footy when the phone rang. It was Peter Jackson. He was downstairs and wanted to come up to see me. It was an unexpected visit. I'd had a few more phone calls with Peter over the past month, but we hadn't arranged to meet.

When I opened the door, it was a bit of a surprise. The best way I can describe the look on Peter's face was despair. He sat down and we started talking. 'I need to make this change at Melbourne work, but I'm exhausted, I've run out of ideas,' he said.

Footy is an emotional business, and I could tell he was wedded to Melbourne. It wasn't just a job for him now. I didn't know him very well, but he was obviously at his wits' end and genuinely wanted to rescue the footy club.

He talked about the depth of the problems, including the financial woes and concerns that key players who were coming out of contract, including Jack Watts, might abandon the club.

Somehow, the worse it sounded, the more it interested me. My circumstances had changed and the timing was right. 'I'm going to have another crack at getting you to coach,' he said. We laughed, but that visit was a turning point for me. By the time Peter left the hotel, I had agreed to consider the job.

I made some inquiries of my own. I spoke to Dave Misson, the elite performance manager at Melbourne. Misso and I had worked together when I was coach of the Swans. He's a terrific person and had been an integral part of the medical and fitness team that had been so successful at keeping players relatively injury-free at the Swans.

During 2005 and 2006, we had the lowest injury rate of any club and used fewer players than any other team. Misso had helped create the 'wellness' system behind those figures, where players rated the difficulty of games and training and how sore their major muscles were. Training for each individual was then modified to take that into account, which kept players fresh and reduced soft tissue injuries.

Misso was critical to my decision. We went through the Melbourne list. He told me how he thought certain players could improve, and filled me in on their attitudes. He put their poor performances down to negativity, disunity and a chronic lack of belief.

I didn't want Misso or Peter to sugarcoat the problems and they didn't, they were very open.

Before I went any further, I told Peter Jackson I also had to meet the players' leadership group and ask them a few questions.

I had seen the Demons play many times as part of my commentary duties, but I didn't know the players. At times they had been hard to watch, but it was impossible to fathom from the outside exactly what was going on.

There had been one particular game against the Swans at the SCG in 2012 that had shocked me. Melbourne had lost by 101 points and I was aghast at their lack of run, voice and teamwork.

I had commented at the time that it appeared to be a deeper problem than lack of confidence, and they seemed incapable or unwilling to follow the coach's instructions. I said it couldn't just be Mark Neeld, because the same issues had arisen under their previous coach, Dean Bailey.

Dean had been coach from the start of the 2008 season until round 19 in 2011. The Demons were last on the ladder in 2008 and 2009 as Dean tried to rebuild the team after the retirement of experienced players. In 2010, they were 12th. The following year was a roller-coaster ride on the field, and there was internal division at the club. The Melbourne board sacked Dean after the team lost to Geelong by 186 points, which was the second-biggest losing margin in AFL history. Dean had coached for 83 games and the Demons had won 22 of those.

When things go bad at a football club, it is never one person's fault. I wanted to meet the players and see if they were willing to take some responsibility for the long-term mess their club was in, or just make excuses.

If I was going to seriously contemplate coaching them, I didn't want to go in blind. I had to try to understand what had gone wrong, and establish whether they were willing to listen and do the hard work required to lift their club to a competitive AFL standard.

The mood of the meeting would tell the tale.

We didn't want media scrutiny, so we met at my account-ant's office in South Melbourne. A number of senior players were there including the young captains, Jack Grimes and Jack Trengove, as well as Nathan Jones, Jack Watts, Mitch Clark, Chris Dawes, James Frawley, Colin Garland, Lynden Dunn and Shannon Byrnes, who had played in two premierships at Geelong before he was recruited to Melbourne.

'Be honest with me, give me the reasons why things have gone so bad,' I said to them.

The players were great and owned up to their part in the problems. They said they could have worked harder and they were fed up with losing. They didn't try to blame the former CEO Cameron Schwab, or coaches Dean Bailey or Mark Neeld. They were saying everyone needed to do a better job.

Then Jack Watts spoke up. I hadn't met Jack before, but I knew his story very well, as most AFL followers did. Jack had been the number one draft pick in 2008, but had never become the consistently good player he should be. Instead, he was one of the most maligned players in the competition, criticised in a cruel way I'd rarely seen before. Jack was held up as a symbol of Melbourne's failure and he'd had to bear the unfair weight of that.

Jack looked me in the eye and said, 'Roosy, I just want to be treated like a human being.'

I was rocked by Jack's words. In one simple, powerful sentence, he gave me the insight I needed. It was not something I ever thought I'd hear a player say. For whatever reason, the important relationships at Melbourne were in tatters. There needed to be more nurturing and less negativity.

From my experience at the Swans, I knew how crucial relationships were in football clubs. And they had become increasingly important now players were full-time professionals.

If players didn't feel as if they were valued, listened to, and treated with respect, they didn't want to come to work.

You had to not only value them, but their family too, and at the Swans we'd created an environment where all those relationships were important.

It was an eye-opening meeting and what struck me was the emotion displayed by the Melbourne players. The wounds were raw, both for individuals and the group.

Shannon Byrnes' contribution was telling. I leant on him to talk, as he had been a senior player at Geelong during their premiership reign, so understood how good teams worked.

He believed in the benefits of player empowerment, because it had been implemented at Geelong in a way similar to the Swans. When he was at Geelong, he knew what his role was. 'I really didn't know what role I was supposed to be playing at Melbourne,' Shannon said.

He was terrific, because his views gave me a good comparison and insight into the difference between successful teams such as Geelong and the Swans, and Melbourne.

In the end, there was a blunt message from Mitch Clark, the key forward who had been traded to the Demons from Brisbane. 'Roosy, can you just come and fuckin' coach us?'

As I left, I knew that, more than anything, the job would be about building relationships, cultural change and education. There was trauma that needed to be managed and healed. They wanted direction, to be appreciated and given real responsibility. It was more of a leadership challenge than a coaching challenge, and that's the only reason I considered it.

I came out of that meeting comforted. They had no real experience of a successful club and were saying they were as much to blame as anyone. They had to do things better, but wanted the club to work with them. Jack's words had especially hit a nerve. The message was compelling and I believed I could help the Melbourne players get the best out of themselves.

After the meeting, I received texts from several players, including Nathan Jones, the hard-headed 25-year-old midfielder, who had won the best and fairest award in 2012. There was another from Jack Grimes and one from Jack Trengove, the co-captains. The messages varied, but the theme was similar – they were basically saying, please consider coaching us. They were like a cry for help.

I read them out to my son Dylan. 'Dad, you have to go and coach them,' he said. The players were honest, high-quality people. They deserved a chance.

Money was the last thing discussed with Peter Jackson.

The first time we had met a few months previously, Peter had sent me an offer of a five-year contract, and I had flatly rejected it. When I did decide to take the job in early September, it only took 24 hours to sort out the contract and the pay. The lure was the opportunity to drive cultural change at the club and oversee the rebuild. I had the opportunity to put all I'd learned at the Swans into practice in a new environment. I had the experience and knew the model to follow.

I told Peter I would have to bring in my own assistant coaches. That was crucial. I wouldn't have accepted the job if I hadn't been able to bring in people I knew well and had worked with at the Swans – including Ben Mathews, Brett Allison, Daniel McPherson and George Stone. I didn't have time to train assistants in my methods – we had to hit the ground running. Also, because my role was to have an overarching focus on leadership and people management, I needed great assistant coaches to carry out the more technical day-to-day tasks.

And we had agreed on a coaching succession plan, which really sealed it. I wanted to drive change and put the fundamentals in place, but I wasn't interested in a long-term contract.

From day one the Melbourne job was different to the Sydney job.

I was never going to coach for longer than three years because I really didn't see myself as a 'football coach' at that stage. I had finished being a football coach. I was drawn to the Melbourne job because it was about leadership, and because I believed in succession planning.

Still, people wanted to know why I didn't want to coach long-term. For me, it was simple – it just wasn't something I wanted to do for an extended period.

On Friday, 6 September, we held a news conference to announce I would coach Melbourne for two years, with the option of a third year.

We didn't promise a quick fix for the club that had been languishing for years. Peter told the media we had to change the culture, development standards and the leadership right across the board. A few weeks earlier, Glen Bartlett had replaced Don McLardy as president, so there was new blood in all the senior positions.

I said there had been several pivotal moments in my decision – the ending of the association with Sydney, meeting the players, and the succession plan.

'I want to set the direction for the club. I would love to hold another (premiership) cup up, but for me it's about setting these guys on a path so for the next five to seven years they will know who their senior coaches will be,' I said.

The coaching succession plan interested the media. Such a plan had still only happened at the Swans and Collingwood. I said we'd appoint a senior assistant who would be groomed to take over the head coach's role. 'I think that's a real positive, as players will have a really clear understanding of where this football club is going.'

I was honest about the challenge ahead. Melbourne hadn't

played finals since 2006, and had won 34 games out of more than 150 played in the previous seven seasons. They had beaten a top-eight side only once in the past four years.

In 2013, the season just gone, they had won two games of 22, and their percentage was 56 per cent, a measure of the fact they'd been thrashed most weeks. I thought they were better than their record in 2013. My goal was to set high standards and make them as competitive as we could, as fast as possible.

Nearly 12,000 Melbourne members had left the club in the previous two years, frustrated at the lack of fight from their team. We wanted to give the fans hope, but there was no magic formula. Everyone at Melbourne had experienced pain, but I said we'd be doing our best to ensure the players put out a good product on the field.

'It is going to be difficult, it is going to be hard, but get on board, there is a direction now for the football club and hopefully the players are excited, we know where we're going. It might take a while to get there, but we know our direction, and that's important.'

Both Peter and I made it plain we wanted to lay the planks for success, but it was a long-term plan and we'd be very happy if someone else took the glory when we'd gone.

Realistically, success was unlikely to come in a hurry. The team had won two games in 2013; to play in the finals you generally need to win at least 12 games, so that improvement would take some time. We first had to focus on rebuilding and mending the club, rather than any thought of premierships.

The coaching notes I'd written 15 years before were pulled out of my desk drawer again. I'd tested them over eight years at the Sydney Swans and knew they were still relevant. Now they would be put into action once more, but this time with a club and a team at rock bottom.

I could never have taken on the mammoth task of turning around Melbourne without the experience of all that came before.

CHAPTER 14

Taking charge

Before the Melbourne players went on their post-season leave in early September 2013, we called them to a meeting at the club. I hadn't met most of them, and wanted to give the guys a strong message about the future, reassuring words to take with them as they went their separate ways for two months.

It had been another traumatic year for the players. Their coach, CEO and president had all departed and they'd won only two games. For many of them, 2013 was the latest in a series of nightmare years. In 2012, the much-loved former player and president, Jim Stynes, had died of cancer, and there had been a cloud hanging over the club due to allegations of tanking games.

For several years, their own fans had booed and jeered them after losses. The club was considered a basket case and the constant troubles sat heavily on the players.

I knew from my meeting with the leadership group in late August that the squad was disgruntled, mentally scarred and sick of the derision. I believe as many as 10 players would have walked away if they had been out of contract. That's how shattered they were.

My aim was to create an atmosphere of stability and

certainty, and reinforce to the players they were the most important people in the footy club. It was a theme Melbourne CEO, Peter Jackson, had emphasised when he announced the sacking of coach Mark Neeld in mid-2013. Peter said it was his responsibility to ensure players saw a future at the club. 'As a club, we have to convince them that this is a place they want to be,' he said.

That was my starting point. I stood in front of the group, holding a sheet of paper. It was my pledge to them, an outline of what we would provide for the players.

'Boys, this is my commitment to you: you will know your role, every one of you will know what you're here to do. Our expectations will be really clear.

'You'll be valued. We'll have a set game plan and we'll train hard.

'You'll all choose the leadership group, and be involved in setting up our behaviours, team rules, standards and discipline. Your leadership group will drive the success.

'We're going to build and repair relationships, because that's the only way we can create strong bonds. We're in this together.'

There's a fairly common philosophy in sport that the coach has to keep his distance from the players, so he can make the hard decisions. I think that's outdated and it had never been my way. I wasn't saying I'd be best mates with every player, but I gave them a promise I'd get to know them, care about them, and be honest and upfront with them.

I would listen and treat them with respect. AFL footy is a tough business and you're not going to get far if you don't have genuinely strong relationships. I was drawing on what I'd learned during my eight and a half seasons as coach of the Swans.

Then the players left for the off-season break. I hoped they had a more positive view of the future and would come back ready to give it everything.

While the players were away for around two months, there was a lot to do. The priority was to get my coaching and support staff in place. I had a commitment from Peter Jackson that I could bring in my own assistant coaches, because I needed people who already understood the things I valued, on and off the field.

Over the next month, we employed Ben Mathews, George Stone, Brett Allison and Daniel McPherson. I had worked or played with each of them at the Swans. I had strong relationships with them all and they knew my strategies.

To be honest, I wouldn't have taken the Melbourne job had they not been able to come with me. It was going to be hard enough to get to know the players quickly; I didn't have time to get to know coaches too, or teach them my expectations.

Ben Mathews, in charge of the midfield, was a great role model for the Melbourne players. He came to the Swans from Corowa/Rutherglen on the NSW/Victoria border in the mid-1990s. By his own admission, he was a working-class midfielder, but he played almost 200 games, including the Swans' 2005 premiership. During that time, he curbed some of the most highly rated midfielders in the competition, including Gary Ablett. Ben has an incredible understanding of what it takes to be an AFL midfielder and he was the perfect person to school Melbourne's young group of on-ballers.

We appointed George Stone as a development coach. He is a great friend and one of the most respected assistant coaches in football. In 2013, he received a lifetime achievement award from the AFL Coaches Association, and it couldn't have gone to a more deserving person.

George knows the ingredients to win premierships. He's

been involved in six flags – 1986, 1988, 1989 and 1991 with Hawthorn, and 2005 and 2012 with the Swans. When Tadhg Kennelly arrived at the Swans from Ireland as an athletic 19-year-old with raw talent but no AFL skills, George transformed him into one of the most skilful players in the game and an integral member of the 2005 premiership side.

Brett Allison, a dual premiership player at North Melbourne, was appointed head of development. Brett, who worked at the Swans and Kangaroos in development, has a great eye for upcoming talent and a very good rapport with young players.

Daniel McPherson was our final coaching appointment and we put him in charge of the Demons' forward line. I had played at the Swans with 'Frosty', as he's known, in the 1996 Grand Final. He had then worked with the NSW/ACT under-18 team and in development at the Swans.

They all understood what it takes to be successful and how hard you have to work. They also had great people skills. Those appointments were a shortcut for me. It was going to be a harder job than when I took over at Sydney, because I had to spend a lot of time getting to know the players. Knowing the coaches well was crucial.

We were also fortunate that Jade Rawlings, who had been an assistant under Mark Neeld since late 2011, remained at the club. Jade, who had played at Hawthorn, Western Bulldogs and North Melbourne during a 148-game career, was the backline coach and had been in charge of the group for two years.

You spend so much time with the coaching group, at training, games and travelling interstate. I felt the dynamic was right. At the Swans, I'd learned you need to have assistants who are strong-minded and will challenge you, but in a spirit of co-operation. There should be vigorous debate about training, game plan, leadership and team selection, but you need to walk out of any meeting united by a common purpose.

If I got outvoted at match committee on a player selection, I accepted it – it wasn't *my* team. Players sometimes didn't believe me when I told them I didn't make all the decisions, but it was true.

The pieces of the puzzle were slotting into place. Josh Mahoney, who had been at the Demons as an assistant coach since 2008, was reaffirmed in the crucial role of manager, football operations.

Josh had an interesting playing career, which gave him a great background. He had been drafted by Collingwood and made his debut in 1997. At the end of 1998, he was traded to the Western Bulldogs and then delisted a couple of years later. He didn't give up footy, but played in the VFL. Then, in the 2004 pre-season draft, he was picked up by Port Adelaide. At 26, he was back in the AFL and he went on to play in Port Adelaide's premiership side. It's a great story of persistence from a player who prided himself on defensive pressure.

Todd Viney was also a key member of our staff, as manager player personnel. His role was a link between the coaches, development staff and recruitment, which was headed by Jason Taylor. Todd had been a champion player at the Demons, twice winning the best and fairest, and was captain in 1998 and 1999. He worked as an assistant coach at Hawthorn during their 2008 premiership year, but had been back in the Melbourne football department since 2010.

Jade, Josh and Todd's experience at the Demons was invaluable to our new coaching group, and they gave us terrific insight into the players.

But it was also important for the players to know that the

new coaching group carried no baggage. We were prepared to look at them with fresh eyes and give everyone a chance.

Dave Misson, who'd worked with me at the Swans, was overseeing fitness, which meant we had a head start on the track. He knew how we had trained at Sydney, was familiar with the drills, and had strong ideas to improve the players.

Under Peter Jackson and president Glen Bartlett, the club had put a sound structure in place and was heading in the right direction.

Glen had been appointed in August and was an excellent president. He had played a few games for West Coast in 1987, but was mostly known as an outstanding leader for West Perth in the West Australian Football League. He then had a successful career in the law in Perth and Melbourne and had joined the Demons board just three months before, in mid-2013.

He was low-profile, very steady and understood the behind-the-scenes role a good board should play. He was prepared to let Peter be CEO, and Peter's experience in footy clubs meant he gave me the support and leeway I needed to do my job.

Turning around Melbourne, or any club or organisation, is a group effort. We were going to teach the players to execute their role on the field, but the philosophy of playing your role was just as important for the off-field crew as we revamped the club.

There is a misconception about footy clubs that the CEO or the president or the coach is the most important person. My strong view is that every role is important.

If you'd asked Leigh Matthews what worked for him when he coached the Brisbane Lions to three premierships, I'm sure he'd say it was that he had football manager Graeme 'Gubby' Allen as his right-hand man and Michael Voss as captain.

At Sydney, we wouldn't have had a premiership in 2005 without the support of chairman Richard Colless, Andrew Ireland's efforts as head of football and Rick Barham's recruiting.

Any good club is the same. If you look at the history of footy clubs, as soon as any of those crucial relationships turn seriously pear-shaped, the place fractures and the coach rarely survives.

Peter Jackson and Glen Bartlett weren't just employing me to coach. They knew I would bring other talented people to the footy club. I had good people around me and it was vital I listen to them and take advice. That harked back to two of the coaching notes I had written in 1998: **Surround yourself with coaches and personnel you know and respect** and **Be prepared to listen to advice from advisers.** You need to have people you trust, people you want to go into battle with, in all positions.

I also referred to another of my coaching notes: **Coach's attitude will rub off on the players.** That wasn't just about me. That related to George Stone's attitude and Ben Mathews' attitude – to all of us. If we didn't appear relaxed and positive, players would adopt the same mentality. It was important the players saw us working together as a coaching team, with a genuine care for each other.

The final pieces of the puzzle were still to come – the make-up of the team and the game plan.

There was positive news a couple of weeks after I started, when Jack Watts decided to re-sign with the club on a three-year contract. I'd met with Jack, assured him I wanted him to stay and he was a big part of my plans. Jack was versatile, and could play in the forward line, defence or on the ball.

He bore the brunt of so much flak, but I believed part of the problem was he'd never been given a defined role in the team.

I explained that I saw him playing mostly as a big-bodied midfielder, and he liked the idea. He told the club website the fact I was now coach had been a significant factor in his decision to stay. Jack was relieved and happy, and looking forward to the new year. It was a good start.

But there were plenty of other concerns when we assessed the playing list.

The starting point for the coaching group was to sit down for four full days and watch every minute of several 2013 games. We watched how they played and what their habits were. That gave us a good feel for where they were as a playing group.

Some statistics told the tale too. In 2013, we had gone into our attacking zone on average only 40 times per game and most teams we played had gone into their forward line at least 18 more times than us. We could never win games if we didn't get more drive from the middle of the ground.

It was obvious the team needed extra quality midfielders, so that became our primary goal during the trade period in October. We had to find midfield depth, and players who could run hard both offensively and defensively, to be competitive. Our standout midfielder was Nathan Jones, an aggressive stoppage player, but he needed much more support.

We had reasonable stocks of tall players, with Tom McDonald, James Frawley, Chris Dawes and Jesse Hogan, a budding teenage star, who had played VFL for our reserves at Casey Scorpions and won the best and fairest there.

One of the first calls I made when I got the job was to player manager Liam Pickering, who looked after Western Bulldogs midfielder Daniel Cross. The Bulldogs had delisted Cross, but I loved his hardness and his leadership qualities. He had a reputation as one of the most disciplined team players in the competition. I told Liam I saw a role for Daniel at the Demons, so Crossy came to us in November as a delisted free agent. He turned out to be a very important asset.

Todd Viney and Jason Taylor had a really good handle on the midfield options and we also targeted Adelaide midfielder Bernie Vince. When I was at the Swans, we had tried to get Bernie to Sydney, so I had met him and watched his career. Then we found out he might be available and we pounced.

Bernie was 28, but the sort of experienced midfield leader we needed. Bernie won Adelaide's best and fairest in 2009 and was a lively, confident player. I was rapt to get Bernie, as he came from a great culture at Adelaide. His qualities as a role model came to be as valuable as his ball-winning skills. He was a great pick-up, and we were able to get him via a draft pick received as compensation for Colin Sylvia's departure to Fremantle.

Because we had finished second-last on the ladder, we were allocated pick two in the draft, so we put that on the table in the trade period. It was the same approach I had taken at the Swans, ready to forgo the unknown quantity of a player in the draft for a more experienced player who could immediately fill a gap in our team.

We did a deal with the GWS Giants, securing young midfielder Dom Tyson, draft pick number nine, and a late draft pick, in exchange for picks two and 20.

When Bernie Vince and Daniel Cross turned up at the start of pre-season training, they made an extraordinary contribution. They had a significant impact on emerging players such as Jack Viney and Jesse Hogan, setting a great example for them to follow with their elite training and preparation habits.

Our simple plan was to trade for experienced players and add some young talent through the national draft. We used draft pick nine to select Christian Salem, an explosive, classy young midfielder from Hampton in Melbourne's southern beachside area. With the late draft pick, the club took a bit of a punt and selected Brighton Grammar boy Jayden Hunt.

At the end of the trade and draft periods, we had nine new players on our primary list and had achieved most of our short-term aims. The players were due back for training in early November. Everything was in place, and all the coaches were excited to get stuck into it.

But first impressions aren't always what you hope . . . As often happens at the start of pre-season, there were a number of players who'd had surgery or were injured and they couldn't get on the training track yet.

So it was a small but enthusiastic group at our first training session, at our ground on Punt Road. The coaches were pretty gung-ho too.

We decided to do some lane work, which is a simple drill, where you have two groups of players who kick it to each other and run to the other end. It's about the easiest drill there is, but we didn't have enough players to do anything more complicated.

At one end, Rohan Bail kicked it to our ruckman, Jack Fitzpatrick. We watched wide-eyed as Fitzy ran towards the ball, then let it slip through his fingers and smash him in the nose. I looked over at George Stone and he looked at me. Okay, so Jack has dropped an easy mark. That happens . . . But then Fitzy picked the ball up, tried to kick it on his left foot. It snicked the outside of his boot and rolled sideways about eight metres.

The players killed themselves laughing and it was definitely one of the funniest things I'd ever seen at training. An hour or so later, when we'd finished the session, George said drily, 'Gee, this is going to be interesting.'

During those first few months, the coaches were on a mission to get to know the players, flaws and all. We had to understand them, and their strengths and weaknesses, so we could work out what roles they were suited to and how we could get the best out of them.

I told the assistant coaches they didn't need to sit in their offices – that I'd much rather they work out in the gym with the players or take them for coffee. They should do anything they could to spend time with the guys and build strong relationships.

We needed to watch how they trained, how they behaved in the gym, to find out who had good habits and who needed guidance. We wanted to know about their life away from football, anything that might help us to help them.

On the training track, we impressed upon the players that we had to strengthen the defensive side of their game first. We concentrated on contested ball drills, running drills, and drills to help us transition the ball down the field.

As it was when I started at the Swans, the emphasis was on winning your own ball, and getting it back off the opposition as quickly as possible. My philosophy hadn't changed – I still believed the foundation of game style had to be built on defence. Anyone can tackle, anyone can chase – defence was about effort, not talent, and that's what we had to bring to the Demons' game.

When I took over, Melbourne had averaged about 110 points a game against them in 2013 and lost 20 of 22 games. You can't win games of footy leaking that many points to the opposition every week.

It was three years since I'd coached the Swans and people often asked me if the game had altered in that time. Maybe it had in some ways, but we put a huge emphasis on what hadn't changed: the teams that worked hardest generated success; the teams that won their own ball still had the most success; and good defensive teams were generally winning teams.

That was the strategy and there was also an understanding that it wasn't going to turn around quickly. There was no magic wand for a team that was so far behind the top levels of the competition.

As coaches, we knew we were going to cop criticism and abuse for our defensive style. But we held firm. The first part of the plan was teaching the players to be more competitive, so opposition teams couldn't just run all over them and score at will. We tried to keep it simple.

The psychological component was also a big focus for a playing group down on confidence and carrying scars. There was a lot of time spent pumping up the players and trying to convince them they were better than they thought they were.

Bernie Vince and Daniel Cross were a great influence. I asked them to speak up and tell their new teammates that they were training hard and their work habits were as good as they'd seen at the Crows or the Dogs. We spent plenty of time on positive reinforcement. We continually reinforced that what happened last year had happened and had no bearing on what we did from now on.

Before Christmas, we turned our attention to rebuilding the team's culture. I remained a strong believer in the Leading Teams approach, which had been employed so successfully at the Swans from 2002 onwards.

The experience at Sydney had confirmed my beliefs that it didn't matter what club it was, there had to be a commitment to leadership. We had to define expected behaviours and lift standards and they had to be followed through. These concepts mattered more than anything.

The team's success had to be driven by the culture, not by the talent level. That was the only way to achieve more consistent performance.

We took the playing group to Sorrento on the Mornington Peninsula for a leadership camp, run by Leading Teams' facilitators, firstly Kraig Grime and then former Western Bulldogs and Carlton player Jim Plunkett.

The experience, from a behaviour and leadership perspective, was dramatically different with Melbourne, compared to the Swans. It was just as powerful and the expected behaviours, values and standards the Melbourne players came up with were similar, relating to effort, courage, teamwork and discipline. But the educational phase was quite a contrast at the Demons, because the group was not as advanced as the Sydney squad – there was no doubt about that.

When I took over at the Swans at the end of 2002, the playing group had played finals nearly every year since 1996, so they knew what success looked like and understood what it took to produce winning performances.

At Melbourne, we were starting almost from scratch. The group was evolving and we couldn't lump everything on them at once. The process was confronting at times and Melbourne players, especially the young ones, weren't quite ready for all of it.

They had to be shown a bit more love.

In a supportive environment, the Melbourne players had to find their own way, and then work out how to live and breathe totally new standards and habits.

It was an interesting time for the coaching staff. Most of us had been through the program before, we knew how it worked and knew its benefits. It was tempting to show the players the shortcuts, but we resisted. They had to find the answers themselves.

It's like doing your kids' homework for them – in the end, you're not doing them any favours.

We knew the program would work, but as coaches we had to stop ourselves from rushing the Melbourne players. I would have loved to hurry them, given the pressure the club was under from the media and fans. But that would have corrupted the process. We knew it would work to change the culture, but we had to be patient.

And we were still getting to know the players, so we had to see who would emerge as the best leaders under this new model. We didn't know who would be the Demons' equivalent of the Swans' Stuey Maxfield, the one who would relentlessly drive the behaviours of the group.

We did a fantastic exercise in one session during the pre-season, where we asked the players to pick the team now, based on those who best upheld our new behaviours.

It was a really helpful exercise for the coaches. When we looked at the players' choices, we were surprised at some of the names in the team. But it gave us a strong idea of the players they valued as teammates, those they saw as good characters with the right values.

As part of the Leading Teams exercise, the players had to vote for a new leadership group. At the end of the 2013 season, Jack Trengove, who had been co-captain with Jack Grimes since 2012, had decided to relinquish the role. Trenners had been just 20 years old when he was appointed captain. His form had dropped during the two seasons he was at the helm and he admitted it was a burden. He quite rightly wanted to concentrate on improving his form.

Back in 2012, when Melbourne had named Jack Grimes, then 22, and Jack Trengove as captains, I had expressed concern during my commentary role. They seemed too inexperienced to have that responsibility. I felt for both of them, because at 20 and 22 they should have been in the position of normal young players, working on their own game and learning from the senior players, before they became leaders.

Under our new system, the players voted in an open forum for a six-man leadership group. They chose James Frawley, Mitch Clark, Colin Garland, Jack Trengove, Jack Grimes and Nathan Jones, who had won the best and fairest that year.

As coaches, we had to choose the captains and there were two standouts to lead the club – Grimes and 26-year-old Jones. They were named in January 2014 as the new co-captains.

Jack Grimes had embraced the changes at the club. He didn't hide the fact that he had struggled with the pressure of captaincy until that point, but had learned from it and grown as a leader.

I was very impressed with Nathan over the pre-season. As I got to know him, I realised his work ethic was second to none and he was such a competitor – always up for the challenge.

Not only was he best and fairest in 2012 and 2013, he was also best team man in 2013. He had played consistently well in a very poor team and had the sort of never-say-die spirit I loved. He never backed down from anything and loved to argue and debate with the coaching staff. It was all in the cause of getting better and helping to change the footy club.

But choosing the leaders and captains was just part of the task at Melbourne. We had to spend a lot of time educating the group and the leaders, going over and over the behaviours so everyone was really clear. They had to learn to live them, not just mouth them. We had set high standards but had to make sure the players took responsibility and owned them.

As round one drew close, I predicted my biggest challenge

in the coaches' box would be to bury the ghosts of the past. Would the players have confidence and place trust in each other? I knew there were bruises and wounds from the battering they had taken in the past few years. They wouldn't heal overnight. It was only human nature.

The group had shown a genuine desire to learn and improve during a gruelling pre-season. They had listened, shown good attitude and trained well. But how would that measure up in the pressure cooker of a game? That was the big mystery and we were about to find out.

CHAPTER 15

The mental scars

After four months on the training track, the 2014 NAB Challenge pre-season competition was an early chance to test the waters and see how far the Melbourne players had come. The three practice games turned out to be a microcosm of the year ahead – a mix of all that was good, and all that remained bad, about the team.

We played Richmond in the first match and had a nervous start. We kicked seven behinds before we scored our first goal. But the boys got a run on and, while the game was a tussle, we won by 14 points. It was an indication we had made some improvement on the back of our hard work over the summer.

Our second pre-season game was against Geelong, in Alice Springs. The Cats jumped us in the first quarter, but to our players' credit, they didn't drop their heads. We lost, but it showed the scars of recent seasons had not completely robbed them of resilience.

But the final pre-season game was a massive reality check. We played the 2013 premiers, Hawthorn, and were thrashed by 110 points. At one stage, they scored 10 consecutive goals. There was no pressure, no resistance, no real contest.

At the club's season launch a week later, I publicly thanked Hawthorn coach, Alastair Clarkson, for teaching the Melbourne players a valuable football lesson. 'What we found out was, as much as we have improved, if we want to take on the best teams and not do what we've learned and worked on, we'll get belted,' I said in my speech to the players, their families and a room full of hundreds of the Melbourne faithful.

That last game had exposed us. If the players fell back into old habits, nothing would change. 'We will not be able to compete with the worst teams in the competition, let alone the best,' I warned. It was a stark message on the eve of the home and away season. If we did the basics over and over again, we were capable of competing. But we still had a very long way to go and there was not going to be a quick fix.

As round one approached, we had more challenges. Our three first-choice tall forwards, Mitch Clark, Chris Dawes and Jesse Hogan, were all injured. Our forward line was decimated and would be cobbled together without any of our key attacking players.

When I accepted the head coach role in September 2013, I said at the media conference that better results would take time and I was happy to take the hits until then. It didn't take long.

In the first game, we took on St Kilda and it played out as a battle between two struggling sides. We had our chances and sent the ball into our forward line more often than the Saints, but we couldn't capitalise and went down by 17 points. It wasn't what we had wanted, but there was no shame.

In round two, we took on the West Coast Eagles in a Sunday afternoon match at the MCG. The Eagles had finished 13th in 2013, so we went into the contest confident we had a reasonable chance.

But what followed was a shock. By quarter time, the Eagles had scored six goals and we'd scored one behind.

In the coaches' box, we were stunned. It was as if nothing we had talked about for the past five months had been absorbed.

Almost every time there was a stoppage in our forward line, the Eagles would win the ball and then stream down the field, unchallenged, to score. In most AFL games, a team goals from a defensive stoppage a few times over four quarters; in this match, West Coast were scoring after virtually every one, taking it straight down the ground.

Our players were frozen. Their effort, from where we watched in the grandstand, was nowhere near the standard required to win any game in the AFL. We were beaten by 93 points, **4.6 (30) to 18.15 (123)**.

It was difficult to watch. The players were fit enough, they had trained well, but they weren't able to translate that preparation into the game. As soon as the Eagles kicked a few goals and the scoreboard looked lopsided, they had reverted to old habits.

When we couldn't score, it became a potent issue on the field. You could see it on their faces, 'Here we go again, another loss.' Their level of engagement and involvement in the game dropped dramatically and their body language was negative.

I've no doubt they thought the new coaching regime would solve their problems, that all they needed to do was run down the race to win. We had to make them realise their own efforts would determine the outcome, not what the coaching staff did.

During that thrashing by West Coast, I started to fully understand how beaten down the players had been by the previous few years. Dozens of losses, jeers from their own fans, a pasting by the media, harsh words from their coaches – it all added up to terrible self-esteem.

We had to do serious remedial work on the group's mind-set. I had wondered if the ghosts of the past would impact the new season and I had my answer. The mental scars were real and they were deep.

We could talk all we liked about game plans, defence, stoppage set-ups and ball movement, but it wouldn't make a difference until we tackled their fear of losing and their chronic lack of belief in themselves and each other.

I didn't yell or scream at the players after the loss. I only rarely broke my coaching rule – **After game, don't fly off the handle. If too emotional say nothing, wait till Monday** – and this wasn't the time to start.

The players and staff told me that in recent seasons the team had received more than their fair share of tongue-lashings and they obviously hadn't helped the situation.

As hard as it was, as coaches our job was to separate the emotion from the loss and look at the underlying reasons. We had to find solutions, not give them a spray.

I had dinner with George Stone, Ben Mathews and our wives that night and we were still in shock at the lack of fight from the players. It was a big eye-opener for all of us – evidence we had even more work to do than we'd imagined.

The playing group and the coaches met at the club the next day for our regular Monday match review. It was one of the most difficult, but ultimately one of the most important, meetings during my time at Melbourne.

The truth had to be laid bare. I said to them: 'Guys, I don't care if you win or not, all we want you to do is try. We just need effort.

'No one expects us to win, so let's forget the scoreboard and just focus on what maximum effort looks like. That's all I want from you, to give maximum effort.'

To the coaches, it had appeared they weren't trying, but when we delved into it, that wasn't fair. The problem was they didn't actually know *how* to give maximum effort. Their understanding of how to play a premiership standard of AFL footy was very limited, because they had never been taught the work rate that is required.

I wondered how they had even won two games the previous year, they were so far off the level the game demanded. It was back to square one. We spent a lot of time explaining what sort of running and work rate was needed to have any chance of winning.

We showed them the GPS tracking data from the West Coast game. The best data came from Daniel Cross, who was 31, and had been delisted by the Western Bulldogs at the end of 2013. We'd picked him up because he was a total professional and we knew he'd be a great role model for the young players.

He was our oldest player, but he had run 15 kilometres during that game, further than any of our young midfielders. His GPS compared to the majority of his Melbourne teammates was ridiculous. There was an enormous disparity between how hard he had run on the ground and what the others had put out. That was purely through effort and because he understood what it took to genuinely compete.

I pointed out some simple equations to the players. 'If you run 13 kilometres a game and your opponent runs 14.5 kilometres a game, what is the likely outcome?' I pointed out the obvious: 'So, you're going to have to push yourselves and run a lot more. We're going to find out what you're really capable of.'

They had to run, with purpose. They had to run to defend their opponent, and also run back the other way, so we had a chance to transition the ball into attack.

We told them not to fret about the scoreboard and not to worry about how many games we were going to win. All they had to worry about was working hard and their role.

The irony is that, in poor teams, players go outside their role more often. When things are going bad, the better players think it's honourable to try to do more. A player like co-captain Nathan Jones says, 'Shit, I know I'm not supposed to be at this stoppage, but if I don't get this clearance, no one will.'

There was a big problem with trust. We wanted them to start trusting their teammate would be at that stoppage and trusting their teammate could win the ball.

If one player went outside his role and turned up at that stoppage, that might mean there was no one covering an opposition player in another area of the ground. Everyone would be out of position and the system broke down. That was what had happened at the forward stoppages against the Eagles and allowed them to score so many easy goals.

The Melbourne players wanted to do the right thing, but they didn't yet know how to work hard enough, or play for each other.

It was important to reassure the players that the coaches would work with them, that we would never give up on them. We were there for the long haul.

Nathan Jones, one of the players who always gave 100 per cent effort, walked past me in the corridor after we had lost again the following week against the GWS Giants and said, 'We're shit.'

I said, 'Mate, don't worry about it. I'm not going any-where, just relax, we'll get through it.'

They felt disappointed in themselves and a bit guilty, as if they'd let down the coaching staff. In the face of that, we deliberately kept the mood as positive as possible to show we were up for the fight.

But it's not easy losing and that's why the combination of coaches was so important. You can't have any out-of-control egos or any outliers – we had to be solid and stick tight. There was a massive focus on educating the group and we had to be on the same page about the way to teach players, and the way forward.

As well, we had to get inside the players' heads. I had so many intense conversations with Nathan, and guys like Jack Grimes, Jack Trengove and Jack Watts, the ones who had been there for years and had been through significant trauma in footy terms.

We had to talk about their wounds and face the issues head-on. I met with them every week and we spoke about their mindset and the baggage they carried. When I look back, we definitely needed to go through a long process. It was the start of a three-year program where we worked very hard, with all our players, on the mental side of the game. I still believe that the mental side is largely undeveloped in the AFL, and elite sport generally. Athletes and coaches spend hours and hours on skills and the physical aspects of sport, and don't devote enough time to developing the power of the mind and self belief.

At Melbourne we made it a focus through sports psychologist Dave Williams and Tami Roos, who taught the players to meditate and visualise. Dave and Tami were integral to the team's development and improvement over the next three years.

Dave worked individually with players on a range of issues, including their self-doubt. Tami's meditation was designed to give the players a way to focus on the present, and not dwell on what had happened in the past.

Tami introduced a catchphrase that became really important during games. If things had gone badly on the field, she suggested the players focus on the word 'reset', as a way of getting themselves into the present moment and acting constructively.

We had observed how the guys would slump and drop their heads when they made a mistake, or the opposition got a run-on. Now, using the word 'reset' as a cue to stay in the present, they could put it behind them and only worry about the next contest. It became a powerful tool for the players.

The visualisation was also a way to change their mind-set. They went through a process, under Tami's guidance, where they 'saw' themselves doing positive things on the field before they went out to play.

I also showed them numerous videos emphasising the power of the mind, including one featuring Conor McGregor, the Irish mixed martial artist who has been the UFC (Ultimate Fighting Championship) Lightweight Champion and Featherweight Champion. McGregor came from a working-class family in Ireland, and started an apprenticeship as a plumber. But he wanted to be a champion fighter and began visualising over and over again how he would hold the UFC championship belt.

We made Tami's meditation and visualisation sessions compulsory at the Demons because I knew they could bene-fit the team. There were two sessions – one during the week, and another two hours before every game.

When we got to the ground, I would speak to the players in the coaches' room, giving them the main message for the day.

Tami would then take the group for a 15-minute session, building on the themes I had spoken about.

For example, I might say that in the match we had to stop the opposition taking the ball through the middle corridor of the ground. So Tami would take that message and guide the players to help them focus on that key part of our plan.

The meditation and visualisation became the starting point for their pre-game preparation.

At the Swans, Tami taught many of the players to meditate, but it was never compulsory. But the game was now more physically and mentally demanding than ever, so we decided to make meditation and visualisation an integral part of our week.

Changes were implemented off and on field. We worked on mindset off the field, and moved players around on the field to give us more steel. We sent regular full-back James Frawley to the forward line to give us a target and we switched high-flying half-forward Jeremy Howe to defence.

As well, Chris Dawes recovered from injury and came back into the side for our round four match against Carlton. Neither team had won a game yet and our players chased and tackled with more intent than I'd seen. Carlton wasted their chances and kicked five behinds in a row in the last term.

If I'm brutally honest, Carlton had the ascendancy in that final quarter, but, because they kept missing goals, our players didn't slump or hang their heads. They didn't stop playing their roles, they didn't go back into their shells and their body language held up.

James Frawley played really well up forward and once again Nathan Jones was one of our best, doing the grunt work in the midfield. We won by four goals, the first time Melbourne had beaten Carlton since 2007.

The players received the reward for carrying out the jobs we'd asked them to do. We weren't bereft of talent, we had the ability from day one to play some good football, but it was a matter of staying on task and keeping their minds focused during games.

Finally, there was a bit of relief and they could belt out,

'It's a grand old flag'. There was a sense of, *Thank God, we won a game, we're making a bit of progress.*

But it wasn't a huge confidence boost. Their main emotion seemed to be disbelief that they'd actually won and we had to closely point out to them the things they'd done well.

It didn't help that the media focused on how bad the opposition were. I used to joke with the players that every time we beat a team, it was because the opposition had its worst game ever.

Throughout that first season, we asked the players to do things that were unfamiliar to them, as we re-educated them with a team-first ethos. In the game against Carlton we asked Nathan to run with the Blues' best midfielder, Marc Murphy.

Nathan is a fantastic player and had been the club champion the previous two years. He's a born competitor, with a fantastic work ethic and a huge heart. Before I took over, his style was simply to hunt the ball aggressively at every stoppage, rack up 30 possessions and play bloody good footy. He was a stoppage animal.

But he'd never been shown what we believed was the right way to play team-oriented footy. We had to make sure his competitiveness was directed toward the team's aim and wasn't focused on how many possessions he got.

It was a significant change in approach for him. For the past few years, he had run onto the field expecting to get beaten every week. He had gone into survival mode. His thinking was, 'I'm going to get to every stoppage and if I can win enough of the ball, hopefully I'll help the team. But even if we lose, I can walk off with my head held high.'

We had to change that. There were many discussions with him, insisting it wasn't his role to be at every stoppage. He had never previously been asked to go head-to-head with the opposition's best player, to beat him and curb his influence.

That game against Carlton was pivotal for Nathan and for the group. We set our best player to play on their best player, to beat their best player.

Our view was that if Nathan could do that, it would educate him and send a message to the rest of our players – if it's good enough for our captain to be a run-with player today, then it's good enough for everyone to try to beat their man.

Nathan had to lead the way and show he could play a different role. We wanted to create an honest midfield group that could run two ways, defend and attack, and make it hard for the opposition.

If he bought into it, it was a powerful message to his peers.

He's a strong character and we had plenty of vigorous debates about it. He came off the ground after tagging Marc Murphy and there was general agreement among the coaches that he had beaten the Carlton star and was the best player on the ground.

'Mate, that's the best game you've played,' I said to him.

But he looked at me, shook his head and said, 'No, it's not.'

I insisted it was, but his perception, at that stage, was different. He still had to get used to the idea that disposal numbers weren't the measure of success in our new play-book.

I came to have huge respect and affection for Nathan. He's such a fighter, sets very high standards for himself and always wants to improve. He loves the Melbourne Football Club and will do anything to see it succeed.

The senior midfielders we had recruited to the club, Bernie Vince and Daniel Cross, were also important and understood what we were trying to do. Their example to the players was paramount and they were incredibly good for the footy club.

They both did jobs on the best opposition players and Crossy was a beacon in how to play AFL football at a high level. His effort week in and week out on game day was extraordinary.

I didn't want to saturate the Melbourne players with stories about the Swans' best players, because it would get boring for them, and for me too, so we used Crossy as an example of someone who always put the team first and did his job.

We played the Swans a couple of weeks after the win against Carlton. We lost by 10 goals, but in the second quarter we kept Sydney to just three points.

After the game, I emphasised how well they had performed during that 30 minutes of football, to keep one of the top teams in the competition almost scoreless. The next step was to be more consistent and bring that effort in all four quarters of the game. We had great quarters and halves, but mostly we couldn't do it for the whole game.

One of the main things I noticed coaching Melbourne in that first year is that an AFL game is very long. When I was coaching the Swans, I had never felt that, because the two-hour time span often allowed us to get back in the game if we were behind.

But that wasn't the case with Melbourne. We might be in front by a point with 20 minutes to go, but we'd end up losing by six goals. I knew we could play good football, we just couldn't do it for 120 minutes. It was a sign they didn't yet have the strength of mind and the necessary resilience to stick it out.

The staff that had been at the club for a few years, such as Jade Rawlings and Josh Mahoney, kept our spirits high. If we got down on ourselves in that first difficult year, they would reassure the new coaches how far the group had come. 'Guys, we used to come in at half time 15 goals behind, this is much better,' Jade would say. He was terrific at keeping the coaching group on track.

That game against the Swans gave us the chance to teach the players another lesson. One of our key learning tools was showing game vision, especially of other teams who played the way we admired.

We wanted to be a contested football team, a hard team, and wanted to be able to transition quickly into defensive and offensive positions. That required relentless running and a willingness to react quickly.

I remember showing the group vision of Swans midfielder Kieren Jack, taken during the game against us. At a centre bounce, Kieren had started in the square. The ball moved into our forward line, and Kieren was there. He beat all the Melbourne midfielders to the contest.

He won the ball, kicked it towards the middle of the ground and kept running. He beat all our midfielders to a stoppage up the ground, on the Swans' half-forward flank. He got the ball again in his own attacking area and the Swans ended up kicking a goal.

'That is why they're a good team, that is the standard required,' I said to them.

Based on GPS data, I estimated the Swans midfielders collectively ran an extra four or five kilometres a game, compared to our midfielders.

Our players had a tendency to be lazy and react slowly when their opponent started running, and let him get too far before they started chasing. I showed them vision. 'Guys, if you had reacted smartly and got on to that player more quickly, what do you think he would have done?'

They would answer, 'Oh, he would have stopped running, because I was there and he wasn't free.'

We were trying to convince them that if they ran hard for 10 metres straight away, they would probably have stopped their opponent running further and getting the ball.

Instead, most of the time our players hesitated, dilly-dallied, and their opponent moved 20 metres away and kept running, because he was on his own. Our player would then hop to it, and chase his opponent for 100 metres, instead of 10 metres. My point was – run hard early into a defensive position and you'll actually save energy.

There are not many players who will keep running offensively if they are not in the clear and don't think they're going to get the ball. Our players could change their opponent's mindset by shutting him down really quickly.

But we had to go over that so many times and it took a long time to convince them to change their behaviour and switch on. It was about attitude – they had to be willing to run and ready to do it.

Their slow reaction time was a result of bad habits. They hesitated because they hoped the opposition might mis-kick, turn the ball over, and then they'd be in a good offensive position. With that mindset, we would only ever beat lowly teams.

'You can beat bad teams by allowing them to give you the ball back,' I told them. 'But good teams aren't going to give you the ball back. You've got to *get* it back off good teams.

'I want you to be right on your man when they kick the ball to him and when they handball it to him.

'If you don't run to get there, he'll get the ball and then you have to chase tails all day.'

That's why we had been so easy to score against. In 2013, they had lost by an average of 10 goals in their 20 defeats. Essendon beat them by 148 points and North Melbourne by 122. Our starting point was at least to dramatically reduce the scale of the losses.

I couldn't speak highly enough of our defenders, led by Lynden Dunn and Colin Garland, in that first year. They did their best to beat their opponents one-on-one. But, like the midfielders, they needed to understand their role required both defence and attack.

When they got the ball, they were so relieved, they'd just go back and kick it, and wouldn't transition into offensive mode to help the team score. They'd just kick it down the line, it would boomerang back, and they'd be in defence mode again. It was the same with the forwards – they had to learn to make second and third efforts, to tackle and lock the ball in our attacking zone.

The messages started sinking in and in round seven we played Adelaide at their home ground, before a partisan crowd of 44,000 screaming Crows fans. It was a nail-biter, but we held on to win by three points, the first time the Demons had won in Adelaide for 12 years. It had been a tough few months and I was so happy for the players and the staff.

The defensive development was most exciting. We had kept the Crows to 67 points, their lowest total of the season, and that had given us the opportunity to win. The dramatic improvement in our defence meant we had more control of games and were far more competitive.

We had another clutch win, against Essendon in round 13. With less than a minute to play, we were five points down, when Bernie Vince laid a brilliant tackle in defence. The ball spilled free and then, through a chain of handball and short passes involving 10 of our players, it landed in the hands of young midfielder Christian Salem, 25 metres from goal. He kicked straight and we were one point ahead with only 20 seconds to play.

It was the best passage of play I'd seen from the boys all year, exactly the sort of transitional running we wanted from them. The victory gave them a glimpse of what they were capable of. They could do it, but not as consistently as we needed. For a young group learning new ways, it was hard to sustain and too often they were out-worked by the other team.

That was our fourth, and final, win for the season. From that point on, we lost 10 games in succession.

It was hard going. Because I had experience with the Sydney Swans, I knew it was important not to waver or change the game plan. I had faith the processes we'd put in place would eventually work. I told football manager Josh Mahoney that if I had been a first-year, novice coach, it would have been almost impossible to stand firm under the mounting pressure.

The biggest challenge of being an AFL coach, as opposed to being the CEO of a large corporate entity, is that everything you do is pored over so publicly. The concepts of change management are the same, whether it is business or footy, but coaches have to make every change under the glare of the media spotlight.

You don't have time to get it right behind the scenes. Every move is closely scrutinised and critiqued and the pressure weighs heavily, from your fans and from the media. You can't say, 'Boys, we've got 10 weeks where no one is going to see us play these teams, so let's slowly build up and then reveal ourselves to the world.' The scrutiny starts from day one.

In reality, a team like Melbourne, that had won two games and lost 20 in 2013, and won only four the year before that, probably needs half a year of losing by 100 points, then 90 points, then 80, 50, 20, and so on.

If you were running a business, that's the way the graph would go – you'd start to slowly turn around your losses and start making a small profit a year later. But the expectation in footy is that you should win from the get-go, no matter how much restructuring you're going through.

I didn't like losing 10 games in a row, I got annoyed,

but I didn't let that out on the players. Part of the reason Melbourne hired me was because I had done the job before and I'd withstood sustained criticism before. At the Swans in 2005, we had most of the footy world bagging our style and we'd held firm to win the premiership.

Despite the difficulties, we couldn't get too distracted by the week-to-week results. We had to hold on to the concepts we believed in, around the game plan, leadership, accepted behaviours and the team ethos. My coaching notes, the 25 points I'd written down when I finished playing, were a constant reminder of the approach I had to take, no matter how frustrating it got.

It's like building a house. The footy clubs that dig the trench, pour the concrete in, put up a strong framework and then lay the bricks, are the clubs that are successful over a long period of time. The footy clubs that want to build quickly with flimsy materials, put a swimming pool in the back yard, with a spa and a tennis court, they're the ones that fall down.

So in a sense, as hard as that first year was, we were taking time to build from the ground up, with a solid foundation. As a coaching group, we weren't there for our own egos, we were only there because we thought we could help the players.

There wasn't a day when I went home thinking, *What a bunch of no-hopers!* It was never us and them, all the coaches were fully committed to the players.

Losing the last 10 games simply reinforced that our job was to educate, to teach and to persevere.

CHAPTER 16
Reclaiming the lost years

The most crucial years in any player's career are those between the ages of 18 and 22.

Over nearly four decades as a player and coach, I formed a strong belief that if young footballers aren't put through a quality development program at an AFL club, it's unlikely they'll have a long and successful career.

One of the most significant challenges during my three years at Melbourne was to reinvent a number of players who, in my view, had been mishandled for five years.

Players such as Jack Watts, Jack Grimes, Jack Trengove, Max Gawn, Jeremy Howe, Sam Blease, Jack Fitzpatrick, Luke Tapscott, Rohan Bail and even Nathan Jones not only had mental scars, they had big holes in their football armoury.

It wasn't their fault, but resulted from the lack of development in those crucial early years. Some had been held up as the great hopes of a struggling football club and sent into battle in the AFL before they were fully equipped. It was no wonder they struggled.

At the club's 2014 season launch, a few months after I started as coach, I made it clear that wouldn't happen again. 'To the young players, what I want to say is, you are not the saviours of this football club,' I said.

'Too often in the past, unfortunately, this football club has put up these young blokes as the saviours of the club. They are not here to be the saviours. They are here to learn, to listen, to develop and eventually, if they do that, they'll get good habits and become very successful players. That's the role.'

It was a pointed message. The development of our youngsters would be dramatically different under my watch.

Our big 19-year-old forward, Jesse Hogan, was not expected to rescue the club, nor were talented midfielders Christian Salem and Dom Tyson. We would never put that pressure on them. We had an obligation to nurture and educate them, so they had the best opportunity to have a fruitful career.

The majority of teenagers drafted to AFL clubs come out of the TAC Cup under-18 competition in Victoria, or the elite under-age competitions in South Australia and Western Australia.

There are varying degrees of talent among draftees, but the common factor is they can all win the ball. However, they've rarely been well educated in the defensive side of the game at the elite junior level.

In my experience, many young footballers arrive in the AFL with habits that are detrimental when they play at the top level. If those habits aren't changed during the next few years – if they're not taught to play a hard, accountable, style of football – it's very difficult to fix later on.

From my earliest days at Fitzroy in the 1980s, role models like our best player, Garry Wilson, had taught me you had to train to your absolute limit and really earn your stripes before you got a run in the senior team. I put that into action when I became coach of the Swans.

It didn't matter if you were Jarrad McVeigh, who was the number five pick in the 2002 draft and a great ball winner at junior level, or Kieren Jack, who took up footy as a teenager and only made it to the Swans via the rookie list. They were put through the same development process, schooled in the same way, and they ended up being co-captains of the Swans.

Both Macca and Kieren learned that to get a senior game under the Sydney system, they had to tackle, chase, smother and beat their opponent. They honed those skills in our reserves team for several years. It didn't matter how long it took, they stayed there until they could consistently do the things we valued.

Even when they did play seniors, the education process continued. They had to tag superstar midfielders such as Ben Cousins and Gary Ablett, so they could learn how to beat the best players. It was all about teaching them what we termed the 'right way' to play and I know they both appreciated it later. That development helped them evolve into leaders and premiership players.

I honestly believe it's counter-productive to rush young players into senior football before they're ready.

You can develop your best talent in the Victorian Football League (VFL), or the North East Australian Football League (NEAFL). It's a myth that draftees should get a taste of senior football as soon as possible. You need to follow a defined process, to give young players an opportunity to compete when they do play senior footy.

That's my philosophy, but it wasn't everyone's way.

At Melbourne, they had taken the approach that the best method to improve the team, and build excitement for the fans, was to throw the talented youngsters into the senior team not long after they arrived at the club.

Regardless of their form in the reserves, they would get a senior game because they were talented, high draft picks.

There was a view that if you gave them senior experience as soon as possible, they'd find their way through, and once they'd played around 50 or 60 games, they'd be good AFL footballers.

Then, once the team collectively had players with a certain number of games, the wins would start to flow. The philosophy was, 'Let's just keep playing them and history tells us if we have enough players who've played 78 games, we'll win.'

The system went against the principles I had based my coaching on. I could sense when I got to Melbourne that the players aged between 18 and 22 were floundering.

Former Melbourne captain and broadcaster Garry Lyon had mentioned that fact in 2013, the year before I arrived, when the team won only two games. Garry said the most worrying aspect of the Demons' decline was the lack of player development, and the drop in confidence among the group. He said players such as Jack Watts and Jack Trengove were shadows of their former selves.

Jack Watts was the most obvious and public example of Melbourne's woes.

A few years earlier, I'd witnessed the Melbourne system in action. Melbourne finished last in 2008, so they had the first pick in the draft and they selected Jack. He was touted as the shining light for a club, and a fan base, craving success.

Jack is a great athlete and was a talented basketball player and footballer at a young age. But when he was drafted, he was still 17 years old and doing year 11 at Brighton Grammar in Melbourne.

In June 2009, in the annual Queen's Birthday fixture against Collingwood – one of the most watched and hotly contested games every season – Melbourne decided it was the right time to unveil their prized 18-year-old schoolboy recruit.

It was round 11 and the Demons had won only one game

to that point, but here was a reason to come to the MCG and get excited about the club's future.

Russel Howcroft, a Melbourne-based television and advertising executive best known as a panellist on the ABC program *The Gruen Transfer*, was a Demons' board member at the time. He has since admitted that Jack's selection was largely based on marketing for the Demons, not physical readiness or form.

The club president at the time, Jim Stynes, sent a mass text message to supporters, urging them to make sure they came along to watch Jack make his debut. Coach Dean Bailey said the game was an important opportunity for us to 'wheel out our No. 1 draft pick'.

In the first few minutes, Jack – still a skinny year 12 student – was given a very unfriendly welcome to senior football, when he was gang-tackled by three of Collingwood's toughest competitors, Nick Maxwell, Heath Shaw and Shane O'Bree. He ended the day with three kicks and five handballs.

I was at the game and appalled by what I saw. The starting point for Jack's career was miles away from what I believed was best for a young player, or for the team.

Playing too soon is even tougher if you are part of a struggling side, as Jack was. At the Swans, we gave Dan Hannebery a few senior games while he was still at school, doing year 12 at Xavier College in Melbourne. But he was able to come in and play a bit-part role on a half-forward flank, with experienced, tough players providing support around him.

Jack was done no favours when he was thrust onto the MCG before he had been taught to play in a way that would stand up to the heat of the toughest competition.

Players like Jack Watts and Jack Trengove should have had a solid educational phase in the Demons' VFL team, Casey Scorpions, to set up their senior careers.

When I arrived at Melbourne, our coaching group was faced with the task of trying to rebuild the careers of a number of players. The big question was – did we have a group of poor players, or was their under-achievement due to a lack of development?

I would love to have coached Jack Grimes, Jack Trengove, Jack Watts, Sam Blease, Nathan Jones and the other boys when they were 18 and first came to the club. They were such high-quality people. We wanted to try to make up for the lost years and give them a chance to show us what they were capable of under our new system.

We had named Nathan Jones co-captain with Jack Grimes in 2014 and he said he thought there was real hope for Wattsy and other players to improve once we set up the revamped coaching structure.

Jonesy believed the weight of expectation and pressure on Jack in particular had been unfair and played a big part in his slow development. During the five seasons since his 2009 debut, Jack had become a very public whipping boy, a symbol of the club's failure to make any progress.

Bernie Vince, who was recruited from Adelaide, noticed it. He said that, as soon as the team started to struggle, he couldn't work out why all the talk was about how bad Jack Watts was.

I had so many people ask how Jack could possibly cope with the constant criticism. It was something I was keen to find out when I started the job. It was interesting to get to know Jack and discover he had actually stood up to the relentless bagging pretty well, outwardly at least.

If it had been me under that pressure, I would have left the country and gone to Hawaii. But in my first meetings with Jack, I found he was a resilient kid. Fortunately, he has a happy gene.

Despite everything, he loved the footy club and loved his teammates. He reminded me of Micky O'Loughlin, who was one of the most popular players at the Swans because of his infectious nature and his ability to get on with everyone.

Jack genuinely enjoyed being around the footy club and that enabled him to keep fronting up week after week, even when his situation was so challenging.

Jack is one of the nicest people you'll ever meet, but he did have a long way to go to become 100 per cent professional in the mould of former Swans captain Brett Kirk, or his outstanding young Melbourne teammate, Jack Viney.

We set about building Jack's confidence on the field. I started by saying I didn't expect him to suddenly become a star player. All we wanted was more consistency and application. We were trying to give him direction, to educate and support him, but also hold him accountable to team rules.

I could see the talent that made him so highly regarded as a junior. It was still there, but if I had to sum up Wattsy's problem, it was that he had never found his best on-field position.

He had been moved around the ground a lot. He was not quite big enough to be a key position player in defence or attack; we thought he'd become a big-bodied midfielder, but in the first year we also played him in the forward line.

He was 23 and didn't have a set role. He was lost. I have to admit we didn't really help him at first, because it was genuinely challenging to work out where he played best.

He had good games on the wing and in attack, but he still mixed them with poor games. With Wattsy, I probably went against my own philosophy, 'Know your role, play your role', because it took time to work out his strengths.

George Stone and I always felt it would be much easier for Wattsy when the team got stronger. There are players who build the foundation of your team and there are players who come in, like Jack Gunston did at Hawthorn, and provide the class and cream on top. Watts is a player of that kind.

When we had taught and coached everyone to be better, then Jack Watts would be better too because he'd have more opportunities. The question was, could we get to that point as a footy club and get Wattsy there with us?

With the ball in hand, he was as good as any player I'd seen, but he was still a work-in-progress and he was frustrating at times.

As much as we tried to help Jack, he also had to take responsibility for his own career. It took him a bit longer to work on his deficiencies and become more committed to the game than we had hoped. That happy-go-lucky, laconic nature was a strong point, but also his weak point at times.

We had to push him to train harder and meet the standards we demanded. He was out of the team early in 2015 and again at the end of the year.

I had a frank discussion with Jack at the end of 2015, because I was genuinely worried he might never reach his potential at Melbourne. We met at a café in Port Melbourne and I asked him if he wanted to be traded. 'This is not about whether I want to trade you, it's about whether you want to go,' I said.

I told him I was really concerned about his future and that he deserved to reach his potential and play good footy, wherever that might be.

To his credit, Jack wanted to stay and keep playing at Melbourne. I was rapt, as was Simon Goodwin, the senior coaching assistant who had been appointed to succeed me as coach at the end of 2016.

The real turning point for a player only comes when they decide to make it happen. His slump in 2015 was a catalyst for Jack to say, *Enough is enough.*

In 2016, my third and last year as coach, Jack blossomed, playing mainly as a half-forward. He was pivotal in four or five wins, including a game against the Gold Coast Suns where he kicked the match-winning goal.

He was our second-highest goal-kicker for the year, with 38 goals, and had the most score involvements of any player in the team. He came fifth in the best and fairest, his highest placing ever. We'd got to a certain level as a team, which allowed Jack to show his worth and perform at his best. He was a valuable member of the team, not its saviour.

Jack's case illustrates the challenge for a number of players at Melbourne. He was the highest-profile problem, but there were many other players with similar issues.

Jack Grimes and Jack Trengove, appointed co-captains in 2012, both struggled under the weight of that leadership role. Grimes was 22 when he was made captain and Trenners was 20, the youngest captain in the history of the AFL, or its previous incarnation, the VFL, which was formed in 1877.

There's a good reason why there had never been a captain so young. It was the same as throwing 18-year-old Jack Watts to the wolves against Collingwood in the Queen's Birthday game. They were put up as the messiahs when they were still finding their own feet in the AFL. I think they knew they weren't ready to be captains, but of course they were honoured and wouldn't turn it down.

They are both fantastic young men, had excellent training habits and were good players. But, understandably at that age, they had little real idea about the responsibilities of leadership. They needed to be shown the way by more senior players, but most of them had left the club.

I really felt for those two boys, because they should have been in the position of normal 20- or 22-year-olds, working on their own game, before they developed into leaders. They weren't yet mature enough to handle all that was put on their young shoulders.

Trengove, who was the number two draft pick in the 2009 draft, wisely stood down from the captaincy role at the end of 2013 to concentrate on developing his own footy. Jack Grimes remained co-captain, with Nathan Jones, for a year, until we made Nathan the stand-alone captain in 2015.

Their careers struck obstacles. Jack Trengove was sidelined by a serious foot injury in 2014 and 2015 and didn't return to the field until the middle of 2016.

Jack Grimes played in our reserves in 2016, before being delisted. I can't say enough about the attitude he showed in his last season at the club. It wasn't easy for him, going from captain in 2014 to playing for Casey. It's hard to describe exactly where it had gone wrong, but he found it hard to read the intricacies and subtleties of the game at AFL level.

Grimes had missed out during those crucial development years. Being appointed captain at 22 meant he had to help others first, and couldn't concentrate on his own learning.

Sadly, there were a number of players who weren't able to make it through under our new system. Over the course of the three years, we turned over nearly 30 players out of 44 on the list, and much of the change was due to the lack of development those players received between the ages of 18 and 22. The majority of players weren't able to overcome that.

Before I left Melbourne, I got both Jack Grimes and Jack Trengove into my office. I told them never to underestimate the impact they'd had on the footy club.

I hope Jack Grimes understands he played an important role as captain and continued to do that when he stepped down. He still drove the group to improve, drove his own high standards and drove the performance of our Casey

Scorpions reserves team in the VFL. He is a great role model and he was significant in helping to turn the club around in the three years I was there.

On the positive side, our ruckman Max Gawn, who was named All-Australian in 2016, was able to evolve into one of the competition's best players under our new development regime.

Max was drafted in 2009 and had played 17 games to the start of 2014. He was desperate to make his mark in the senior team and thought he deserved to be picked, but we made him wait.

He got pretty cranky about it at times and told us it was unfair. But he had to do his time in the reserves until he showed us he could play team footy and do all the little things we valued. He had to stop worrying about why he wasn't in the team and concentrate on earning his chance, no matter how the senior team was going.

There was a general attitude among the reserves players in 2014 that all they had to do was wait for the senior team to lose, and for someone to play poorly, so they could get their opportunity. If they didn't get selected, they'd get churlish. They actually didn't want senior success and it was an attitude we had to get rid of.

We wanted to instil good long-term habits, so the young players had to really prove themselves before they were elevated, even if that meant an under-performing player stayed in the senior team. Gifting games to the young guys didn't set them up well for the longer term.

That was a real juggling act and created a challenging environment at times, but we were determined to educate them in a way that some of the older players hadn't been.

Todd Viney, manager of player personnel and a former club captain, was frustrated in those early days, concerned we kept a few players in the senior team who didn't always uphold our standards and values, particularly around hardness at the contest and perseverance.

But we didn't yet have 22 players who could do that, so we had to wait until players learned the ropes in the reserves. We were on the same page, but the frustration boiled over for each of us at times.

In 2014, Max Gawn played nine games and then, in 2015, he didn't get a senior game until round 10. Two weeks later, playing Geelong at their home ground, Max had a breakout performance. He had 44 hit-outs, and was best on ground as we won by four goals in a huge upset against a team that had belted us so often.

One of the Cats' favourite sons, Corey Enright, was playing his 300th game, but with Max leading the way, we'd shocked Geelong. It was a huge morale-boost. The players, and Max in particular, got enormous belief from that win. They were starting to realise they could compete with the best.

It was a defining game for Max. From that point on, he went from strength to strength, because he had the right foundations. In the 2016 pre-season, Max trained the house down and got super fit. The rewards flowed during the season, as he became the AFL's number-one-ranked ruckman. Both Max and the team reaped the benefits of making him do those hard yards.

By 2016, the turnaround in the attitude of the guys playing for Casey in the VFL was remarkable. They were really engaged, keen to play as well as they could, and they understood how our development program worked. They felt valued and felt they were playing their part in a club that was going somewhere. There was real camaraderie and spirit amongst the entire playing group.

It reinforced to me the importance of making all 44 players on the list feel valued, even when only 22 can play in the senior team.

Assistant coaches Justin Plapp, Brett Allison and Daniel McPherson, who oversaw the Casey program, worked hard to create a similar environment there to the one we had for the senior players at Melbourne.

When players weren't selected for the senior side and went to Casey, they didn't feel like they were going 'down'. They were still very much part of the Melbourne Football Club. We were one club with a common purpose, moving forward together.

We had all done the hard yards and the tide was starting to turn.

CHAPTER 17

The tide has turned

We ended the 2015 season, and began the 2016 season, with games against the star-studded Greater Western Sydney Giants. We were all keen to test ourselves against the Giants, who boasted more than 20 players selected in the first round of the national draft over the previous few years. They were stocked with A+ talent.

In our final game of 2015, we scored a four-goal win over them and in the first match of 2016 we got home by two points at the MCG. We were down by three goals at three-quarter time, but kicked six goals in the final term to run over the top of the Giants.

In my mind, they were two of the most symbolic wins during my tenure.

As I began my last season as coach, those victories signalled we had transformed the talent level of the Melbourne team over the course of three pre-seasons, by bringing in nearly 30 new players. It was a notice to the footy world that we had started to assemble a team with genuine talent and genuine depth. We had developed and educated them to stand up against the best.

At the end of 2015, we had recruited one of the Giants' talented young players, Tomas Bugg, to add more punch to our midfield. During the 2016 pre-season, Tom told us that GWS had gone into the last game of 2015 thinking, 'We've played Melbourne before and we're going to kill them.'

Tom said his teammates had been surprised at how good we were and how much we had improved over the course of 2015. We were earning respect.

Those wins were a tick for our development program. They also provided more evidence for my long-held opinion that you can build a team in a variety of ways, not just through high draft picks. Our side had been constructed with a few top draft picks, a group of players we'd brought in through targeted recruiting and trading, and others we'd developed and nurtured in our reserves. As well, changing our culture and behaviours had played a crucial part in the improvement, along with a strong, consistent game plan.

You put them all together and you can start to compete.

What made those wins even more promising was that we were also, on average, the youngest team in the competition during 2016, at 23 years and 270 days. The only other team with an average age under 24 was the Brisbane Lions.

However, as always with so many young players in the side, it's never going to be a smooth upward trajectory. In round three, we took on North Melbourne, in Tasmania. It was a horror start – at quarter time the Kangaroos had scored eight goals and we had managed to scramble two goals.

In the coaches' box, I was worried. 'Oh no, is this the same sort of Melbourne team, maybe we haven't improved much after all?' But we stayed positive with the players at quarter time, telling them things hadn't gone our way, but we were going okay and to keep at it.

And then, in the second quarter, through hardness and toughness, we stormed back into the game with a nine-goal term.

In that 30 minutes of football, I had proof the mental scars that had affected the team during the past two seasons had finally healed. In 2014, we would have lost that game by 100 points, but the 2016 version of the Melbourne footy team fought back and ended up losing by only five points.

In the past, being six goals behind at quarter time would have messed with their heads. They would have looked at the scoreboard and told themselves, 'We're so far behind, we're no good.' They would have dropped their heads, retreated into their shells, and that attitude would have dictated how they played.

It showed me they were no longer worried about the margin. They believed they could get back into the contest. The ghosts had gone. Even though we didn't win, the mood afterwards was really positive, from the directors and staff and the players.

The buoyant mood showed we all felt the same thing – we were finally a different Melbourne team, with different talent. They were going to make their own history, no longer burdened.

We had rebuilt our midfield, with talented players such as Bugg, Dom Tyson and Bernie Vince coming in through trades, and Christian Salem, Christian Petracca, Angus Brayshaw and big-bodied inside midfielder, Clayton Oliver, through the national draft.

As the 2016 season rolled on, I was really pleased how a number of players had developed. Led by our hard-working captain, Nathan Jones, the players had fully embraced our new system.

Jack Viney, who was a father–son selection in the 2012 draft, had come on in leaps and bounds. In 2015, he finished second in our best and fairest count behind Bernie Vince, even though Jack missed six games with a broken leg.

Early on, Jack's attitude to everything he did, on the field and off, was like a bull in a china shop. Fearless and flint-hard in the contest, he knew only one way to go about it. But Jack had matured and become really thoughtful about his footy. He was more considerate of the team and wanted to get the best out of other people. He could win the ball, but also play run-with roles on the opposition's best play-ers when we needed, so he was very significant to the team's evolution.

I was also rapt with the way Neville Jetta had improved. He fell out of favour in 2013, but in the last game of that season I watched from the stands as he did a shut-down job on Western Bulldogs player Luke Dahlhaus. When I took the coaching job, we decided to re-draft him as a rookie and helped him develop as a defender, with a role to play on the opposition's best small forward. He ended up being top 10 in our best and fairest in 2014, and again in 2016, and is an important leader at the club.

I'm a big fan of Nev. I loved his work rate, his ability to use the ball effectively, and the way he stuck to his task. He was also incredibly competitive, very coachable, and quick to embrace new concepts – whether they were about play-ing one-on-one, assisting his teammates, or transition from defensive to attacking mode.

I felt Neville was one of the most underrated players in the competition and certainly one of the most underrated players I've ever coached, right up there with the Swans' fan-tastic small defender Nick Smith.

There was a strong feeling in 2016 that the club was head-ing in the right direction. We still had plenty of work to do, but everything was slotting into place.

Too many people think you can flick a switch and change a club's fortunes overnight. I wish you could, but that's not the way it works. It takes time to implement changes that are going to be worthwhile and lasting.

When I was appointed to the Melbourne job, my prime aim had been to set up a system that would leave the Demons in good shape, in a position to play finals for a sustained five-, six-, seven-, eight-year period of success. We were getting there.

One of the most critical decisions was the appointment of Simon Goodwin as my successor. I initially met Simon in 2014, during my first year as coach. It was an informal meeting, as it was with the other prospective coaches we spoke to.

Within an hour, I was fairly certain we had our next senior coach. Simon spent most of the time talking about building success through culture and team behaviours. He had previously worked with leadership consultants Leading Teams when his coach at the Crows, Neil Craig, had brought them to the club.

Simon firmly believed in their method of player empowerment, leadership groups and accountability. They were the aspects that separated him from other coaches we interviewed, who had come in and talked about their ideas on stoppages, and kick-ins, and game plans.

In mid-September 2014, we announced Simon would join the club in the role of 'senior assistant coach', to eventually take over as head coach after a two-year apprenticeship.

Simon was a champion Adelaide Crows player, who played 275 games and captained the club from 2008 to 2010. He played in two premierships with the Crows and was their best and fairest on three occasions. He had spent the previous four seasons as an assistant coach at Essendon.

His appointment was the final piece in the off-field puzzle, and we began a succession process similar to the one that had happened at the Swans when John Longmire took over from me at the end of 2010. I was confident it would be as seamless for the Melbourne players as it had been for the Swans.

In 2015, Simon was a line coach, overseeing the midfield, and concentrated on building relationships at the club. But in 2016 he had a much broader, hands-on role to make sure the changeover at the end of the season would be smooth. We were really keen for Simon to do as much as possible, so the club could continue on the same path when I left, with no right-turns.

He conducted the pre-season training sessions and coached during the pre-season competition. The players had to hear his voice and really get to know him and his style. We discussed game plans a lot and were on the same page. But if I was slightly doubtful about a game plan issue, it didn't worry me and it was his call. I was very mindful that he was soon going to be head coach and the players needed to stay on the same path.

During the home and away season, he took the helm at the coaches' post-game review meetings every Monday and set up the training schedule and game plan meetings with the players.

I still managed dealings with the leadership group, oversaw the culture and behaviours and looked after relationships with the medical, fitness staff and players.

Goody ran a lot of the educational component during the week, then on game day I was head coach and spoke to the players before the game and at the breaks. But it was a collective effort, with Simon and the other assistant coaches – Jade Rawlings, Ben Mathews, Brendan McCartney and Daniel McPherson – contributing all the time. That was the way it had always been when I coached.

There was plenty of talk during the pre-season competition, when Goody coached the team, that we had become more attacking. We had, but it was part of our natural progression. In 2016, we were finally able to put all three phases of the game – contest, defence, and offence – together.

It highlighted the fact that you have to meticulously build a new game plan, and it's not instant.

In the first year, we had concentrated on improving our contested ball numbers, winning the football, not fumbling and more efficient tackling. We had worked hard to stem the flow of opposition goals and conceded five goals fewer per game in 2014 than we had in 2013.

In the second year, we continued that emphasis, but added defensive mechanisms and then added offensive mechanisms after that. In 2016, or year three, everyone was talking about our offence. But really, it was the first time we'd been able to drive all three phases of the game – and even add in a few tricks.

The tricks are the 'add-ons', that might help you kick an extra goal or two – extra players such as the half-forwards at the stoppages, or players coming off the back of the square at centre bounces.

It clicked in rounds four and five, when we beat Collingwood by nearly six goals and then Richmond by a similar margin. It was the first time since rounds 13 and 14 in 2011 that Melbourne had won two games in a row. For nearly five years, the Demons had never been able to back up from a win, but we had finally done it.

It was another sign we had a harder edge, both mentally and physically. We had made mistakes and Richmond had started closing on us, but we had steadied and won.

Max Gawn was outstanding that day, with 47 hit-outs as he continued to develop into the best ruckman in the competition, and Jack Viney, with a club record 23 contested possessions, had willed us to the line.

During the middle part of the season, we were up and down, but there were no mental demons. We dished out beatings to a few teams, including the Gold Coast Suns and Brisbane, and lost to teams that were more advanced than us. At times we were getting beaten because we were young, or because other teams were simply more talented than us at this stage.

But we were now very much a middle-of-the-rung team. When I took over in 2013, we were bottom of the pile. Former Victorian Premier and Hawthorn president Jeff Kennett, who loves a bold statement, had suggested at one stage that Melbourne no longer deserved to be in the AFL and should be relegated to the Victorian Football League.

So, we'd gone from being a VFL team (in Jeff's eyes) to a bottom-of-the-ladder AFL team and now we were holding our own in the mid-rank of the competition. We had a more consistent output and had improved significantly. Our fans came to games no longer expecting the worst. They knew they would see maximum effort from the players, whatever the outcome.

There was no better feeling than our win over Hawthorn in round 20. We came up against them when they were on a nine-game winning streak and on top of the AFL ladder. They had won the past three premierships and had been belting our players around for years. Melbourne hadn't beaten Hawthorn for more than nine seasons, since round eight in 2006. Our captain, Nathan Jones, had played Hawthorn 13 times and never been on the winning side until that day.

We were a goal up at three-quarter time, but Hawthorn sneaked in front early in the last term. We didn't panic – we kicked the last five goals of the match to beat them by 29 points. The last 15 minutes of the game was the best football I'd seen us play.

There was so much excitement in the group after that memorable win. They had put in a massive effort and earned a huge reward. The players, such as Jonesy, who had been there for many years felt they finally stood for something and were really proud.

It was the sort of win, achieved with 10 players who had notched up less than 50 games, that could bond the players and drive them into the future. Every player had done his part. For the first time in my coaching career, I gave best and fairest votes to all 22 players on our team, because they all deserved to be acknowledged for carrying out their roles.

We had nine wins for the season, the most for Melbourne since 2006. And it was no fluke. We went to Adelaide the next weekend, kicked eight unanswered goals early in the game and beat Port Adelaide by 40 points. We had 10 wins and 10 losses, with two games to play.

The milestones kept coming. It was the first time since 2010 Melbourne had won three games in a row. They were important steps forward for a young group of players who were growing as a unit together. 'It sets up the belief for the group and trust in each other,' I said after the match.

In theory, we were in finals contention, but it was a long shot. We had to win our last two games and also rely on other results going our way.

In round 22, we played Carlton, who had lost the previous nine games. After all the build-up, we ran out of steam. We went down by 20 points. The following week, against Geelong at Skilled Stadium, my final game as coach, we hit an even bigger wall. We were trounced, by 111 points, which was the biggest losing margin during my coaching career.

There is no doubt it was disappointing and really tough to watch. Everyone was down and I didn't really say much to the players after the game. I knew we were better than that, but I could see they were exhausted.

I hoped that loss was the catalyst to drive the players over the summer. As far as we had come, we still had to improve to get to where we wanted.

For me personally, it was a message that it was time to move on. I'd done the job and now it was time for a younger coach, for Goody, to put on the finishing touches and hopefully get the success everyone craves.

Despite the shock of that last loss, I was confident we had built the foundations for success in the next few years. We had grown enormously, but the last two games showed us we were not yet quite good enough to be a finals team.

There were reasons for that. In the AFL Prospectus, the publication produced every year by Champion Data, the statistics showed that in 11 games during 2016 we were the youngest team in the competition. Also, on average over the whole year, we were the youngest team. In the round 22 loss to Carlton, the average age of our players was 23 years and 18 days – half a year younger than any other team playing in the competition that day, and nearly two and a half years younger than Carlton's average age.

Our 22 players had an average of 60 games, while Carlton's averaged 91. As the prospectus states, 'Youth and lack of experience is unpredictable and ordinary performances shouldn't be a shock . . . Ten wins at a percentage of 98, and a finish of 11th with that youth is nothing to scoff at.'

While we still had a way to go, over three years we had significantly changed our personnel and overhauled the way we played. Our percentage – which the prospectus states is one of the most effective ways to judge how a team is tracking – had gone from 54 per cent in 2013 to 98 per cent in 2016.

In effect, in 2013 the Demons were having their score almost doubled every week – that was what a percentage of 54 told us. Three years later, with a percentage of 98, we were almost breaking even. In pure mathematical terms, we were close to 100 per cent better. We were averaging nearly four more goals per game and conceding five fewer.

Other statistics also told a positive tale. When I arrived in 2013, Melbourne averaged 23 fewer contested possessions per game than their opposition. In 2016, we averaged five more than our opposition, the first time Melbourne had been in the positive since Champion Data, who provide the official AFL statistics, began recording that stat in 1999.

In 2013, when they won only two games, Melbourne had averaged 79 fewer disposals than their opposition per game. By 2016, we had transformed that stat and averaged 31 more disposals per game than the opposition. It was a turnaround of more than 100 possessions per game. The players had learned how to win the ball.

There was one last function for me as head coach – the best and fairest award night at the Crown Palladium in the first week of September. It was a great evening, with Jack Viney a very deserving winner of the Keith 'Bluey' Truscott medal, following on from his dad Todd, who won in 1993 and 1998.

The lifelong Demons fans in attendance made it clear they weren't focused on our last loss in 2016, but on a bright future. So many people came up and thanked me for what we had achieved over the past three years.

It was a reminder to me how, collectively, everyone had done an incredible job to drag the footy club out of the depths of despair. From chairman Glen Bartlett, to CEO Peter Jackson, to all staff and players, everyone had worked so hard to win back respect and create real hope for the years ahead.

I could walk away satisfied I'd done everything I set out to do three years earlier. When success comes for the Melbourne Football Club – as I know it will – I'll be as happy as anyone.

Despite the difficulties, setbacks and criticism, we had not wavered from our plans and our beliefs. As it was at the Swans a decade earlier, that is the key to long-term success.

In an industry where the football media reacts day-to-day looking for headlines and there is far too little thoughtful analysis, the only way forward is to focus on putting the right environment in place. For me, that is the biggest lesson of a lifetime in football.

When I look back, the best thing I ever did was write down my 25 coaching points in 1998, just after I finished playing. They were always in my desk drawer and always my guide, no matter where I went. Because they were written down, I stuck to them. They held me accountable and ensured I had empathy with the players.

I'd encourage any young sporting coach or corporate leader to write a list of what they do, and don't, like about the leaders around them. That list meant I stuck to my principles and resisted the pressure to alter course when things didn't immediately work out the way I would have liked.

There is no more public, or more pressured, environment than AFL football. The coaches who listen to outside voices and waver from their own beliefs are the ones who don't make it. The leaders who stick to their processes, who hold firm and hang on for the inevitable bumps, are the ones who eventually get rewards. Live and die on your own blueprint, not someone else's. Build strong relationships and form bonds with the people who are in it with you.

Two months after I finished coaching, an email arrived from Robbie Jackson, the head strength and conditioning coach at Melbourne. Robbie has worked at a number of different

National Rugby League and AFL clubs and is one of the best in Australian sport. Better than I can, Robbie explained everything I valued and everything I tried to achieve as a coach.

I can't thank him enough for allowing me to reproduce his message here.

EMAIL FROM ROBBIE JACKSON, 5 November 2016
Lately I've been speaking to interns, students, coaches and even corporates, and one of the common questions I get after the session is, 'What's the difference between the coaches you've had?'

To be completely honest, I had never really given it much thought, and would often just answer with, 'Oh, they are all pretty similar with their own quirks', and then move on to the next question.

That was until earlier this week when I was speaking to a bunch of strength & conditioning interns – and one of the things I discussed was the mistakes I made early, and the most important lessons I have gained from these experiences.

I would always tell students to make sure they have the piece of paper, but also to get practical experience with real teams, athletes etc., any way that you can. Volunteer, assist . . . go out of your way to put yourself in these places and be around athletes, coaches and in the sporting environment, as there are lessons you just can't learn from a book or lecture.

I then went on to explain that early in my career I was the 'bad cop' – the 'tough guy' S&C staff who would demand perfection. I would penalise players for being one minute late, would give physical penalties for not hitting targets and demanded buy-in from every single player. I got results.

Neil Craig once said to me, 'You may not be liked, but they certainly respect you.' At the time, I considered that as mission accomplished. The mantra at the time was, 'It's not about being liked, it's about being respected', and to that end I certainly felt I was as good a coach as I could be.

Enter Paul Roos.

Now, without wanting to inflate your ego, you've actually had a profound effect on my personality and thus – coaching. You walked into the club and one of your key messages was, 'Clubs are built on relationships – between coaches, between players, between football and admin.' You made a point [to] us all: 'Know each other, have a conversation, actually show some care about each other, 'cos we are going to have ups and downs but the only thing that'll make you get up and help your teammate, put your body on the line, work that extra hour . . . is knowing that they would do the same for you and that you care.'

I really took that on board, Roosy . . . and I actively started to take more of an interest in what the players were doing outside of footy, whether they were single or in a relationship, did they have siblings, what are their hobbies, do they want kids in the future, are they studying, what do their parents do for work, and what sort of music did they grow up listening to. Everything I could do to understand more about what makes these 'players' real 'people'.

The result is, and it's funny that it is the guys who have been delisted or moved on in the last few years who have actually expressed this to me the most – that many of the players state that they highly respect me for my coaching and diligence, my OCD behaviours and exacting standards . . . but more so, they like me for caring about them, taking the time to message them, congratulate or commiserate, inviting them into my house to tackle extra sessions, or just to catch up for a feed.

My point is this, when I look back I have learned from many coaches . . . and as an S&C coach each has taught me separate lessons that have stuck with me, but I can roughly summarise each in one key point –

Craig Bellamy – you demand respect through your actions and living the standards you expect your athletes to follow.

Brad Arthur – always have a plan . . . but be damn sure you have a plan B and C because things can/will change at any second.

Ross Lyon – work harder than anyone else . . . you don't have to be the most talented if you are willing to put in work and leave it all on the line.

Mark Neeld – pressure makes diamonds . . . but it also creates earthquakes . . . be very clear that the pressure you are under or applying doesn't cause a fracture.

Neil Craig – the mind controls the body, and never let any sports scientist convince you otherwise.

Which then brings me to you, Roosy . . . and I am going to paraphrase but this is essentially how I summed up the most important lesson I have learned from you as a coach.

'Win their hearts, and you will win the battle.'

This lesson has not only improved my coaching career, but my life as well. I am far more open to having real conversations with complete strangers, workmates etc. and not wondering what it is they are seeking/want, or what can I gain from this interaction – I am simply trying to understand people better. I don't need to yell to enforce or intimidate players anymore, I can (quietly) express my disappointment, sometimes with a simple look, and they will realise they have let me down . . . not held up their end of our agreement.

I used to get so frustrated with [Christian] Petracca and yet after showing [him] genuine care, he once messaged me at the end of the day to let me know he was disappointed in himself for the way he behaved in the gym, being a distraction to others, and that he felt he'd let himself and me down, when I have been telling everyone how much he had improved.

I received a message from Nathan [Jones] during the year noting how much I had changed in [the] last couple of years, and that although he still loved that I had exact standards and 'didn't tolerate any shit'. . . that he and the playing group felt genuinely cared for and that I had become more of a teammate and less of a 'stiff'.

All of this, across so many players on the list, I actually credit to your focus on behaviours and relationships. You modelled the behaviour that you wanted players and staff to exhibit, and I think your farewell speech at the MCG was testament to that, when you went to great lengths to thank admin staff and how they are critical to the success of the club.

I'll wrap this up before it turns into a thesis . . . but when coaches/interns/anyone who will listen now ask me, 'What's the difference between the coaches you've had?' I am still going to say, 'Oh, they are all pretty similar with their own quirks . . . but . . . the greatest lesson I've learned from them is that all coaching should begin with understanding the true importance of building relationships.'

So, thanks Roosy – I am a better coach, friend, husband, mentor and member of society thanks to your time at Melbourne Football Club.

Postscript

Hardly a day goes by that I'm not asked when, or if, I'll go back to coaching an AFL side.

I understand why people ask, but for me the question is not relevant to how I see my future.

Just because you've had success at something, that doesn't mean you want to do it all the time, or for the rest of your working life. There are so many other things I'm keen to throw myself into.

Tami, Dylan, Tyler and I have loved being intimately involved with two AFL clubs. We will be forever grateful for the experiences we had, and the people we became close to, at both the Sydney Swans and Melbourne.

But even when I took the Melbourne job in 2013, as I said at the time, it was because I saw it as a role centred around leadership and people management, rather than just football coaching.

Don't get me wrong – I absolutely love the game of Australian football, and love my role analysing and commentating for both television and radio. I have strong opinions about how the game should be played, how players should be developed, and how clubs should be run, and I'm happy to share them. But AFL coaching is a highly scrutinised, high-pressured occupation, and it gets more intense every year.

I was interested to hear former Essendon coach James Hird say that he believes the pressure and stress faced by AFL coaches is mostly unhealthy.

My main priority has always been to maintain a work/life balance, and I believe I was able to achieve that most of the time when I was coaching. I made sure my family was part of the club and part of the job. I meditated every day, which helped me to cope with the demands.

But I believe it's becoming harder and harder for coaches to achieve that balance in their lives, as the media scrutiny of football becomes more brutal, and generally more negative. Just look at the anxiety and tension etched on the face of any senior coach during a game. It's such a highly competitive, tough game, so coaches, players and senior club administrators can never be complacent for a moment. It is all-consuming.

I believe there isn't enough understanding in the football media, or the wider community, of how demanding the AFL competition is, and how difficult it is to win games of football. It's so easy to criticise, and to me that shows a complete lack of respect for the quality of the competition.

So one of the things I'd like to do, now that I'm part of the media myself, is to give followers of the sport genuine insight into what it is like for players and for coaches.

As well, I believe that so many of the life skills I learned as a player and coach over 30 years are transferable to other aspects of life besides football. From here on, I'd like to spend more time sharing those insights. I want to try to take that wisdom, all the lessons from my AFL experience, and translate that to the corporate world, the education system, and to families as well.

From my experience, a good football club does certain things very well: they have open and honest discussions, and practice direct communication, and they do it better than most non-sporting organisations.

Good football clubs act quickly to address issues, there and then. They hold each other accountable to a set of behaviours, and then give honest feedback around those behaviours.

Performance is measured so immediately that there is no other way. Good football clubs find solutions, based on their values, rather than focusing on problems. They help their players develop so they can see the solutions for themselves.

These are lessons I believe many businesses and individuals could learn and implement.

So how will we spread these messages, and educate the wider community, about the importance of communication and relationship-building?

Tami and I have set up a business, the Roos Synergy, which is centred around wellness, leadership, work/life balance, meditation, and the power of the mind.

We're presenting to corporations, helping them to establish behaviours and implement mechanisms so they genuinely live those values every day.

We ask some simple questions.

Would your company, your organisation or your family be better off if you were better communicators?

Would you be better off if you were focused on solutions?

Would you be better off if you established a positive environment?

Would you be better off if you had good work/life balance?

Would you be better off if you were able to integrate wellness practices such as meditation into your workplace?

The Roos Synergy is taking the knowledge gained through our sporting life, and through our family life, and melding it together to help individuals and corporations be more fulfilled and successful.

There might not be any premiership medallions, but we're very excited about this next phase of our lives.

Acknowledgements

To Nick Fordham for encouraging me to write this book, a great manager and a great mate.

To Samantha Sainsbury and all the people at Penguin Random House for making it possible. It was a pleasure to work with you all and see this book come to fruition.

A special thanks to Jen McAsey for writing the book with me. Jen and the Cordell family have been incredible friends for many years now, and not only did she help write the book but our families shared many of the wonderful experiences contained within it. The ease with which the book was written is a testament to the relationship that Jen and I have formed over many years. What an amazing job Jen did translating over 30 years of experiences into a fluid, incredibly well-written account of that journey, and the book would not be what it is without her invaluable influence and expertise.

To Rob Jackson, thank you for the incredible email and, secondly, for allowing me to use it in the book. As leaders, we often don't get enough feedback. To read what you wrote and the impact that I had on your life was very humbling and meant the world to me. Thank you very much.

When writing a book at 54 years of age you realise how many people have an influence on your life. Every experience is relevant, both positive and negative, and there are many, many people that contribute to your journey.

To my mum, dad, brother and sister, who shaped my early years, thank you for the experiences we had together as a family.

As I look back now, I was so fortunate to go to the Fitzroy Football Club. To all the players, coaches and staff, I cannot thank you enough for the incredibly positive messages and the lessons I learned in my 15 years at the club.

The move to Sydney was life-changing, and the 2005 Premiership will forever be a highlight of my working life. Well done and thank you to the many people who contributed to that historic victory, and for the many lessons I learned along the way. Whilst the Premiership was clearly a highlight, the culture we were able to build at the Sydney Swans is something that we can all be proud of, and has led to lifelong friendships.

To the Melbourne Football Club, and in particular the players, I cannot thank you enough for teaching me about leading from the heart, resilience and courage. To coach a team that had only won two games in the previous year required me to draw upon every bit of skill and experience I had gained in 30-plus years of football. Once again I could not have done this without all the staff. A great organisation requires that everyone plays their role. No person can do it by themselves. I look forward to watching the Melbourne Demons' success.

To Tami, Dylan and Tyler, we made the choice to do everything together as a family. This certainly made the lows a lot more bearable but, more importantly, the highs are something we will cherish and share forever. Family is, has been, and will always be my number one priority.

Index